SPOKANE BOULDERING

IN MEMORY OF:
ALEX RICE
ANDREW BOWER
ANNA DVORAK
DAVID STEPHANS
JESS ROSKELLEY

Spokane Bouldering by Shane Collins and Nate Lynch
©2022 Sharp End Publishing, LLC
All rights reserved. This book or any part thereof may not be reproduced in any form without written permission from the publisher.

Published and distributed by:

Sharp End Publishing, LLC
PO Box 1613
Boulder, CO 80306
303-444-2698
www.sharpendbooks.com

ISBN: 978-0-9657079-6-1

Printed in USA

Cover Image: Kristin W. on Scarlett Johansson V5 | Photo by Ben Bolt

READ THIS BEFORE USING THIS BOOK:
WARNING!

Climbing is a very dangerous activity. Take all precautions and evaluate your ability carefully. Use judgment rather than the opinions represented in this book. The publisher and author assume no responsibility for injury or death resulting from the use of this book. This book is based on opinions. Do not rely on information, descriptions, or difficulty ratings as these are entirely subjective. If you are unwilling to assume complete responsibility for your safety, do not use this guidebook.

THE AUTHORS AND PUBLISHER EXPRESSLY DISCLAIM ALL REPRESENTATIONS AND WARRANTIES REGARDING THIS GUIDE, THE ACCURACY OF THE INFORMATION HEREIN, AND THE RESULTS OF YOUR USE HEREOF, INCLUDING WITHOUT LIMITATION, IMPLIED WARRANTIES OF MERCHANTABILITY AND FITNESS FOR A PARTICULAR PURPOSE. THE USER ASSUMES ALL RISK ASSOCIATED WITH THE USE OF THIS GUIDE.

It is your responsibility to take care of yourself while climbing. Seek a professional instructor or guide if you are unsure of your ability to handle any circumstances that may arise. This guide is not intended as an instructional manual.

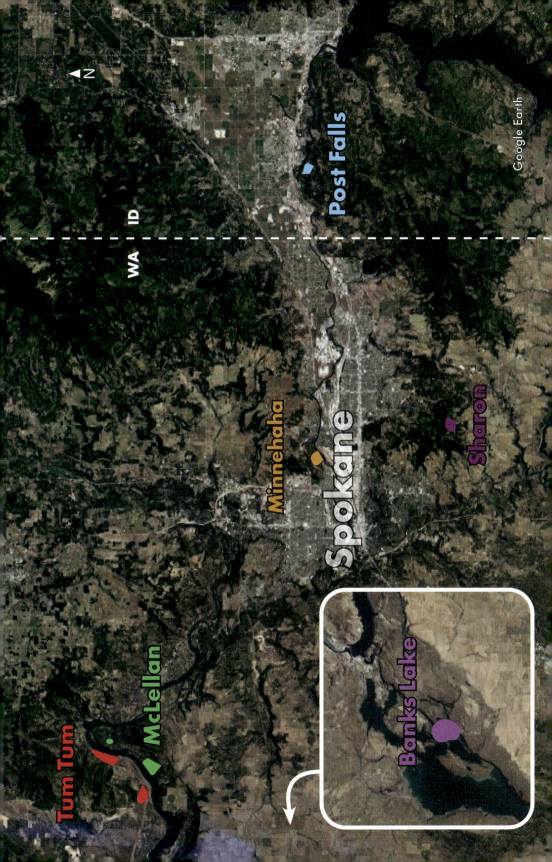

Cam F. on McLove Handles (V3).

TABLE OF CONTENTS

INTRODUCTION: 7

BEST OF SPOKANE: 20

McLELLAN: 21
    IVY AREA: 26
    DAVE'S GRAVEL: 40
    THE GLEN: 58
    THE HOOD: 74
    THE COMMONS: 84
    LOST & FOUND: 102
    FERN GULLIES: 111

TUM TUM: 114
    LOWER EAST SIDE: 117
    THE HAIRPIN: 118
    CORONA BOULDERS: 125
    CRAIGLANDIA: 126
    HIGH BOULDERS: 139
    LOWER WEST END: 140
    UPPER WEST END: 152
    CORKSCREW CANYON: 162

ROCKS OF SHARON: 166

MINNEHAHA: 174
    MINNEHAHA PARK: 177
    LOWER BEACON HILL: 188
    BEACON HILL: 190
    UPPER BEACON HILL: 195

POST FALLS: 196
    SPILLWAY: 197
    DEATH FALL WALL: 202
    FAR OUT: 204

BANKS LAKE: 206
    NORTHRUP CANYON: 208
    NORTHRUP POINT: 215
    HIGHWAY ROCK BOULDERS: 216
    SUPERBLOOM AREA: 218
    LANDSLIDE & BEACHHOUSE: 219

QR LIBRARY: 220

INDEX: 225

SPOKANE'S PREMIER CLIMBING GYM & YOGA STUDIO EST. 1995

Located conveniently downtown in Spokane's historical armory. We offer 12,000 sq. ft. of climbing terrain including two large bouldering areas and 40 ft. tall top roping and lead climbing walls. Our goal is to provide a fun, safe and friendly environment for beginners and experienced climbers to enjoy everything climbing has to offer.

WILDWALLS.COM | 509-455-9596

202 W. 2ND AVE
SPOKANE, WA 99201

Steve M. on Propaganda Project

FOREWORD

SPOKANE BOULDERING

by Bob Loomis

The German climber, one of the greatest of the 20th century, Hermann Bühl once wrote "There is probably nothing finer than to climb free and unencumbered by equipment, reveling in the gymnastic upward movement, like Preuss or a Düfler before you, relying only upon yourself, keeping a sharp eye on things, feeling the rock beneath your feet and fingertips." Though Bühl expressed himself in the form of what we would today call free soloing or that form of bouldering known as high-balling, his words are just as appropriately applied to all forms of bouldering, no matter how common the boulder problem.

Bouldering is a form of artistic expression, more akin to a dance than to sports such as basketball or football. But it is also athletic movement as Bühl stated—a form of gymnastic movement. Indeed, high end bouldering involves high-level athleticism that can only be achieved by years of disciplined, consistent training, together with sharp kinesthetic awareness and mental focus. Additionally, for boulder problems beyond a certain height, one must balance awareness and focus with a willingness to accept the potential for serious injury or even death. One has only to consider John Gill's bouldering ascent of *The Thimble* in the Black Hills of South Dakota in the early 1960s (now rated hard 5.12), before the guardrail was removed, to appreciate this aspect of bouldering.

High-end bouldering does indeed require intense preparation and effort, along with perseverance—a willingness to fall off a problem repeatedly. But bouldering can also be playful, a simple creative achievement involving artistry and wit. In other words, it can be almost anything the practitioner wishes it to be. Some pursue bouldering as an end in itself with laser-like, single-minded devotion, but for others it is a romp on the rocks mixed with friends and laughter.

I learned that bouldering can be fun, intense, athletic, challenging, and at times downright scary when as a teenager in the early 1970s I had a chance to boulder for a day with one of this region's finest climbers, Chris Kopczynski. I had only started climbing a year or two prior and associated climbing with a rope and a belayer. Chris, a highly accomplished alpinist, with difficult ascents from California's Yosemite Valley to British Columbia's Rockies, provided a different perspective. On that day, his tutelage proved that bouldering was

Nate L. on Middle of the Pack (V8).

an important tool in building strength and technique for longer and more difficult rock, ice, and alpine ascents in the many ranges I would soon visit. A strong athlete, he has always been armed with a ready smile, wit, self-deprecating humor, and integrity.

It was customary at the time to show up at Minnehaha rain or shine on Saturdays—unless one was sick or out of town—and climb with whoever showed up. The region's climbing community was so small with Minnehaha the de facto meeting place, that everyone was on a first name basis. As a young novice climber, I was eager, so I showed up that Saturday morning extra early, the air still chilly with dew on the grass. I did not have to wait long until a car pulled up and out hopped Chris who promptly introduced himself and asked if I wanted to boulder with him.

Knowing of Chris by reputation I eagerly said yes. What followed was a half day of swiftly moving from one boulder problem to another of increasing difficulty, several of which would now be classified as high-ball problems. This was well before the time of crash pads, spotters, chalk, brushing holds, sticky rubber, etc. Chalk was not used by Spokane climbers at the time—we did not know better. If it was hot and our fingers were sweaty, we simply wiped our hands on our pants or rubbed our fingers in the dirt before climbing. But chalk was being used in Colorado, and controversially being introduced in places like Yosemite. Chris climbed first and while he scampered down the backside of the problem, I would do my best to follow—thankfully, most of the time succeeding. Several times he watched me climb and made suggestions on how I could move more smoothly, extend my reach, achieve greater balance and equilibrium before making the next move, and use my feet better. In one morning with him I was introduced to the world of bouldering. It was fun and foundational. That Saturday left a positive impression on me that exists today almost five decades later. I will forever owe him a debt of gratitude for what he taught a young, insecure, but eager teenager. Every young climber should have a mentor or two like him.

Shane Collins (left) with Bob Loomis (right).

Shane C. on The War Room (V4).

Along the way that morning, Chris regaled me with stories of great climbers, some of whom I had heard about, but most strangers to me, who had built their climbing prowess on regular bouldering—climbers such as Royal Robbins, Yvon Chouinard, Chuck Pratt, and John Roskelley, etc. One name in particular stood out—John Gill, who, as any devotee of the history of bouldering will know, single-handedly, and often by himself, raised the standards of bouldering from perhaps 5.8 in the early 1950s to 5.13 by the middle of the 1960s. Gill used the "B" (for "bouldering) system that he devised to rate boulder problems. A B1 problem was something someone else besides himself could climb. A B2 problem was something only he could climb. A B3 problem was something he could not yet climb. That was it—pretty simple! If he eventually climbed a B3 then it was downrated to B2. If someone repeated a B2, then it was downrated to B1. Now boulder problems are rated using the "V" system invented by John "Vermin" Sherman in the 1990s.

Much later I aspired to climb some of Gill's problems so made a few trips to Devil's Lake, Horsetooth Reservoir, the Jenny Lake boulders, and some of the problems around Pueblo, Colorado. I managed to climb a few, but most I could not. Memories of working problems like the *Center Overhang* on Red Cross Rock, which is featured in Pat Ament's inspiring work *Master of Rock: The Biography of John Gill*—a Gill B2 later downrated to B1 will stay with me the rest of my days (I was never able to climb it clean). What I did learn from those days following in Gill's footsteps was humility and respect for his intense athletic preparation, mental focus, gymnastic ability, and visionary eye for problems. His boulder problems still stand the test of time and regularly beat back some of the world's finest. Later, I was honored to meet Gill himself, and was impressed by his humility, quiet demeanor, encyclopedic knowledge of climbing history, and impeccable ethics.

So, reader, whether you are an experienced climber or new to bouldering, there will be something for you in this guidebook. This book is a welcome addition to climbing in the Inland Empire. Devour its pages, fill your mind with imagination, be inspired, and go out and challenge yourself. You will be blessed with some of the finest days you will ever have on the rocks and create memories that will endure for the rest of your life!

Bob Loomis

Cierra G. on Fungus Among Us (V3).
Photo by George Hughbanks

INTRODUCTION

*"She may not look like much,
But she's got it where it counts, kid"*

-Han Solo

SPOKANE

The Millennium Falcon is the most iconic ship in the American imagination—trust me, I'm going somewhere with this.

The external cockpit pod sneaking off the right side of the ship and the fork-shaped "mouth" left over from the missing Auxiliary Ship component has not only popularized the otherwise forgettable YT-1300f light freighter but more importantly has given it a permanent place in our culture. We feel a chill crawl up our skin as the screen shows the familiar silhouette appear from dark space pinpricked with constellations. Then the vessel dips, upon a magical cue from the bright and dramatically strung Star Wars theme. We feel nostalgia as the characters we know travel through space in the beloved bucket of bolts.

Sorry, bucket of bolts? It's easy to forget that this ship is no perfect specimen. Nearly every passenger has something negative to say about the Millennium Falcon. How can this be? From an aesthetic point of view, it looks the equivalent of a concrete building that an apprentice architect (with a severe budget limit) put together, but it can dance through an asteroid field and fend off clusters of TIE fighters—no sweat! Yes, almost every time the ship isn't flying, Chewbacca or Han are working on an endless number of issues resulting in sparking electronics and belching steam. But...remember when it shot out freaking Darth Vader! Also, let's not forget that whole Kessel run thing! No matter the flair or feats accomplished, the MIllennium Falcon is not a world (shall we say galaxy?) class ship. This begs the question: should it be less beloved or more?

Enter the bouldering around Spokane. We aren't sure what you may have heard of the rock in Spokane. Likely nothing. Maybe whispers that it's sharp. Perhaps that the locals are notorious sandbaggers. Even dirty rumors that it's all choss. Whatever you heard, it could be the truth, but definitely not the whole truth. Yes, things aren't perfect. The boulders don't shine with chalk on every hold, don't offer a consistently friendly texture, or reside at the end of groomed trails. Nevertheless, they offer a place to create memories, to challenge ability, to fail often, and to succeed with relish. We even think some may be the best we've climbed.

As George Lucas taught us through a seemingly bummy spaceship—even though something isn't packaged to impress, isn't shiny and new, isn't the biggest or sleakest, it in no way means that it won't become your favorite. In fact, it's hard to feel any of that when busy enjoying time outdoors, exploring the beauty, and realizing that much like the Millennium Falcon, this place is one of a kind.

HISTORY

Modern climbing, in one fashion or another, has been a part of the Spokane area since the 1920s. Back when railroad workers traveled from the oddest parts of the globe to work in Spokane's expanding rail system and industry, workers would flee the loud movement of steel to a quiet, nature-y reprieve. The ability to be completely surrounded by mountains, rivers, cliffs, and boulders near the city is a prized feature of this eastern part of the state. It's a secret that Eastern Washington has kept close to it's chest.

George H. Headwound Cave (V4).
Photo by Jon Jonckers.

The secret, of course, was shared and these areas started being utilized as a training ground. There were groups of climbers who, in preparation for the big walls of Yosemite, would head out to nearby rock and scurry up and down every feature, crack, and ledge—mostly in what we'd today consider heavy duty hiking boots. Even with cumbersome equipment and questionable protection these people grandfathered modern climbing in the Spokane Area. Top alpinists like John Roskelley would use these areas as training grounds for the hardest climbs in the world. Subsequently these areas produced some of the strongest climbers including John's son Jess who held the world record for being the youngest American to climb Mt. Everest.

Places covered with walls of rock like Minnehaha, Dishman-Mica, Mirabeau Parkway, Q'emiln Park, Liberty Park, Lincoln Park, and Cliff Drive within city limits were the first explored and still inspire new climbers to push themselves and push each other. It's easy to see why people were drawn to these areas: lush, trail-less pockets of hills covered with ponderosas, scattered with sporadic embossed granite and basalt—areas seemingly undisturbed by the human footprint, as if they are waiting for adventurous souls to wander through and explore.

Sometimes I wonder if climbers back in the day thought that those places would turn into the places they are now. Don't get me wrong: Minnehaha is one of my favorite places but because of its accessibility, it attracts garbage, graffiti, and damage. Before places like this became popular, they would have evoked a unique and memorable experience. But I don't think those experiences are lost. Although it may take viewing them through a different lens to fully appreciate.

That's the Catch-22 of writing a guidebook to invite more people. The possibility of losing beauty through more traffic is real, but sharing the experience and the places we love with others outweighs the possible downsides. That being said, keep in mind that respecting these areas while we're out climbing cannot be understated—but we'll get to that part. The point is that climbing shouldn't be about gatekeeping or keeping secrets. If I get to enjoy something, you get to enjoy it too because the world we live in belongs to everyone.

The history of climbing in the Eastern Washington area isn't much different than other places. It was a part of the ever-growing progression that grew across the globe in the early 20th century. However, what makes our history stand out is the people and the culture it has developed.

When preparing this book, we talked to the

SPOKANE BOULDERING | 11

Chelsea M. on *The Legend of Red O'Kelly* (V5).

our climbing days we won't look back and talk about the grades or the specifics of the climbs, we'll look back at the people that were there with us. The encouragement we give to one another, the jokes and loving jabs, the laughs shared, the shwamping through the thick grass and tall trees (and the subsequent tick check and removal), the relationships made, the good days and the bad.

This pure spirit propelled itself forward in a massive push in the 90s and early 2000s with people like Adam Healy, Arden Pete, Brett Jessen, Cole Allen, Serra Barron, Dmitry Kalashnikov, George Hughbanks, Johnny Goicoechea, Mike Bokino, Spencer Davy, and countless others. These climbers took it upon themselves to scout every rock face and keep discovering. Legend has it that not a single rock, good or bad, pleasant or painful, easy or hard, went untouched by this wave of young, strong climbers. The grit and the heart of bouldering that was inherited from the early developers was the spark for the modern development and growth of climbing in our very special area.

people who know it best, including the authors of other local guidebooks—Bob Loomis and Marty Bland. During our time together, the biggest takeaways had little to do with the rock itself. In fact, names of climbs, grades, ascent details, beta, and technique were hardly mentioned. The real backbone of climbing in Eastern Washington is the spirit and the soul of adventure. It requires grit, sacrifice, and passion. These local rocks produce a bold, strong, and tenacious type of rock climber. Climbers like Jess Roskelley, Alex Rice, and Andrew Bower. People who would seek the outdoors for the sake of the outdoors. People who felt that it wasn't just about climbing, but rather about the grueling approach, the falling and getting back up, the torn skin, the long days, pushing yourself that extra bit. It's about being alone in the woods as a form of reflection. It is about the experience itself. Most of these people have come and gone, but the area is still the same and wants the same of us. More importantly, this area has given us a community—a shared love that turns strangers into close friends.

In one of our talks, Bob said that at the end of

ETHICS

We don't need to spend a lot of time talking about the ethics of going into the hills, parks, and open environments. Our assumption and our hope is that we are all acutely aware of the decades of irreversible damage done to our planet and, in turn, are mindful of our impact. So we'll skip to the the plea.

This is a plea to be aware of your surroundings. This land doesn't belong to you or me or anyone else; it's something we share (just like Earth itself) and it's absolutely something that one person can ruin for the rest. The best fight against the continuing damage to nature and the potential loss of access is to shoulder the cause on our own. This is much more than a "Pack it in, pack it out" mentality because there will always be people who simply don't care. It's up to people like us to steward these areas in hopes of keeping them safe, clean and intact.

On one of my first visits to McLellan, I got a

little lost and stumbled into a field with rocks that looked completely new, untouched and beautiful. As a dumb-dummy that didn't know any better and had no idea of the area's history, I thought that I must have been the first climber in that area. That was an amazing feeling even though it couldn't have been further from any type of truth. The feeling equipped me with a desire to explore more, to develop and seek out more of that same feeling. Our hope is for every climber to have a feeling like this when they go outside. On the other side, I have visited areas completely covered in bottles, wrappers, graffiti and even man-made structures that eliminated any feeling of discovery, excitement or exploration—substantially cheapening the experience as a whole.

As climbers, we have an obligation to help pave the way to cultivate and maintain our local recreation areas. We do this through a mindfulness, with the understanding that people have been there before us, people will be there after us, and all are entitled to that "brand new" feeling of discovery.

So that's the plea: let's all use these areas for the shared gift that they are. Let's protect them from garbage by keeping a bag in our car and packing out trash. Let's cool it with the excessive tick marks and chalk on holds you'll never use. Let's leave the earth where the earth is—if there's a tree blocking a super dope top-out, respect the tree and leave it (to be honest, it could fall over soon, anyway). Let's behave like we're not the only people out there—because we're not. We don't need music and yelling in our bouldering sessions. People out for a day hike, a mountain bike ride, or a walk with their dog are also enjoying these areas and deserve to experience it without distractions.

Last but not least, we're all in this together and things only get worse if we don't do anything. This is why the authors of this book are going in with you. **IF YOU TAKE A PICTURE OF YOUR FULL GARBAGE BAG FROM CLIMBING AREAS, WE'LL BUY YOU A BEER AS A THANK YOU. WE HOPE TO BUY A LOT OF BEER.**

Dmitri K. getting bucked on *Fat Boy Slim* Project. Photo by Serra B.

BACKGROUND

So why did we write this book anyway? Both of us (us being Nate and Shane, nice to meet you) have been climbing locally in the Eastern Washington area for over 10 years. There's often been talk that someone should write a guidebook. After years with no movement, we started documenting the rocks that we became familiar with. The project actually started as an app. A location-based app for climbers to go out to an area and see the rocks that were around them based on gps, and allowing them to document problems that would then be crowdsourced to other users. This project failed in its infancy for two reasons. The first being that the areas needing the most direction and guidance also didn't have cellular service. The user would have to constantly download the content to a phone which could be more data than the device could store. Secondly, unless we launched with a nearly complete database, the possibility for multiple postings by multiple climbers with conflicting ideas was severe. If no one did the research, it could be anyone making uneducated guesses on past ascents. After a few heated discussions over these concerns, we pivoted.

Nate L. on Proxima Nova (V3)

understand if you disagree with them.

Now let's shift back to outer space. Halley's Comet is the only periodic comet that can regularly be seen from Earth by the naked eye. It takes about 75 years for the comet to orbit around the sun, and so at least once (twice for the lucky ones) in someone's lifetime, they'll be able to look up and spot it in the night sky. I remember hearing John Green talk about Halley's comet on his podcast. In talking about revisionist history he mentioned that we don't technically know the correct name of Halley's Comet. It's been called Hallie's, Halley's, and even Holly's Comet and that's because the astronomer for whom this comet is named, spelled his own surname variously as Halley, Hallie, and Holly. I'm not one to judge because once, when I was 26 years old, I managed to lose my keys for 8 days, but regardless, I think we probably all feel confident that we can spell our names the same way each time. Anyway, the last time Halley's Comet passed by Earth was 1986. Four orbits around the sun earlier, in 1682, the astronomer Edmond Halley figured out this comet's elliptical patterns and named it after himself, correctly predicting it's repeating passes in the future. But this couldn't have been the first time Halley's Comet was seen. There's evidence that people found out about the comet over 2000 years ago. *The Talmud* references a moving star that appears once in 70 years. That's kinda the point. Humans are very quick to "discover" things that were already learned. All of this to say, while Edmond Halley was not the first to discover the comet in 1682, he did record and name the comet that we know today. Things are very similar in the bouldering system of naming and classifying rocks. While climbing itself isn't new, naming

We decided to direct our energy to the book: to comprehensively collect knowledge of the area, cross-reference the history through many, many interviews with people all over the globe that climbed here before we were born. We pieced together the best way for climbers to navigate the areas, identify the rocks, and have a base to grow from.

Is it perfect? Nope. Is it accurate? In the ways that accuracy matters, absolutely. This book will guide you to the boulders, identify them and break down the possible ways to climb them, and leave the rest up to you. Our biggest challenges are the least important. Names and grades have always been and will always be a pain point for some climbers. This book is not for that climber. If we've placed something in the book as a V5 and you are convinced it's a V4 or V6, that's okay. This is meant to be a guide for the majority rather than the granular. We've made the grades as accurate as possible based on multiple reports from different climbers. We

Mollie A. on Mollie's Run (V1)

climbs wasn't a very widespread practice for many years. Something that we now call *Voodoo Magic* was simply just called "That one V4 over there." In writing a guidebook for these rocks, we agreed that we didn't want to have any general, unknown, or vague classifications for each problem, so everything here has a name. This is done with the respectful understanding that it's possible (read: likely) that these rocks have been called something different over various generations. We've collected the most agreed upon and historic monikers to ensure that everything listed is named.

An interesting part of our very special climbing areas are the inconsistencies that time reveals. There are periods of time where groups of people or individuals will climb something followed by a "dark period" where it seems like no one visited that area. As you can imagine, this makes identifying boulders by name quite difficult. Something that was climbed once in 1979 and unnamed was then climbed in 1996 and given a name that was forgotten by the time it was climbed again in 2003 and then changed once more upon being "found" by eager, and as mentioned before, very dumb authors claiming to be some sort of "first acsenionist" in 2013 (yes, us). We've tried very hard to track down the early boulderers to make sure we got our history right and give credit where credit is due.

This turned out to be the most difficult part of the process as memories from 25 years ago aren't as exact as they once were. Also, some people critical to the growth of bouldering in the area had, understandably, no interest in returning an absurd amount of texts, emails, and phone calls. That said, both of the authors are overwhelmingly grateful for the time and the patience given by Bob Loomis, Marty Bland, George Hughbanks, Arden Pete, Adam Healy, Johnny Goicoechea, Dmitry Kalashnikov, and Drew Schick for answering a billion questions at ungodly hours. There are undoubtedly going to be some inconsistencies in names, but our goal is to respect the history, even if some of the people are long gone, passed, or don't care in the slightest what people are calling a rock. There are many gaps in what we uncovered, but we also refuse to publish a book without identifying each boulder with a name for the sake of clarity moving forward. That means

Nate L. on *Unorthodox* (V6)

everything has a name whether legitimately christened by the true first ascensionist, poached by a random kid with no knowledge of the history, or labeled en masse by two guidebook authors with no imagination and an aversion to climbing "unknown" problems. If you're reading this after noticing an error in our research, we deeply apologize and will do our best to correct anything substantial brought to our attention in a future revision. Feel free to reach out on our website at *https:/spokanebouldering.com* or shoot us an email at *spokanebouldering@gmail.com* with any praises or criticisms.

SO YOU'RE NEW TO CLIMBING, EH?

I remember one night when I met up with one of my non-climber friends at a brewery to hang out and happened to run into some people that I've climbed with a few times. We talked about climbing for a little bit and then said our goodbyes. Once it was back to just my friend and me, he said "I didn't understand any of those words you were saying back there." This is a really good point. Climbers, when talking about climbing, tend to use many words that simply don't mean anything to the layperson. This would be a terrible reading experience for someone unfamiliar with these words and terms and because we will be referencing them a lot throughout this book, we're going to list words and their meaning here to give you a key in unlocking this wacky language of "Climber-speak."

PROBLEM: This is what climbers call a named path up a short rock through some self-important sense of "solving" the potentially cryptic sequence of movements required. Despite this, we tend to ask for beta (see below) from others after no more than two attempts at climbing said problem.

SEND: To successfully complete a problem by climbing from the designated start to standing on top of the rock.

MANTEL: The precarious bit of movement required to transition from a mostly vertical part of rock to a mostly horizontal piece of rock. Much like climbing onto a counter sans stepping stool.

DROP KNEE: A technique for limber climbers where feet are placed on opposing footholds and one knee is brought inward and down along with an ever-critical subtle hip swivel. Through some phenomena of physics and black magic this ligament-threatening position can help secure you on the rock for further hand movement.

HEEL HOOK: Using your heel on a hold and engaging your hamstring to help you balance, rest, or make upward progress.

CAMPUS: The act of climbing without the use of feet. What one would do on monkey bars (Not recommend on slabby rock).

PUMP/PUMPY: The strength-sapping rush of blood to forearms that renders climbing difficult. Can at times feel debilitating.

CRIMP: A small hold. Generally something smaller than the first pad of a finger. The definition slides depending on grade, so be wary.

SLOPER: Typically a hold that is angled at less than horizontal and/or rounded.

SIDE PULL: Fairly straightforward, this is a sideways-facing hold that faces away from the center of your body usually grabbed thumb up.

GASTON: Not clear in name at all, this is a sideways-facing hold that faces towards the center of your body. Used with thumb down. Imagine opening a pair of sliding doors simultaneously.

EDGE: A flat hold somewhere between a crimp and a jug. Typically flat (horizontal).

JUG: A large hold typically incut (better than horizontal). Definition of jug varies with the difficulty of a climb.

SMEAR: A foot technique where the heel is dropped and as much of the bottom of the shoe as possible is pressed into the rock. This relies on rock texture and stickiness of rubber, rather than a conventional hold to stand on.

SPOT: The act of standing ready below a climber to ensure when they fall they land on the pad, and do not do so head first. Keeping fingers together is best for your digit health (Spoons not forks!).

BETA: The sequence of movement for hands and feet used to climb a problem. This varies considerably from person to person depending on many physical characteristics. Don't let anyone tell you that you used the wrong beta. Beta is subjective. Unless it involves a drop knee, then it clearly is the superior beta, while campusing is the worst. We jest (but seriously though).

SLAB(BY): Any rock that is less than vertical.

STEEP: Vertical is not steep. Once a rock achieves an overhung state, it can then be called steep.

CHOSS: Rock that is crumbly. Also used loosely to describe rock that is not good in some way.

SPOKANE BOULDERING | 17

HOW TO USE

A sample spread from inside the guide.

HOW DOES THIS BOOK WORK?

This book is broken up into six chapters, one for each area. Each chapter starts with a little bit about the area, a donut chart breakdown of the quantity of climbs by grade, and a map of the area or zone.

The book proceeds through each problem numerically, starting over for each chapter. The title for each climb includes its number, name, grade, and star rating. The number correlates to the maps as well as lined pictures of the rocks indicating problem location and general path. The V-grade designates (subjectively) how difficult the problem is to complete.

The V scale is the most common North American way to grade difficulty. Grades range from V0 for very easy (think climbing a stone ladder) up to V17 (the hardest climb in Spokane maxes at 12, so no sweat). The higher the V, the more difficult the climb will be. These numbers are subjective with many variables and factors that need to be considered. Weather, height, preference, style, and how many Oreos you ate on the approach can all affect how difficult a climb may feel on

any given day (we find three Oreos to be best, two if double-stuff). If you climb a V3, there are some V4s that you'll be able to climb and some V2s may seem impossible. That's just the way it goes, so don't put too much weight into the grades.

After the name and V-grade you'll see a Star Rating Scale. This Star Rating Scale starts at one star signifying "This is a Good Climb, you should do it if you're close," and goes up to three stars indicating "This is one of the best climbs and cannot be missed." Ratings are based on movement, hold quality, location, aesthetics, and sometimes landing (along with a possible pinch of personal cognitive bias).

You'll see a little checkbox next to each problem name, as well. This is for you to keep track and record your progress through the area if you're into that sort of thing.

Alright I think that's everything, let's go climb.

18 | INTRODUCTION

Romancing the Stone overlooking the Spokane River and Tum Tum.

SPOKANE BOULDERING BY DIFFICULTY

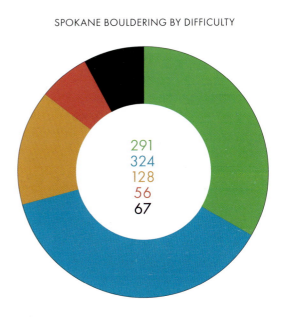

291
324
128
56
67

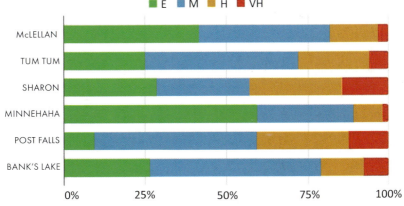

SPOKANE BOULDERING | 19

BEST OF...

V0

- **WALLFLOWER** ★★ THE COMMONS
- **ROOKIE MOVE** ★★ THE GLEN
- **MANDIBLE MANTEL** ★★★ LOST AND FOUND
- **JENGA** ★★ DAVE'S GRAVEL

V1

- **THE TRAVERSE** ★★ MINNEHAHA PARK
- **MR. WHO** ★★ IVY AREA
- **MADE IN THE MANOR** ★★★ CORKSCREW CANYON
- **GREEN CRACK** ★★ DAVE'S GRAVEL
- **CLASSIC CORNER** ★★★ NORTHRUP CANYON

V2

- **TWO TIERED TO FINISH** ★★★ THE GLEN
- **QUEEN FOR QUEEN** ★★★ THE GLEN
- **SUNNY D** ★★★ THE HOOD
- **SUMMER OF 69** ★★ DAVE'S GRAVEL

V3

- **ROMAINE** ★★★ THE HOOD
- **REASONABLE DOUBT** ★★ THE GLEN
- **PROXIMA NOVA** ★★★ UPPER WEST END
- **PROPAGANDA** ★★★ DAVE'S GRAVEL
- **McLOVE HANDLES** ★★★ LOST AND FOUND

V4

- **VOODOO MAGIC** ★★★ LOST AND FOUND
- **THE MOLAR RIGHT** ★★★ LOST AND FOUND
- **THRUTCHY MADNESS** ★★★ LOWER WEST END
- **THE OGRE** ★★ THE GLEN
- **SALIVATE** ★★★ SPILLWAY

V5

- **WIDOWMAKER** ★★★ UPPER WEST END
- **TOP BOY** ★★★ CORKSCREW CANYON
- **THE LEGEND OF RED O'KELLEY** ★★★ CRAIGLANDIA
- **SCARLETT JOHANSSON** ★★★ THE HOOD
- **LIGHTWORK** ★★ THE GLEN

V6

- **THE PROW** ★★★ LOWER WEST END
- **SMOKEY'S** ★★★ MINNEHAHA PARK
- **MOTHER LOVER** ★★★ BEACON HILL
- **FRANKLINE** ★★★ THE HOOD
- **ARDEN'S MIDDLE FINGER OF FURY** ★★★ THE GLEN

V7

- **FAIRWINDS** ★★★ IVY AREA
- **CARVER** ★★★ THE COMMONS
- **BAIT AND SWITCH** ★★★ THE COMMONS
- **BIG DIPPER** ★★ THE HOOD

V8

- **WAHEELA** ★★★ FERN GULLIES
- **PAPA TORTILLA** ★★★ HIGHWAY ROCK BOULDERS
- **FEROCIOUS FRED** ★★★ THE COMMONS
- **COLLECTIVE MIND** ★★★ LOWER WEST END

V9

- **MR. WENZEL** ★★★ THE COMMONS
- **CRIME OF PASSION** ★★★ THE COMMONS
- **HEARTBREAKER** ★★★ HEARTBREAKER
- **DEADLINE (EPIC ARÊTE)** ★★★ IVY AREA
- **CATCHING FEELINGS** ★★★ THE GLEN

V10

- **THE SPADE** ★★ UPPER WEST END
- **NEW WAVE ROOKIE** ★★ IVY AREA
- **A HORSE WITH NO NAME** ★★ NORTHRUP CANYON

V11

- **LOVE TAKER** ★★ HEARTBREAKER
- **ELEVATION** ★★ NORTHRUP CANYON

V12

- **THE ELITIST** ★★★ UPPER WEST END

McLELLAN

Kristin W. on Queen for Queen (V2).
Photo by Ben Boldt

McLELLAN

An aerial view of McLellan showcases a handful of tidy-looking sun-exposed mounds of granite sprawling southwest from the Spokane River. On the ground level and surrounded by these rocks, you're met with apparently endless corridors, gullies, meadows, and plateaus with panoramic vistas over the river.

Honestly, our first time (and many times after) at McLellan we became quite turned around and lost—a common event among most climbers that have visited the area. Once you become more familiar, the looming walls on either side have a way of popping you right back out into a familiar area as soon as you feel on the brink of discovery. With a sense of adventure and a spirit of exploration, the navigation becomes less complicated.

Once you take to the "trails" and head into the rocks and canyons, the terrain is quite refreshing and meandering. Much different from its across-the-river neighbor Tum Tum, most of the areas are relatively flat and accessible with a smattering of small hills. For what this area offers in a pleasant roaming experience, it demands in other areas. Most notably, the condition of the rock in McLellan is akin to your laundry. You clean it, you use it, you leave it, and if you want to use it again, you'll likely need to clean it again. In short, this rock can get dirty. Essentially, this rock can become covered in ostensibly adhesive lichen and delaminating evergreen moss in less time than it takes to say the words "ostensibly" and "delaminating." This is in no way meant to be a deterrent for you to climb in McLellan. Even with the necessary cleaning involved (seriously, bring brushes), McLellan is an outstanding area close to Spokane with a considerable number of quality and enjoyable problems.

McLellan boasts an interesting and diversified landscape. From the tall, vertical faces covered in silvery lines of bolts at the sport climbing crags to the bulging elephant-sized boulders peeking throughout the needle- and pinecone-covered woods, climbers of all abilities will be able to find a problem or a rock that matches their style, sending them home with a smile on their face.

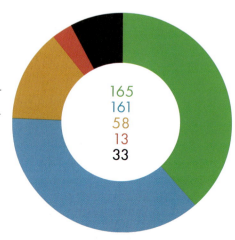

165
161
58
13
33

22 | McLELLAN

DRIVING DIRECTIONS

Probably the most useless part of a guidebook being published in 2022 are detailed instructions on how to get to a large state park when you could just type "Fisk State Park" in your navigation app and have exact directions to the large parking lot, but we're going to do this anyway.

First, just to be exact, coordinates for parking are expressed as QR codes to pin-point their position. If you're driving from Spokane, take a left at the 9 Mile Dam off Nine Mile Road onto Charles Road. Five miles after the dam, take a left onto South Bank Road. About four miles down this road, keep an eye out on your right side for a yellow spray-painted smiley face rock welcoming you to the McLellan Area. This road will turn into a gravel road about three miles down. At 12.9 miles from the dam, you'll be at the Ivy Area. You can park on the side of the road at the Discovery Pass sign. At 13.2 miles, you'll see the entrance to the "Fisk Day Use Area." Warm up those fingers, it's bouldering time!

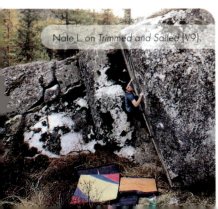

SPOKANE BOULDERING | 23

ARDEN'S McLELLAN CIRCUIT

My favorite climbing circuit features safe landings, plenty of traverses, plenty of vertical gain, scary stuff, not scary stuff, the best crack in Spokane, hard slabs, and is close enough to the car to observe it being burgled. Enjoy!

START IN THE COMMONS

- ☐ Mantel Wall - at least 6 variations + the lip traverse
- ☐ *The Evolving Nature of Flakes* - downclimb the 5.8 dihedral
- ☐ Warm-Up Wall
- ☐ *Layback Dihedral*
- ☐ *Golden Ratio*
- ☐ Traverse left to right from the back of Head Wound Cave - finish by topping out the prow, walking off right. Cross the road.
- ☐ *Party Animal, The Triangle, Party Rock*
- ☐ Cross the road again to *Saintly Sam.*
- ☐ Cross road again, climb The Diamond Slab up 5 feet, move left to blunt arête, thrutch to top. Downclimb the right edge of Diamond Slab, back to center.
- ☐ Attempt the center of Diamond Slab without using either side arêtes.
- ☐ Foot slips one move from the top, slide down entire slab, hit pad, and tumble into bushes.
- ☐ Tape up and jam the *Best Crack in Spokane.*
- ☐ Attempt to get feet off the ground on north end of Best Crack boulder for the Nth time - fail. "I'M A HORRIBLE CLIMBER WHY IS THIS SO HARD?!"
- ☐ Walk back across road, do *Forbidden Bucket* with the cheat-stone start (or do it without the stone but I've not been able to yet). Downclimb 5.8 Dihedral.
- ☐ *Crime of Passion*
- ☐ Walk right, climb up the sport climb that Steve Moss soloed.
- ☐ Downclimb same route because that topout looks dicey. Steve is a god!
- ☐ Go through the notch to this climb's right do *Soul Shine, Soulstice,* and *The War Room* on your way to...
- ☐ *Middle Finger of Fury*
- ☐ Go through Hallway of Impossibles into The Glen counter-clockwise beginning with *Hot Rod Banana.*
- ☐ Unnamed Climb either topping out through moss or horseshoe (up over back down)
- ☐ Go to other side of The Glen, doing another horseshoe underneath the hard sport climb in *Cakes and Ales.*
- ☐ Ascend out of the back of the Glen to *Two Tiered to Finish.*

Arden Pete
Photo by Jon Jonckers

- ☐ *Two Stories*
- ☐ Walk behind *2 Tiered* into Found Wall gully/canyon, Climb the 3 climbs on The Molar.
- ☐ Topout 4 Fathom Wall, just right of the Molar.
- ☐ *Rest at the Y*
- ☐ *Voodoo Magic*
- ☐ Attempt to Climb the right side of Highball Slab Project - the 25' techy slab towards the Sunshine Wall.
- ☐ Get to the top, look down at my one pad and no friends spotting me, give half-ass attempt at the top, jump to my pad and roll off the edge. "Why am I such a coward? Why am I too cheap to have a second pad? I hate me! This slab is hot and I'm out of water, I have to run back to the parking to get more water. I suck!"
- ☐ Towards The Hood, stopping to do the run start and some other stuff in the sunny open area of the Sunshine Wall.
- ☐ Climb the fun problem *Romaine* to the right in the notch past the boulder.
- ☐ Dropping into The Hood, turn left to *Scar Jo* and *Always Climb Up.*
- ☐ Climb the handcrack further up the hallway. Downclimb the chimney behind it.
- ☐ Head down The Hood to the pond and climb *New American Classic* and *Zulu Princess* heading towards the *69YOT.*
- ☐ Climb many good ups on either end of the *69YOT.*
- ☐ *The 69 Year Old Traverse.*
- ☐ *Tara* downhill and left of *69YOT.*
- ☐ Play on the High Times Wall. On your way out of the park, stop in The Ivy Area and play around.

Congratulations! You've completed Arden's McLellan circuit!

24 | McLELLAN

George Hughbanks

CIRCUITS

GEORGE'S McLELLAN CIRCUIT

We'll break up these circuits based on where you're starting and what zones you'll be in. So for this first circuit let's say you're parking in the main parking lot.

- ☐ Hit the trail and start in Dave's Gravel—do a little warming up in the Larry Peterman Area.
- ☐ I always hit the arête on The Propaganda Boulder—a great V3 and a great way to start the day.
- ☐ *Pipedream*
- ☐ Go down into the canyon towards Pack Rat Cave but cut through a small notch to get to *Degradation*.
- ☐ Drop down into Highway 69 and start with the *69 Year Old Traverse* then you can just play around here and get as many ups as you can.
- ☐ Finish out Highway 69 with some hand jams on *Zulu Princess*.
- ☐ Once the back of your hands are good and bloodied, head down to hit *New American Classic* and test the skin on your fingers.
- ☐ Traverse the pond and do the couple problems on The Fungus Wall.
- ☐ Everything on the Chessboard Wall
- ☐ *Flushing a Dead Rooster*

For the second circuit, let's say you're parking or starting from the upper road in The Commons.

For this circuit:

- ☐ Start at Angry Beaver and knock all of these out real quick.
- ☐ Wallflower Rock—do all of these problems except the traverse under the tree, you can skip that if you want. This arête is one of my all time favorites!
- ☐ *Saintly Sam* with the sit-down start
- ☐ Cut up in the notch to hit The War Room problems and *Soulstice*.
- ☐ Do some ups downs in the Hall of the Impossibles.
- ☐ *Run the Jewels*
- ☐ *Two-Tiered to Finish*
- ☐ Cut past the corner of *Two Tiered* and drop to *Voodoo Magic*.
- ☐ Finish out and cool down on Calder's Car Chase rock. Nice work! Now let your arms rest for a bit and take a deserved break.

Congratulations! You've completed George's McLellan Circuits!

SPOKANE BOULDERING | 25

IVY AREA

Entrance Boulder: **1-3**
George's Slab: **4-5**
Deadline / Ivy Arête: **6-11**
Eyebrows and Anus: **12-15**
Emancipation / Retrograde: **16-18**
Mr. Who / The Cube: **19-24**
Huevos Rancheros: **25**
Nazca to Gaza / Ivy League: **26-28**
La Diosa: **29-32**
CHet and CHoulders: **33-34**
Planted: **35**
Order 66: **36-38**
Admiral Thrawn: **39-40**
Lightning Bolt: **41-42**
Tenebrous: **43-44**
Dedos Técnicos: **45-46**
Lakeside Boulders: **47**
Big Boi: **48-49**
Fairwinds: **50-56**
Square's Pace: **57-59**
The Lid / The Louvre: **60-63**
Hello Shorty: **64-65**

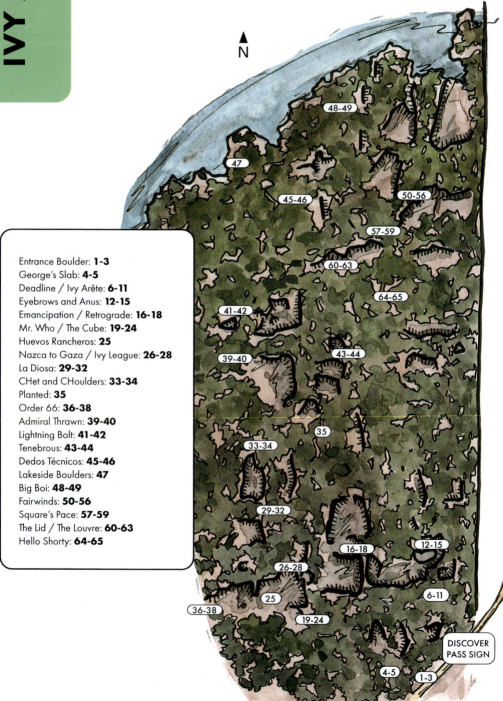

26 | McLELLAN

IVY AREA

Ivy Area Parking

DON'T WORRY: this place isn't named for poison oak in the area—it was first discovered and developed by Arden after his daughter was born and affectionately named after her. The Ivy Area is full of gems and is typically less traveled than it's Cove neighbor. While we have a lot of problems listed here, it's far from comprehensive. Some honorable mentions that aren't listed include a massive rock to the north of Fairwinds that holds some fun-looking highballs, the lakeside boulders that are a bit of a mystery, a hard-looking project with a terrible landing just below *Lightning Bolt*, a scoopy dihedral-looking tall boy right next to that, a few more climbs on the Dedos Técnicos Wall, more highballs on the Big Boi Boulder and a couple other smaller rocks nearby. While this is a zone with a lot of potential, there are amazing established lines here like the testpiece Deadline (Epic Arête), the always fun Ocean Spray, Admiral Thrawn, The Lid and the stunning Fairwinds. The Ivy Area will provide countless hours of smiles and sends and doesn't disappoint.

ENTRANCE BOULDER

☐ **1. WELCOME TO McLELLAN V1**
Visible immediately off the road from the Discover Pass Sign, this rock is just the beginning. Start this problem on the leftish side of the rock with great lie-back moves to catch the top. Welcome to McLellan.

☐ **2. ENTRANCE RIGHT V1**
You can find this short problem with a couple of fun holds on the right side of the rock.

☐ **3. ENTRANCE CRUISER V1** (NOT PICTURED)
On the back side of Entrance Boulder a shelf with great jugs going up and right serves for a fantastic good time.

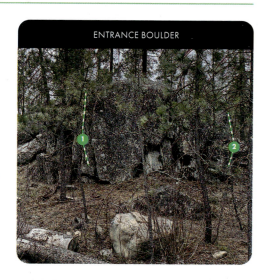
ENTRANCE BOULDER

GEORGE'S SLAB

☐ **4. GEORGE'S SLAB V1 ★★**
You'll find *George's Slab* directly behind and to the north of the entrance boulder. The line trends left up the slabby face. Great moves and super charming.

☐ **5. CORNER HUG V2 ★**
Start low hugging the arête and balance up the blunt arête. Enjoyable and roadside...nothing better!

GEORGE'S SLAB

SPOKANE BOULDERING | 27

Nate L. on New Wave Rookie (V10).

EPIC ARÊTE

☐ 6. SMEG-A-SQUEEZE V8
Start from a sitting position squeezing the fridge-size block. Climb up large blocks to a bit of groveling in a crack to a high finish. Grade unconfirmed.

☐ 7. NEW WAVE ROOKIE V10 ★ ★
Situated on the rock platform, start with hands on crimps in the seam with the bulge out right for feet. Move right and up into the business. Really good movement, and the fall is nowhere as bad as it looks. Trust us. Busting left into a crimp rail from the mid point is an undone alternate variation.
FA Zak Silver

☐ 8. DEADLINE (EPIC ARÊTE) V9 ★ ★ ★
Begin matched on the obvious flat jug. Climb up the proud dual arêtes to a commiting final move. Ultra classic.
FA Alex Fritz

☐ 9. THE SICKLE V5 ★
Left-hand edge, right hand low. Climb up through the crescent rail and over the rounded lip using a bit of magic.

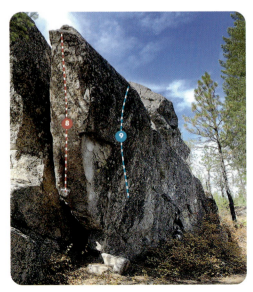

28 | McLELLAN

IVY ARÊTE

☐ **10. VIRGINIA CREEPER V1** ★
Climb the mid-angle slab left of *Ivy Arête*. Might need a brush in one hand for this...
FA Arden Pete

☐ **11. IVY ARÊTE V1** ★★
Climb the obvious tall feature from a stand start. Watch your back for the tree... In case you wanna lean onto it for a rest, that's kosher.
FA Arden Pete

EYEBROWS AND ANUS

☐ **12. TABLE SAW V7**
From a stand start on thin crimps, move right into the crack. Unconfirmed.
FA George Hughbanks

☐ **13. TRIMMED AND SOILED V9** ★★
The sit start to *Eyebrows and Anus*. Start sitting matched on the left-facing crimp rail. Pro Tip: bring your horse butt for this one.
FA Steve Moss

☐ **14. EYEBROWS AND ANUS V8** ★★
Start standing with a small left-hand crimp and a right hand sloper around the corner, climb up to good incuts, a bad pinch, a lunge for the crack, and a slap to the lip—not necessarily in that order.
FA Nate Lynch

IVY ARÊTE

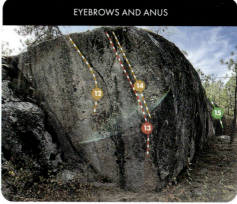

EYEBROWS AND ANUS

Penn B. on *Eyebrows and Anus* (V8).

☐ **15. SAM EAGLE V2** ★
Start this climb in the crack on excellent rock, past the right arête of *Eyebrows and Anus*. Move up into balancy moves on the slab.
FA George Hughbanks

SPOKANE BOULDERING | 29

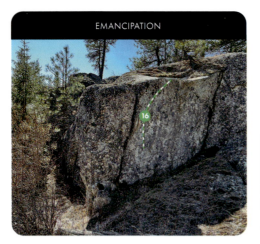

EMANCIPATION

☐ 16. EMANCIPATION V1
Start with the left hand in the crack and the right hand on a small crimp, pop up to the lip and mantel.

☐ 17. EMANCIPATION CORNER V0 (NOT PICTURED)
The opposite side of the crack on *Emancipation* offers a perfect lie-back crack to follow.

RETROGRADE

☐ 18. RETROGRADE V1 ★★
The rock you see when you top out *Emancipation*. Start crouched low on the right side and use the edges trending up left to a great finish—kinda wish this was bigger and longer because it's so good.

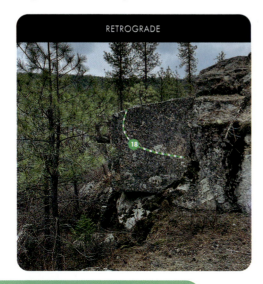

MR. WHO

☐ 19. MR. WHO V1 ★★
Just to the west of The Cube Boulder down the trail is where you'll find this one. Named after the owl that resides in a nearby tree, this problem is a hoot. Add to the "do not skip" list.

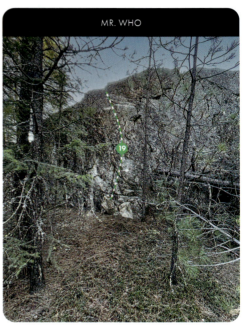

THE CUBE

☐ 20. OCEAN SPRAY V3 ★★★ (NOT PICTURED)
The southern arête of The Cube. Stand start on opposing chest-high holds and head up and right along the spine. Top of the "do not skip" list.
FA George Hughbanks

☐ 21. CUBIC ZIRCONIA V2
On the corner adjacent to the tree, start below the shelf features and make your way up and left through the tree.

☐ **22. GLEAMING THE CUBE V2**
★★
Start as you would for *Cubic Zirconia* and trend right in the seam and wrap it around.

☐ **23. THE CUBICLE V3**
Start on the right side of the front face in the little mouth thingy, using the seam to get to large slopey holds to perch on and continue up. You may want a shirt for the top-out.

☐ **24. GEORGE CUBEBANKS V2**
Slab on the right face of The Cube.

HUEVOS RANCHEROS

☐ **25. HUEVOS RANCHEROS V7** ★
Begin with a head-height left-hand finger lock and a right hand sidepull in the center of the overhang. Move rightward into a good sidepull. From there, trend farther right to top out. Watch out for the detached block at your side.
FA Nate Lynch

NAZCA TO GAZA

☐ **26. NAZCA TO GAZA V2**
Stand start on the corner with two decent neck-highish holds. Trend right and then move up into the broken feature.
FA George Hughbanks

THE CUBE

HUEVOS RANCHEROS

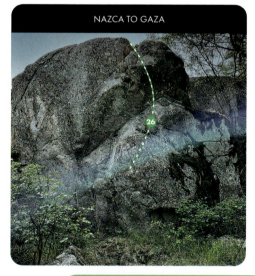

NAZCA TO GAZA

SPOKANE BOULDERING | 31

Alex N. on Huevos Rancheros (V7).

IVY LEAGUE

☐ **27. IVY CREST V3**
Start on the left side on the rock crouched on the low horn, use the bulge face to gain the top.
FA Shane Collins

☐ **28. IVY LEAGUE V2** ★★
Sit start/hug start. Use fun holds and a high crimp to get the slopey top.

LA DIOSA

☐ **29. EGGS ON PLATES V1** ★
Commence on the leftmost side of the wall and follow good jugs up and right to a thin and concerning top.

☐ **30. THE GOD PROJECT**
Middle of the rock with the tree to your back. Tall and seemingly delicate. Looks sick.

☐ **31. LA DIOSA V6** ★★★
Compressing with a good chest-high left sidepull and a slightly lower right hand pinch, use nice sidepulls and incut crimps to gain the finishing jug directly above the start. Take off a grade or two for an early exit right with more hold options.

☐ **32. BEBE STEPS V1**
Typically dirty. Many juggy steps on the right side of the rock.

CHED AND CHOULDERS

☐ **33. THE CHED ARÊTE V3** ★
Sit start under the arête and use good incut holds and some interesting footwork to top the highest point.
FA Shane Collins

☐ **34. THE CHOULDER V1**
Same start as *CHed* but instead of staying under and on the arête, move out right to the face and top in the center of the rock.
FA Shane Collins

SPOKANE BOULDERING | 33

Mollie A. Admiral Thrawn Var. (V2)

PLANTED (NOT PICTURED)

☐ **35. PLANTED V4**
Start crouched in the small open section of rock between two trees with a high left hand and low right hand. Reportedly easy for the grade (depending on how the top goes for you).

ORDER 66

☐ **36. ORDER 66 PROJECT** (NOT PICTURED)
This is a terrifying rock that somebody will inevitably try to climb. We hope that all flailers do not get impaled by the staggering granite point in the landing zone. But hey, if you don't flail you may send a prime piece of stone.

☐ **37. CAPTAIN PHASMA V1**
At the end of the corridor, on the north-facing rocky band, this is the crumbly looking corner. Be careful pulling on these jugs, they might just like...pop off.

☐ **38. THE RANCOR V4**
Start matched on the right-facing sidepull. Bust over to the farthest right seam, move up more seams into a committing bump up to the lip.

ORDER 66

34 | McLELLAN

ADMIRAL THRAWN

☐ 39. ADMIRAL THRAWN V5 ★ ★ ★
From the left end of the shelf, climb up and right. Proceed in compression up the prow. The right side can also be climbed at V2.
FA Shane Collins

☐ 40. BLUE FACE WALL (NOT PICTURED)
A few easy climbs just above the admiral are fun to play on, but rarely climbed.

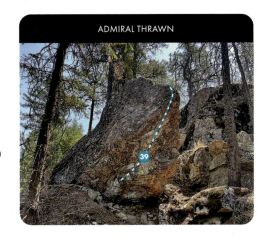

LIGHTNING BOLT

☐ 41. LIGHTNING BOLT V2 ★ ★
Start on the right side matched on the low bulgey thing. Make a few small and delicate moves out left following the seams and top out at the end of the upper seam.

☐ 42. SHEEV V3
Same start as *Lightning Bolt*, but head right on the slopey lip. Move left using the slopers until you think you can rock over.

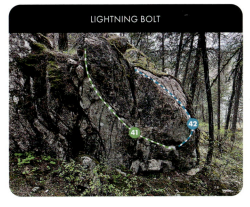

TENEBROUS

☐ 43. TENEBROUS V4 ★ ★
Climb incut edges from a low start in the steep overhang. Good fun.

CHIMERA

☐ 44. CHIMERA V3 ★
Climb the small trailside overhang (sit-down start) into an engaging mantel.

SPOKANE BOULDERING | 35

DEDOS TÉCNICOS

☐ **45. DEDOS TÉCNICOS V3** ★ ★ ★
Start low with right hand in the crook of the right arête and left-hand a touch higher on the left arête. A bit cryptic, but not too difficult once deciphered.

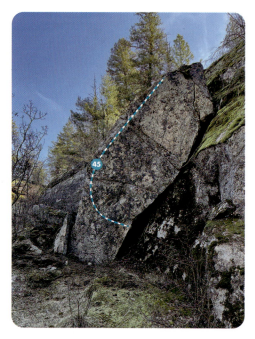

☐ **46. TREMBLE PART 2 PROJECT** (NOT PICTURED)
There are a few lines just around the corner from Dedos. The most obvious possible line with an "uneven" landing looks tough but fun.

LAKESIDE BOULDERS (NOT PICTURED)

☐ **47. LAKESIDE BOULDERS**
The Lakeside boulders are nestled under Dedos Técnicos near the water—this would be a great chill spot to kick it on hot day and an even better spot for someone to bolt that line above the water.

BIG BOI

☐ **48. THE BIG BOI PROJECT** (NOT PICTURED)
Tall face within eyesight of *Perfect*.

☐ **49. PERFECT V1** ★ ★ ★
Start as low as you can on the left side of the dirty crack. Use great big holds and trend up and right.

PERFECT

FAIRWINDS

☐ **50. SHEPARD AND FLOCK PROJECT**
Climb the slightly overhung thin face just left of *Crosswinds*.

☐ **51. CROSSWINDS V6** ★
Start on the left end of the low seam. Move up and right on decent holds into a cruxy finish on toothy pockets.

☐ **52. FAIRWINDS V7** ★ ★ ★
Start left-hand sidepull, right hand undercling. Move up the corner on good edges into a harder move up high. Classic.

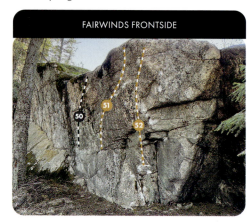

FAIRWINDS FRONTSIDE

36 | McLELLAN

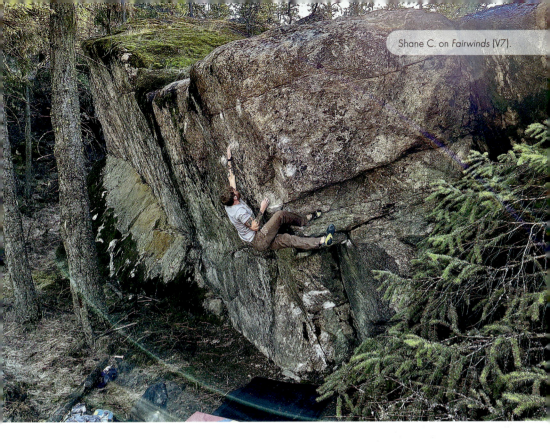

Shane C. on *Fairwinds* (V7).

☐ 53. DIG DUGGED V8 ★ ★ ★
Sit start on the low flat hold. Move up crimps on the arête with a cruxy fall-in move. Fun compression and easy to work.

☐ 54. BREAKING WIND V5 ★
Start low on the obvious incuts. Bust up to thin holds and jugs above.

☐ 55. HEADWINDS V5 ★ ★
Sit start on the low shelf, move into a flake and slot the crack above. It's not over 'til it's over.

☐ 56. TAILWINDS V2 ★
Start with right hand sidepull and left-hand edge in an odd crouch. Pop for the rounded lip above... there is more to do so keep going.
FA Shane Collins

FAIRWINDS BACKSIDE

SPOKANE BOULDERING | 37

Shane C. on *Shark Wrestle* (V4)

SQUARE'S PACE

☐ 57. SQUARE'S PACE LEFT V2
To the left of *KD*, start under the bulgey shield thing with a left-hand undercling and low right hand crimp in the vertical seam and make your way up. By the time you're reading this it's incredibly possible that the flake we're calling the shield is long gone and broken off. If that's the case, hello future!

☐ 58. KEVIN DURANT IS NICE V2
Located just south of the beautiful Fairwinds boulder. If you top out *Fairwinds* you'll see it to your left—two problems on a shelf. Mostly dirty and shunned in the shadow of much nicer rock, this slab follows a neat little seam and just like Kevin Durant...is nice.

SQUARE'S PACE

☐ 59. SHARK WRESTLE V4 ★ (ACTION SHOT ONLY)
Just up the hill from Fairwinds and on the hilly slope sits this delicate climb. Commence all the way right with the tree by your shoulder and a lower-than-you-want left-hand crimp, and chest-high right hand pinch. Balance all the way left with scrunchy and smeary feet to the V-shaped fin with a left-hand sidepull. Using the fin, a crimp on the face, and bad feet, burst to the top and hope.
FA Shane Collins

THE LID

☐ **60. THE LID V2 ★★**

Topping out *Shark Wrestle*, you'll see an interesting-looking rock about a stone's throw ahead of you. Start crouched and pop to the lid feature. Fun!

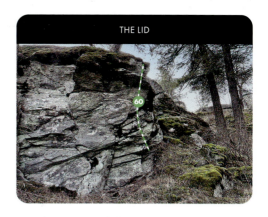

THE LID

THE LOUVRE

☐ **61. DOWN THE BACK V1**

The slab on the left face. Start with a right hand on the arête and a left hand at the bottom of the crescent moon thingy. Wiggle yourself onto the slab and cruise it.

☐ **62. BUT WHO CARES V3**

Not as thuggish as it looks... Should put a smile on your face (that may change to concern while pulling the mantel).

☐ **63. STILL THE LOUVRE V3**

Start with a low left-hand crimp on the face and the right hand on a very small and flexy crimp. Use some great holds to go straight up to the lip...again, the top could be troublesome.

THE LOUVRE

HELLO SHORTY

☐ **64. HELLO SHORTY V2**

Start sitting with left hand in a crack and a good right hand. Move up and then right into the small roof.

☐ **65. GET SHORTY V1**

Climb the corner to the right of *Hello Shorty*.

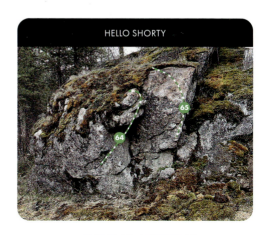

HELLO SHORTY

SPOKANE BOULDERING | 39

DAVE'S GRAVEL

The Larry Peterman Boulder: **1-5**
Corner Store: **6-11**
Submarine Boulder: **12-15**
Propaganda: **16-18**
Bold School: **19-21**
Pipe Dream: **22-26**
Nine Mile Balls / Final Stanza: **27-32**
Top Tier: **33-35**
Paws then Claws: **36**
Tomato Tutu: **37**
Game Over / Space Jam / Prostor's Wall: **38-49**
Kitty Litter: **50-51**
Tara's Wall: **52-56**
Pineapple Pizza / Pinch Project: **57-59**
Highway 69: **60-75**
The Bulge: **76-80**
The Classic: **81-83**
The Pack Rat Cave: **84-87**
High Times Wall: **88-93**

DAVE'S GRAVEL

Named after Dave Stephens—one of the first climbers to start wrestling these pebbles back in the 1960s and who first published a map of the area in 2006. These are the first rocks you'll see in the main parking lots and serve as a sort of entrance to McLellan. Dave's Gravel holds terrific lines like *Bold School, Tara* and the entirety of the long corridor of Highway 69. It also hides the towering overhang that innervates the loins of local strong sport climbers—the always impressive Pack Rat Cave.

LARRY PETERMAN BOULDER

LARRY PETERMAN BOULDER

1. DS STORE V0
Stand/hop start to the edge with the small tree growing out of it. Awkwardly pull up using dirty crimps to top out left. Not the best climb out here, but likely not the worst.
FA David Stephens

2. LARRY'S LEFT HANG V4 ★
Start on the large jug on the left edge of the small roof. Climb up just left of the overhang with a big reach or two.
FA Larry Peterman

3. THE LARRY PETERMAN PROJECT V4 ★★
Start on a flat hip-high jug under the small roof. Power over the bulge with some commiting moves. VARIATION: Start as for *Larry's Left Hang* and traverse into the *Larry Peterman Project*.
FA Larry Peterman

4. PROJECT
Possible project starting on a slopey right hand deep on the right side of the bulge.

5. JENGA V0 ★★
More stable than the name implies, this stack of rocks is an excellent warmup or first boulder problem.
FA Larry Peterman

SPOKANE BOULDERING | 41

CORNER STORE

CORNER STORE

☐ 6. BOWLING BALL V2 ★
Left of *Lil Lip*, start practically lying down with wide opposing sidepulls. Ridiculous, you say? So is your mom (a foot hold broke making this potentially more difficult.)
FA Dan Taylor

☐ 7. LIL LIP LEFT V2 ★
Starting in big flat seam, crank with a high heel or foot to a good crimp in the face of the slab. Adventure seekers continue up, but be warned, it's more lichen than holds. Otherwise, pull your body left and out.

☐ 8. UP FIRST V1 ★
Starting crouched on two underclings on the right hand side, make a move to the cut in the middle of the face to gain the good seam over the lip.

☐ 9. SHAKE SPEAR V3 ★ ★
Starting with sidepulls on either side of the large horn, use good crimps and pinches to pop to a good flat block in the dihedral. Shorter people (like one of the authors) will need to commit to the pop.
FA David Stephens

☐ 10. SOCO AMARETTO LIME V2 ★
Start to the left of *Corner Store* and climb the seam using some balancey gastony action.

☐ 11. CORNER STORE V3 ★ ★ ★
Start standing on opposing sidepulls and sloth to the top in compression. Quite good.
FA Larry Peterman

SUBMARINE BOULDER

SUBMARINE BOULDER

☐ **12. SILENT STEEL V5** ★
Magic your way up the face from a low laydown start on the crimp rail. A lot more fun than it is tall...and it's not very tall.
FA Nate Lynch

☐ **13. RED OCTOBER V3** ★
Make some scrunchy moves from the V-notch and top out.
FA Shane Collins

☐ **14. YELLOW SUBMARINE V2**
Start matched-ish in the pod and follow the seam to the left.

☐ **15. OBELIDEAR V0** ★
Around the corner from *Yellow Sub*, surf the giant holds up and right and top out near the tree.

SPOKANE BOULDERING | 43

PROPAGANDA

☐ **16. PROPAGANDA LEFT V4**
Start hugging the blunt arête with a solid foot. Inch your way to a good hold higher on the vert face and finish it.

☐ **17. PROPAGANDA PROJECT**
Stab for a crimp in the seam at the 8 ft level from your choice of underclings and sidepulls. From there, levitate your way to the lip. Going to be stout.

☐ **18. PROPAGANDA V3 ★★★**
From a stand start on a left-hand undercling and a good right edge, proceed up fun holds and good movement. Instant classic.

Jeremy C. on *Propaganda* (V3).

BOLD SCHOOL

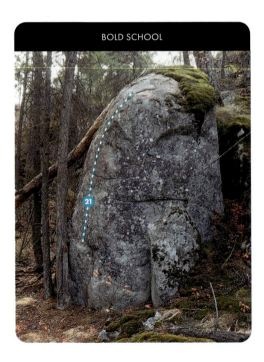

☐ **19. MY FORGOTTEN MAN V1 ★** (NOT PICTURED)
Slab left of the fallen tree. Follow the left-facing (dirty) rail.

☐ **20. 7 LITTLE LIES V4 ★** (NOT PICTURED)
Slab right of the fallen tree.

☐ **21. BOLD SCHOOL V3 ★★**
Start on a chest-high left undercling and a right crimp up to good edges. Don't look down. Top out over the high point.
FA David Stephens

44 | McLELLAN

PIPE DREAM

☐ **22. PIPE DREAM WARMUP V0** (NOT PICTURED)
The small block in front of *Pipe Dream*. Nice to hang on.
FA Larry Peterman

☐ **23. PIPE DREAM ARÊTE PROJECT**
The arête left of *Pipe Dream* was a V5, but has since had a key sidepull and foot break. It will likely still go, but is much harder.

☐ **24. PIPE DREAM V5** ★★
Start at the lowest right end of the angled seam. Follow the seam left with fun moves into a trickier final section.
FA Nick Tansy

☐ **25. PIPE DREAM DIRECT V7** ★★
Start as for *Pipe Dream*. Move right to a distant rounded crimp and continue up. Bring your full wing span for this one.
FA Bryan Franklin

☐ **26. BOWL OF DREAMS V1** ★ (NOT PICTURED)
Start pressed in the scoop, tech up to the lip, and exit left.

Bryan C. on *Pipe Dream* (V5).

NINE MILE BALLS

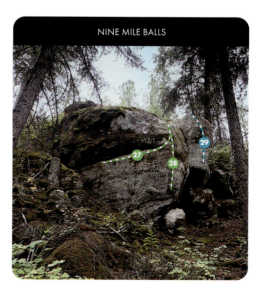

☐ **27. NINE MILE BALLS V2** ★
From the left, traverse through the big seam to the corner and then go up.
FA David Stephens

☐ **28. THE HALFWAY POINT OF NINE MILES BALLS V1**
Start on good holds about head height if you're tall. If you're short, make your way to the good holds somehow. Then climb straight up.
FA Tara Hamm

☐ **29. HOT AND HEAVY V5**
Compress up the detached fridge just right of *Nine Mile Balls* to a few committing moves up high. A little grainy. Detached bulge below is on to start.
FA Nate Lynch

SPOKANE BOULDERING | 45

FINAL STANZA

☐ **30. FINAL STANZA V3** ★
Sit start with left-facing sidepulls. Balance up through decent holds to a reach for the lip.
FA Shane Collins

☐ **31. LUCA BOMB V6** ★★
From a left-facing sidepull climb up and slightly left into high feet and a big balancey reach. Simple but hard. Great fun.
FA Nate Lynch

Shane C. on *Luca Bomb* (V6).

Nate L. on *Final Stanza* (V3).

46 | MCLELLAN

TIGHTEN UP

☐ **32. TIGHTEN UP V4** ★

From a crouch start on low opposing holds, slap up the right-leaning bulge to a stepped lip. There's a little pocket up there somewhere....

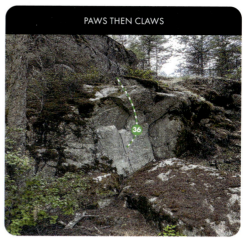

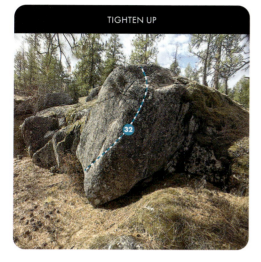

PAWS THEN CLAWS

☐ **36. PAWS THEN CLAWS V2** ★ ★ ★

Small but cryptic. Start matched on the chest-high good edge. Classically difficult.
FA Tara Hamm

TOP TIER

☐ **33. MIND OF A LEMMING V2** ★

Climb the left-facing rail from a layback stand start. Delicate (Cue T-swift).

☐ **34. LEVELS V4** ★

Just to the right and next to the shelf on the far left, start with your hands in the big low seam and make a big move up to the good edge on the left side of the rock. One more big move up to a good slope and then you get to figure out the top! (subtract a grade if you use the tree to top out)

☐ **35. TOP TIER PROJECT**

Nice looking wall with too few holds...or maybe not.

SPOKANE BOULDERING | 47

TOMATO TUTU

☐ **37. TOMATO TUTU V2** ★★
If you've never climbed V2 outside, this is a really good place to start—great holds, cool moves, and a good introduction to trusting your pad placements and spotters because of a serious mantel at the highest center point of the rock.
FA Tara Hamm

GAME 7

☐ **38. GAME OVER V1**
The good, juggy seam on the left side.
FA Tara Hamm

☐ **39. GAME 7 V7** ★
From a stand start, move through thin holds to a massive commiting move to the jug near the tree. This line is tall, proud, and will likely test your head. (We don't mean on the rocks below—please bring pads).
FA Steve Moss

SPACE JAM

☐ **40. QUAD CITY DJ V3** ★★
Start sitting on the low part of the rail in the overhang of this diminutive boulder. Follow the rail and then slap up the lip.

☐ **41. SPACE JAM V5** ★
Sit start to the right of *Quad City DJ* with a low sloper on the corner. Much harder than it initially appears, lol.
FA Nate Lynch

☐ **42. BROKEN ANKLES V2** ★★
Using no hands, work your way up the short slab just right of *Quad City DJ*. Seriously.

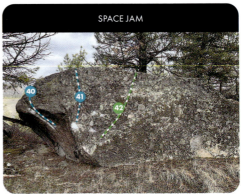

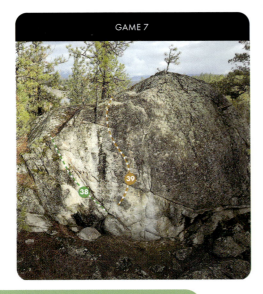

48 | McLELLAN

PROSTOR'S WALL

☐ 43. NAKED PROSTOR V2
Make your way up the far left side of the rock with good underclings and jugs.

☐ 44. PROSTOR'S BACKWARDS HAT V4 ★★
Start on the waist-high jug sidepull and push your way to the left-facing rib with small left and right gastons, and make your way up.

☐ 45. DEGRADATION V5 ★
From a rounded edge and a small undercling make large moves between small holds, finishing with a tough lip encounter.

☐ 46. THE ARROW V4
Start low on a wavy rail at the bottom left-hand section of the arrow. Move your way into the center of the arrow going straight up to top out in the cracks at the tip.

☐ 47. THE ARROW EDGE V4
Start matched on the right side of the arrow and take the arête up inside and over.

☐ 48. LASER RAZOR V5 ★★
Start with two underclings on the right side of the arrow and move delicately up using sharp crimps to top out on the detached block. Highly recommended to not use the arrow as an arête for the left hand. VARIATION *Laser Razor Major*: Instead of moving straight up from the razor hold, continue on sharp crimps up and left, staying away from the arête to add a few grades.

☐ 49. CS V1
Follow the good holds on the far right side of the rock.

SPOKANE BOULDERING | 49

KITTY LITTER

☐ 50. KITTY HAWK V2 ★
Step up the detached slab, grab the jug rail, establish, and get your meat over the lip. Small but good.
FA Tara Hamm

☐ 51. KITTY LITTER V3
On the rightmost side of the boulder, start matched on the corner of the good seam with a couple slaps left, and a few harder slaps right. Top out on slopers uphill to the right.

TARA'S WALL

☐ 52. TODD'S DYNO V4 ★
Starting high on not great, thin, opposing crimps. (I mean, they're really not great). Make one large huck to the lip. Exciting.
FA Tara Hamm

☐ 53. TARA V6 ★★
This is a VERY fun climb. Start in the corner dihedral (the bottom is on for feet). Make your way out right and up the arête on the good sidepull and thinner holds above. VARIATION: Don't use the foot slab for a harder adventure.
FA Tara Hamm

☐ 54. ALL BLUE ROOM V3
On the right side of the arête, sit start on a good sloping jug up to a finger lock in the vertical seam and a left undercling above that.

☐ 55. DANCING WITH MYSELF V6 ★
About 5 feet left of the start of *Tara's Top*, start with opposing crimps and traverse right on terrible garbage-time crimps to large gaston left of the crescent moon. Finish the same as its neighbor.

☐ 56. TARA'S TOP V4 ★
Start with a left-hand gaston on the head-high, right-facing crimp and a right hand sloping gaston. Make your way up to the crescent-moon-shaped rail. Rock over and top out on nice edgy shelves.
FA Tara Hamm

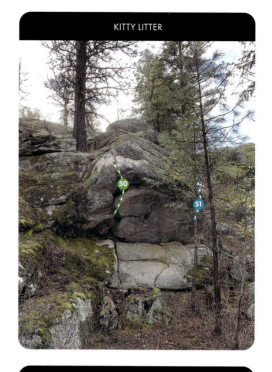

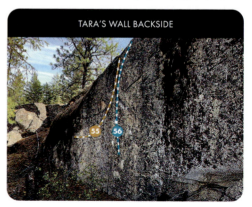

PINEAPPLE PIZZA (NOT PICTURED)

☐ **57. PINEAPPLE PIZZA V0** ★
Good warm-up uphill from *Tara's Top*.

☐ **58. 2 NASTY V2**
A little way to the right of *Pineapple Pizza*. You could climb this...or go do something more fun, like reading the owner's manual for your iron.

PINCH PROJECT

☐ **59. PINCH PROJECT**
Found in the small corridor between *Pineapple 'za* and HWY 69. Begin from a cool pinch, and climb up and right on thin seams.

HIGHWAY 69

This corridor holds a stretch of wall with a large number of moderate and fun climbs. Topped off by a traverse that can start at the far north end, each of these problems can be added onto, climbed into, and transformed to fit just about any climbing level or style. With interesting features and a great landing, this place seems more like a gym wall than an actual rock. It can have a tricky top-out in some areas. Some must-climbs are *Summer of 69*, *Red Scare* and *Pretentious Blog*.

☐ **60. MOBY LIP V5**
Far left of *69*, start on the lip of the whale-shaped feature. Climb up.

☐ **61. THE 69 YEAR OLD TRAVERSE V8** ★
Starting on the *Moby Lip* jug at the farthest left end of the Highway, make about 800 or so moves, travelling right, occasionally up, and occasionally down. Finish as you would for *Pretentious Blog* for the full V8 value. Top out on the swooping finish of *Summer of 69* for a V (just-as-fun) 5.
FA Billy Centenari

☐ **62. PARADOX IN PURPLE V1** ★★
Layback the big crack and head left to jugs. VERY good.

☐ **63. WHISPER AND A CLAMOUR V4** ★
Start on good corner holds in the cracks to the left of the overhanging portion of the wall. Climb up to a tough drive-by.

SPOKANE BOULDERING | 51

HIGHWAY 69 RIGHT SIDE

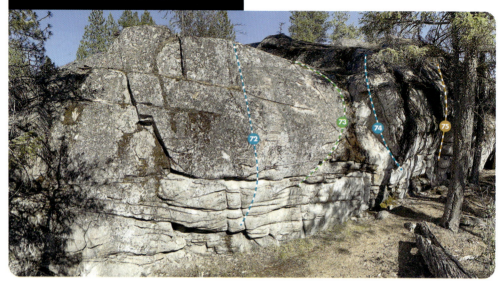

☐ 64. THE DIN V3 ★★
Using a high right hand jug, climb up and under the left-leaning overhang with thin underclings to better holds above. Another great variation is to climb the beginning of *The Din* into the finish of *Red Scare*.

☐ 65. RED SCARE V4 ★★★
Sit start on a curving rail, lunge to chest-high jugs, through a small red sidepull, to another rail and the lip. Another stellar line.

HIGHWAY 69 RIGHT SIDE

☐ 66. SIXTY DINE-O V3 ★
Start on shoulder-high jugs and climb straight up. Big moves, good holds. What more do you want?

☐ 67. SUMMER OF 69 V2 ★★
Start as for *Sixty Dine-o* but climb right up the swooping rail with smeary feet. Best climb at The Highway?

☐ 68. FIGHT OR FLIGHT V4 ★
Starting on the low rounded shelf, move to a right hand gaston, then up through tricky moves.

☐ 69. NONSTOP EGO TRIP V7 ★
Start as for *Pretentious Blog* but climb trending left, implementing a small, smooth crimp.

☐ 70. PRETENTIOUS BLOG V4 ★★
Start on the jug under the overhang, make your way right on sloping pinches to a good edge on the bald sloping face out right, then top-out.
FA Billy Centenari

☐ 71. VLOGS ABOUT CLOGS V0 (NOT PICTURED)
Many variations about 30 feet right of *Pretentious Blog*—all zero-ish.
FA Russ Schultz

☐ 72. GALAXY SMEAR V5 ★
Start on the low, rounded slopey block and make your way up past the bald middle section. Top out right of the tree.
FA Russ Schultz

☐ 73. MATRIARCHAL JESTING V2
With a left-hand slopey sidepull and right hand chest-high undercling, use janky jugs to get yourself on the slab.
FA Billy Centenari

☐ 74. SHERLOCKED V3 ★
Start on two sloping right-sided holds in a sit start position. Head up to good jugs with weird moves in the dihedral.
FA Russ Schultz

☐ 75. ZULU PRINCESS V8 ★
Jam yourself in the bloody crack and ascend. Reportedly excellent.
FA Arden Pete

52 | McLELLAN

Amanda K. on Red Scare (V4).

THE BULGE

☐ **76. CORDUROY SUMMIT V0** (NOT PICTURED)
Around the left end of the wall. Start on a pointy horn and make your way right on blocks. Top out left. Start left for fun variation.

☐ **77. PURPLE PROSE V3**
To the left of the widemouth feature, start on the stuck block using bad holds to gain a delicate top-out.

☐ **78. SOUTH BANK V3**
To the right of the widemouth feature, start on the rail with the right hand undercling and then follow the rail up to right-facing crimps.

☐ **79. LITTLE BULGE PROJECT LEFT**
Tough start on good edges. Make your way up and left on the arête.

☐ **80. LITTLE BULGE PROJECT RIGHT**
Far right line. Start on rounded sloped crimp and use the arête to get to the large seam. Delicate moves on edges gain the top-out.

THE BULGE FRONTSIDE

SPOKANE BOULDERING | 53

THE CLASSIC

☐ 81. NEW AMERICAN CLASSIC V5 ★★★
Sit start with a left-hand sidepull and your right hand on a unique pinch. Power through precise moves with a desperate slap into the undercling. A McLellan classic and a personal favorite.
FA George Hughbanks

☐ 82. CLASSIC RIGHT PROJECT
Potential direct variant.

☐ 83. RENAISSANCE MAN V5 ★
Bust left from a thin right hand on the arête and a left sidepull. Keep it together and top out a few moves later. Traversing all the way to the finish of *New American Classic* bumps up the difficulty.

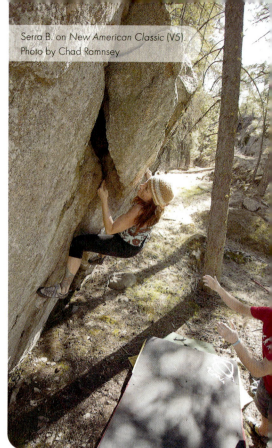

Serra B. on *New American Classic* (V5). Photo by Chad Ramnsey

Nate L. on *Renaissance Man Extension*.

54 | MCLELLAN

Nate L. on *No Lights in the Attic* (V3).

PACK RAT CAVE BOULDERS

☐ 84. ARÊTE POTENTIAL PROJECT
Climb the right-hand arête with compression in seams to a scary-looking rock-over onto the slab above.

☐ 85. CENTER SLAB V2
From a chest-high crimp, climb straight up with easier moves as you get higher.

☐ 86. NO LIGHTS IN THE ATTIC V3 ★
Establish on a head-high undercling, move left to the arête, up and around the corner to the slab, then to the top.

Nate L. on *Hard-On with a Hacksaw* (V4).

☐ 87. HARD-ON WITH A HACKSAW V4 ★★★
Sit start with a left-hand monkey paw undercling and a right hand sloping edge. Move up opposing holds on the bulge with a balancey final act. Jump down or quest up the mossy slab. 10/10, would recommend.
FA Shane Collins

SPOKANE BOULDERING | 55

HIGH TIMES WALL

☐ **88. RED ROVER V3**
Stand start with a foot on the connected bulge. Work up good crimps to incuts in the upper horizontal seam and traverse right to the top.
FA George Hughbanks

☐ **89. GREEN CRACK V1 ★★**
Start on the head-height good jug and make a move left to follow the crack to jugs. Use the dish out right to top it out.
FA George Hughbanks

☐ **90. PURPLE TEETH V6 ★**
In the incut center of the face, start matched on the good edge and move up to small face crimps and an awesome, tiny, two-finger tooth gaston. From there pop to the lip.
FA Nate Lynch

☐ **91. BLUE STEEL V6 ★**
From head-high crimps to the right of the purple teeth, climb up a thin face to slopers and the finishing jugs.

☐ **92. GOLDEN GATE V3 ★★**
On the right side of the wall, start matched on a slightly left-facing crimp rail. Climb to a large jug out left and hug the jutting high arête. Enjoy a delicate top-out. Some big moves or small intermediates on this one—your choice.
FA George Hughbanks

☐ **93. COLOR BLIND V1** (NOT PICTURED)
Doesn't look like much. From a sit start matched on the low edge, ascend the small block opposite the High Times Wall. Could be a knee bar in there...

Dylan H. On Red Rover (V3)

THE GLEN

THE GLEN

Tucked away in the heart of the main area of McLellan, The Glen is home to the widest variety of rock, nestled in one nuggety-gob. From the thrutchfest *Wicked Skengman* to the delicate balance of *Lightwork* to the heartpounding, easyrider highball Three Story Boulder to the popular hang *Chessboard*, you're sure to find a new favorite problem. If you're having an especially low gravity day, give the area strong-guy problem *Catching Feelings* a try...or seven. The Low Glen area only has a few problems listed in this book, but this area is a playground—it has amazing hand cracks, highballs, horseshoes, and traverses, so take some time down here and adventure.

Kristin W. on The Ogre (V4).
Photo by Ben Boldt

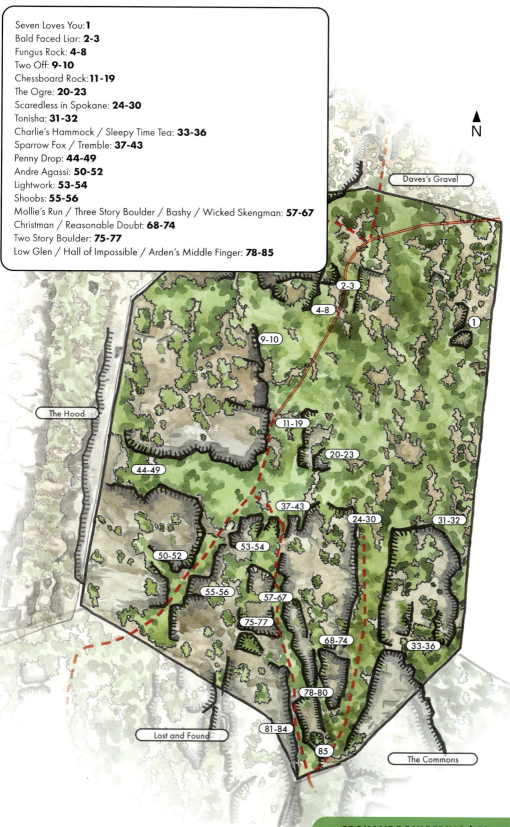

SEVEN LOVES YOU

☐ 1. SEVEN LOVES YOU V5
Starting with two "okay" edges in the deepest part of the incut, cavey part of the rock, slap and work your way to the positive slopers and jugs that traverse to the apex of the boulder. Top out.

BALD FACED LIAR

☐ 2. CASSETTE PLAYER V1
Start on the far left side with an right hand undercling low on the arête and a good jug by the left-side crack. Move up and left using good holds and slots to finish.

☐ 3. BALD FACED LIAR V7 ★
Small in stature but not in difficulty. Start matched on the small rightmost crimp (almost behind the tree) and make moves left with delicate feet. Did someone say tension?

FUNGUS ROCK

☐ 4. QUIZINATOR V2 ★
On the far left side of the boulder, a stand start leads to awkward moves to the top.

☐ 5. FLOOZY V2
Compressing between seams, make your way up and left.

☐ 6. FUNGINEER V2
A fun, high climb to the tree at the top of the crack. A small dihedral marks the start.

☐ 7. FUNGUS AMONG US V3
A mental-testing highball. Bring some pads, k?

☐ 8. 5.11 WORLD V4
Once a 5.11 gear route, the name stays the same sans cord.

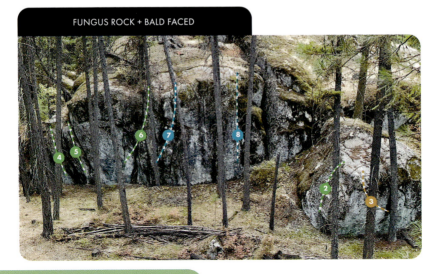

60 | McLELLAN

TWO OFF

☐ **9. THE EDGE TAKES OVER FOR VINNY V2**
From a small edge, climb holds in the crack with some visual exposure to the left.

☐ **10. PARAPLEGIC POTENTIAL V1** (NOT PICTURED)
Just down the hill from *Vinny*, this climb hovers above some sharp loose rocks, but once the middle edge is reached, you should be good. (Should be.)

CHESSBOARD ROCK

The Chessboard Rock sits in a nice open area opposite the popular sport climbing spot, the Morning Wall. A good place to sprawl out, relax and warm up on some quality problems. While the height might make some climbers uneasy, the flat landing area and great holds are an excellent introduction to getting some air under your feet. With a large, slightly unsettling move up high on *Queen for Queen*, these climbs provide a little excitement for low-grade climbing. You can easily access The Glen, Lost & Found, and The Hood from this location.

To get to The Glen, continue past Chessboard and when the trail splits, head left uphill just left of Tremble. To get to Lost & Found, follow the lower right trail at the fork and veer left uphill after the right hand turn to The Sunshine Wall in The Hood.

☐ **11. QUEEN FOR QUEEN V2 ★★★**
Great problem; a little tall. Keep it high and tight for this one.

☐ **12. THE SICILIAN V0**
Center of The Chessboard to the notch. Start building that head game.

☐ **13. CASTLE V1 ★**
Right arête on the Chessboard face.

☐ **14. PETROV DEFENSE V1 ★★**
Commence from a left-hand sidepull/sloper, right hand edge. Climb up and left with some balancy moves, then finish as for *Rookie Move*.

☐ **15. ROOKIE MOVE V0 ★★**
Start on a left sloper/right hand low pinch. Bust up through the big edges. For an extra challenge, start matched on the sloper.

☐ **16. GOOD KNIGHT V1**
The seam to the right of *Rookie Move* is a bit awkward.

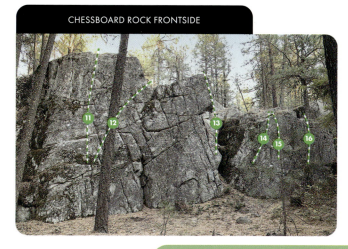

SPOKANE BOULDERING | 61

Nate L. on a Variation of Chessboard Wall.

CHESSBOARD ROCK RIGHT SIDE

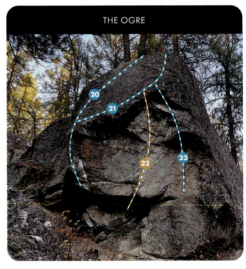

THE OGRE

☐ **17. EASTERN KIDS V2** ★
A low left-hand sidepull on the arête and right hand seam mark the start of this short, bulgey and balancey problem.

☐ **18. WE'RE ALL PAWNS V0**
A right-leaning crack slab that needs a little grooming.

☐ **19. DEEP BLUE V1** ★
Sit start on the corner. A tough sloper on this one.

THE OGRE

☐ **20. FLUSHING A DEAD ROOSTER V3** ★★★
Starting on the far left side on a good jug, make a couple big moves up the arête. Move into the seam leading up and right. Follow the seam to the top.

☐ **21. THE OGRE V4** ★★
Start as for *FADR* but once at the lip, traverse right along increasingly good holds. Rock up with your hands on the largest/farthest chicken head.

☐ **22. CHEEKBONE V6**
From the low fin feature, climb up through thin crimps to good holds at the lip. Top as for *The Ogre*. The crimps on this are a touch fragile...
FA Steve Moss

☐ **23. FAT LIP V3**
Start on the large shelf on the corner. Mantel and proceed to the finish of *The Ogre*.

62 | MCLELLAN

SCAREDLESS IN SPOKANE

☐ **24. SCAREDLESS IN SPOKANE V5** ★

From a stand start climb up the pair of seams on pinches and compression. Fun movement...gets a bit heady up high.
FA George Hughbanks

☐ **25. CUT AND RUN V6** ★★

Start low with opposing sidepulls, move up through neat pinches and a big move to a sloper above.
FA George Hughbanks

☐ **26. MAKE IT HOT V1** ★

From head-height, right-leaning pinches, climb to a horizontal seam and traverse rightward into the finish of *Sunny Sort Of Feeling*. Going straight over is a lot harder.

☐ **27. SUNNY SORT OF FEELING V1** ★★

Start just left of the tree, climbing through cool pods on the slabby bulge. Harder than it first looks.
FA George Hughbanks

☐ **28. TAKING HEAT V4** ★

To the right of the tree, start sitting with a right hand undercling and a small left hand. Crank up to crimps and over the bulge.
FA George Hughbanks

☐ **29. TINY TEMPER V6** ★★★

Start matched on the shoulder-height crimp rail, climb straight up over the rounded lip. Fairly straightforward and fairly hard.
FA Shane Collins

☐ **30. TREE AMIGOS V6** ★

Starts on opposing sidepulls with feet on the bulge. This one might spit you off more than you expect.
FA Dan Taylor

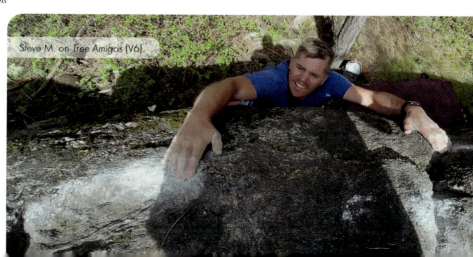

Steve M. on *Tree Amigos* (V6).

TONISHA

☐ 31. TONISHA LEFT V2 ★
Starting on the low good edge, use the ear-shaped jugs on the arête to make your way up.

☐ 32. TONISHA V4
From a good right hand and a left-hand at the bottom of the crimp sidepull, move up the arête to holds on the lip. Traverse left to finish as for *Tonisha Left*.
FA Shane Collins

CHARLIE'S HAMMOCK

☐ 33. CHARLIE'S BANANA HAMMOCK V6 ★★
Start on the right corner of the arête, feet on the detached slab, toss left, mantel (cruxy) straight over the heady bulge.
FA George Hughbanks

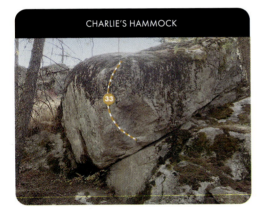

SLEEPY TIME TEA

☐ 34. SLEEPY TIME TEA V4 ★★★
Start standing with a left hand on the arête and a right hand pocket. Follow fun compression moves up the arête until it eases up, and mantel at the apex of the rock.

☐ 35. FORTY WINKS V4 ★
Start matched on the right-facing rail and climb up the face with right-facing sidepulls and gastons. Techy. Traverse into this problem from the start of *Sleepy Time Tea* and you've climbed *Snoozer*. High fives all around.

☐ 36. CATNAPPER V1
Use the right hand arête. Climb to apex and top out.

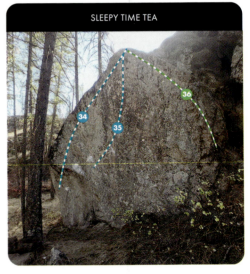

Cam F. on *Forty Winks* (V4).

Nate L. on Pink Wine & Other Vices (V9)

SPARROW FOX

☐ 37. SPARROW FOX V4 ★★★
Climb the tall split face with big moves between fun holds. Kinda looks like a lightning bolt. Fight us if you think it doesn't. A real gem.
FA George Hughbanks

☐ 38. NEAPOLITAN V3 ★★
Matched start on the smooth chest-high jug on the arête. Move up good holds to a high rockover. Continue allllll the way up the slab for a full value adventure.
FA Jeremy Clark

☐ 39. PINK WINE & OTHER VICES V9 ★★
Start on sloping holds in the seam of the overhung face. Move through left-hand crimps, and a large crux move to a sloper above before commiting to the final sequence over a questionable landing. Unconfirmed instant classic.
FA Nate Lynch

☐ 40. BITTER BLOODCLART V8
Starting under the stuck rock, make painful, jammy moves to hug the rock to the finish. Objectively not a fun problem.
FA Shane Collins

SPARROW FOX

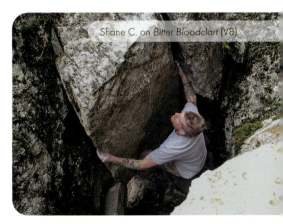

Shane C. on Bitter Bloodclart (V8)

SPOKANE BOULDERING | 65

TREMBLE

☐ 41. CHAPFALLEN V5
Start matched of the left side of the block to the right of *Tremble* in the low notch where the crack meets both rocks. Desperately follow this left arête up and top out directly above. Unconfirmed grade; looks harder.
FA George Hughbanks

☐ 42. TREMBLE V5
Start low in the notch and using some tweaky layback action with a few face edges, follow the center and tallest section of the rock.
FA George Hughbanks

☐ 43. TREMBLE RIGHT PROJECT
Looks doable, we think.

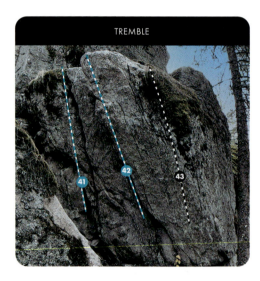
TREMBLE

PENNY DROP

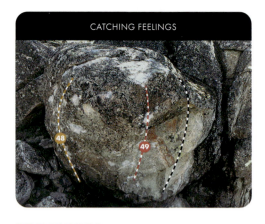
CATCHING FEELINGS

PENNY DROP

☐ 44. THE WRETCH PROJECT (NOT PICTURED)
Possible project on a suspended boulder over a potentially scary fall.... Could use a landing.

☐ 45. FULL SETTINGS RESET V6
From the lowest right jug, climb up and left on the bulge implementing some grainy painful crimps.

☐ 46. A STEP ABOVE PROJECT
A highball project climbing past the sloping edge into very thin territory just down the hill opposite Catching Feelings.

CATCHING FEELINGS

☐ 47. PESTIFEROUS INNERVATIONS V0
(NOT PICTURED)
Climb this small slab when *Catching Feelings* shuts you down. It's just off the left side of the picture. Cleaned and curated for you by the one and only GH.
FA George Hughbanks

☐ 48. THE GIRL NEXT DOOR V8 ★★
Start low, matched on the left-facing jug. Make precise and powerful moves to a commiting finish. Another great testpiece.
FA Bryan Franklin

☐ 49. CATCHING FEELINGS V9 ★★★
From a sit start on two blocky edges, climb up through nice incuts into more technical territory and some committing moves near the end. New school classic.
FA Nate Lynch

66 | McLELLAN

ANDRE AGASSI

☐ **50. ANDRE AGASSI V2** ★
Climb up the left rounded arête to a high finish.

☐ **51. STIFF CHOCOLATE PROJECT**
From high crimps (or low jug on the left) somehow gain the right-facing rail and continue up the tall face.

☐ **52. THE FALL OF TROY V1**
Start from a low jug, climb left and then up on good holds. Tall. If that cool little ear hold is still there, don't trust it too much...

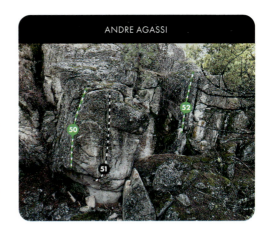

Shane C. on Andre Agassi (V2)

LIGHTWORK

☐ **53. LIGHTWORK V5** ★ ★ ★
Start on the left arête with a rightward-slanting incut and make a big move to the calcium-covered jug (this is easier if you're tall; short beta will add a few crimps). From the good jug follow the seam on the left to an airy and classic top-out. Very cool.
FA Shane Collins

☐ **54. MIDNIGHT CALLER V2**
Start in the middle of the face and head out left to finish as *Lightwork*. Test out the holds on this one, there has been some loose rock.

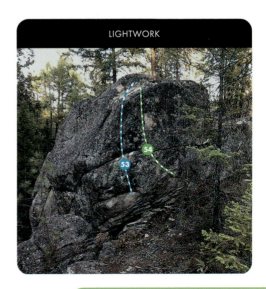

SPOKANE BOULDERING | 67

Justin V. on *Lightwork* (V5).

SHOOBS

☐ 55. SHOOBS V2
A small rock sitting alone at the south edge of The Glen. Start on the right side with a low crimpy shield and terrible feet. Just a couple moves will get you to the top. Doesn't look like much and climbs how it looks.

400 LUX

☐ 56. 400 LUX V1
Starting on the farthest left edge with feet on a slope, traverse from edge to edge to the far right, then head straight up.

MOLLIE'S RUN (NOT PICTURED)

☐ 57. RIGGIN'S RUN V0
Start low on the bottom of the left-trending rail and climb straight up.

☐ 58. MOLLIE'S RUN V1
Start as for *Riggin's Run*, but move left.

SHOOBS

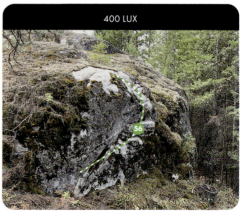

400 LUX

68 | McLELLAN

THREE-STORY BOULDER

☐ 59. THREE STORIES V2 ★ ★
The obvious shelved highball on the east side of the Three-Story Boulder. Good holds and a commiting top make for a great climb.

☐ 60. TALL TALES V3 ★ ★
Stand start this slightly more complex problem just right of *Three Stories*. Joins it's neighbor part way up.

☐ 61. SCARY SLAB LEFT V5 (NOT PICTURED)
There are two slab problems that have been climbed on the NW face of the boulder. Find the hardest way up the slab. Less holds and worse feet for a faster heart rate.
FA Serra Barron

☐ 62. SCARY SLAB RIGHT V4 (NOT PICTURED)
On the west side of the Three Story Boulder, follow thin crimps and slippery feet up the rounded side.
FA Serra Barron

Nate L. cleaning *Three Stories* (V2)

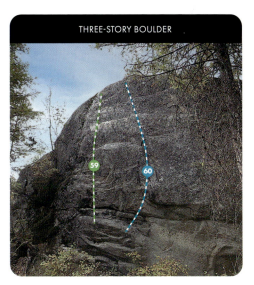

THREE-STORY BOULDER

BASHY

☐ 63. BASHY V5 ★
On the left side of the arête, start with your right hand on a low sloping incut and your left at the head-high sidepull. Using slaps and crimps, compress your way up to a good finish. Neat movement, but a tad sharp until you get it right.

BASHY

☐ 64. UGLY DOG SYMPHONY V2
Would be a cool problem if you didn't have a tree poking your butt.

SPOKANE BOULDERING | 69

WICKED SKENGMAN

☐ 65. PISTOL AND FIST V3 ★
Starting with both hands on a good edge on the farthest left side of the boulder and a good left heel, bust up to the seam and follow it to the top. The good holds are never free of pine needles. Consider yourself warned.

☐ 66. RUN THE JEWELS V2 ★
Start on the lowest jugs in the middle of the steep rock with high feet (not the detached slab). Move left to a great jug, keep heading left on incuts to the top.

☐ 67. WICKED SKENGMAN V5 ★ ★ ★
Start as for *Run the Jewels* but climb up and right to a balancy mantel. It's nice...and tough.

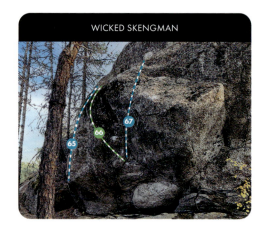

CHRISTMAS IN KEY LARGO

☐ 68. CHRISTMAS IN KEY LARGO V3
Start under the small bottom cut in the rock, move to jam yourself in the dihedral and tweakily birth yourself out to the face and cruise up to a jug finish.

☐ 69. S CARGO V4
To the right of *Key Largo*, use the crimps on the face to move out right and up.

REASONABLE DOUBT

☐ 70. 99 PROBLEMS PROJECT
Great looking holds, terrifying looking top. Needs a good brushin'. Go get 'er.

☐ 71. CAN'T KNOW THE HUSTLE V5 ★
Start on chest-high crimps; make balance moves to a commiting final lunge.

☐ 72. REASONABLE DOUBT V3 ★ ★
Start with your back facing the slanting flat boulder and start with opposing crimps on the chimney-shaped feature. Follow a crimp rail up and right to a balancey insecure top.

☐ 73. FALCON HAWK MOON CHILD V1 ★
Feet on the slab, reach way up from the incuts to a rounded rail above.

☐ 74. HARD KNOCK LIFE V1 (NOT PICTURED)
On the face around the corner from #73. From a left-facing sidepull, good holds and a reach gain the lip.

70 | McLELLAN

Owen S. on *Two Tiered to Finish* (V2).

TWO-STORY BOULDER

☐ 75. TWO TIERED TO FINISH V2 ★★★
Starting in the slot with good underclings, move up through incut holds into more underclings. Trend right to top out with a crux finish.

☐ 76. MOUTHFUL OF LIES V3 ★
Start from the big jugs at head-height, bust up to a rail, on through incuts into the same mantel as *Two Tiered*.

☐ 77. TWO STORIES V5 ★★
From the same big jugs, traverse right to the arête and then proceed up to a delicate top-out.

LOW GLEN

☐ 78. CAKES AND ALE (HORSESHOE) V4
(NOT PICTURED)
This is technically a route, but you climb up and traverse a little and then come back down to make a horseshoe over the dark rock shape on the low face. There's also another horseshoe problem to your back, in between *Rain* and *Hot Rod Banana*. I think Dana Wilson did this first, but can't confirm...but it's there!
FA Adren Pete

☐ 79. RAIN V5 ★★
Start from high holds on the tall face. Quest up the vertical seams on fun grips to a high finish. Stunning.
FA Arden Pete

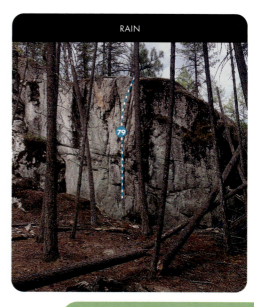

SPOKANE BOULDERING | 71

HALL OF IMPOSSIBLE

☐ 80. HOT ROD BANANA V3
A tall overhung climb on block-shaped and phallic-shaped holds.

☐ 81. HALL OF IMPOSSIBLE PROJECT
(NOT PICTURED)
Everything left of *Hall Monitor* on this wall is a project still. Have at 'em.

☐ 82. HALL MONITOR V8 ★★ (NOT PICTURED)
Establish on the slab with a left-hand undercling. Climb out from under the bulge with a blind hop and up the thin headwall. Climbs much better than it looks.
FA Steve Moss

Cierra G. on *Heiropolis* (V3).
Photo by George Hughbanks

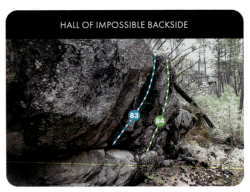

☐ 83. HIERAPOLIS V3 ★
From the dusty edge climb the inside corner with a number of fun holds.

☐ 84. ARCHIMEDES V0
Climb the face over the rotting log.

72 | McLELLAN

Arden P. on *Arden's Middle Finger* (V6).
Photo by Jon Jonckers

ARDEN'S MIDDLE FINGER

☐ 85. ARDEN'S MIDDLE FINGER OF FURY V6 ★★★

Perched above The Hall of Impossible lies a proud boulder with a longstanding area testpiece. Climb the center of the face from obvious crimps. Thin, classic, proud, and heady...and we'll stop there.
FA Arden Pete

SPOKANE BOULDERING | 73

THE HOOD

The Hood is composed of a long, wonderous corridor with towering slabs and intense walls on both sides. Primarily trafficked by shade-seeking route climbers, The Hood is home to the arousing and stiffening *Scarlett Johansson*, the gym-worthy Sunshine Wall problems, the elusive and stupefying *Sic Transit Gloria* and the absolute gem of a climb, *Frankline*. While the routes here take the stage visually, these boulders are standouts regardless and will provide you the filling to the massive, lonely hole in your heart. (omg just kidding.)

The Crow's Nest: **1-3**
Trail Head: **4-8**
Constellation Boulders: **9-15**
Romancing the Stone: **16-18**
Mass Hysteria / Burgled Burgers / Ask Carlos: **19-21**
The Swoop: **22**
Scarlett Johansson: **23-25**
Baby Arête / Kitty Cat Wall: **26-29**
Welcome to the Hood: **30-37**
Sunshine Wall: **38-43**

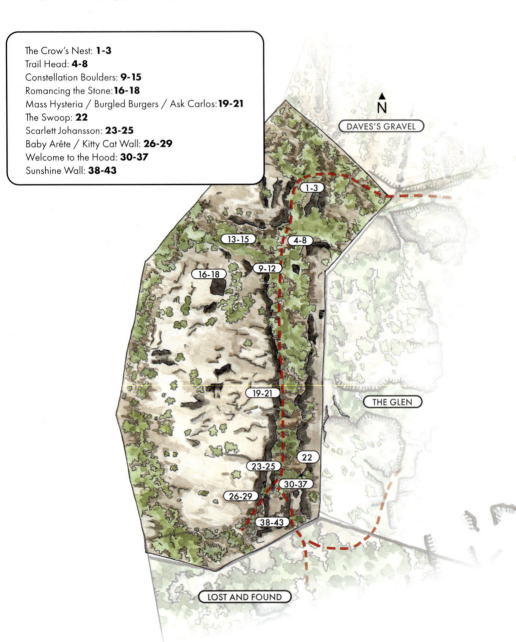

74 | MCLELLAN

Kristin W. on *Scarlett Johansson* (V5).
Photo by Ben Boldt

THE HOOD

CROW'S NEST

☐ **1. VERTICAL MARATHON V0**
Climb the big holds up the low-angle slab. Jugs and smeary feet comprise the last few moves.

☐ **2. CAWWWWDIAC ARREST V4**
From an undercling seam, climb sloping holds over the overhanging bulge.

☐ **3. A CROW NAMED CARL V3**
On the right side of *Caw-diac Arrest*, climb the sloping holds to move out left. Top out hugging the box-shaped block.

TRAIL HEAD

☐ **4. TRAIL HEAD V1 ★★**
Start matched in the jug above the small tree. Climb straight up good incuts.

☐ **5. TONYA HARDLY V4 ★**
Start on *Trail Head* and traverse into *Hat Trick Swayze*.

☐ **6. TWO FACE V1 ★** (NOT PICTURED)
Sit start on good trailside jugs to the left of the red face. Climb up and left.

☐ **7. HAT TRICK SWAYZE V3 ★**
Start left hand in the triangle-shaped sloping undercling and right hand a little higher on a good crimp. Slap up the bare red face and use knobby holds to finish. Fun.
FA Dan Taylor

☐ **8. ABOVE TRAIL HEAD V3**
On the left end of the wall above *Trail Head*, Start on two small crimps. Make your way to a three-finger edge into a sloping top-out. Clean your own adventure.

TRAIL HEAD LEFT SIDE

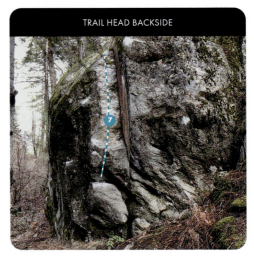
TRAIL HEAD BACKSIDE

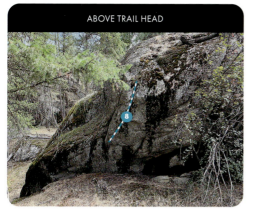

CONSTELLATION BOULDERS

☐ **9. ROUTE WARM-UP ROCK V0** (NOT PICTURED)
Rounded boulder with a number of easy options to get the arms going.

☐ **10. THE ASTRONOMER V2** ★
From a high jug start, move up and right through blocky edges.

☐ **11. FRANKLINE V6** ★ ★ ★
Follow the incut rail up and left from the lowest jug. Continue along small edges to better holds and the top. If the texture was more friendly, it would be 4 stars.
FA Bryan Franklin

☐ **12. PUPPIS V7** ★
Start as for *Frankline* but climb straight up from the end of the rail to a desperate top-out over the bulge.
FA Zak Silver

☐ **13. CAPRICA V3** (NOT PICTURED)
Small compression line across from *Little Dipper*. Unconfirmed.

☐ **14. LITTLE DIPPER V6** ★ ★
Starting matched on the obvious rail, move up and left through incut crimps and onto the bulging lip.
FA Nick Tansy

☐ **15. BIG DIPPER V7** ★ ★
From the right end of the same rail, bust to holds at the lip, then traverse right and top out at the incut holds.
FA Alex Nikolayev

Jeremy C. on *Frankline* (V6).

SPOKANE BOULDERING | 77

ROMANCING THE STONE

☐ 16. GLORY FADES V2
From the left end of the swooping jug climb up to the sloping lip and get on up there.

☐ 17. ROMANCING THE STONE V5 ★★
Start standing with a left hand in the seam and right on a thin sidepull. Move up right through the crimp seam to the top (with some desperate moves). Can be done from a sit with two extra moves for an added grade or three.

☐ 18. SIC TRANSIT GLORIA V7 ★
Start sitting with a right hand on the arête and a left on a small wide sidepull. Power your way up to the horizontal and easier climbing above.
FA Shane Collins

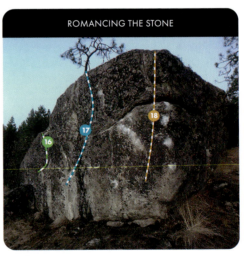

MASS HYSTERIA

☐ 19. MASS HYSTERIA V9
Intially bolted as a route by George Hughbanks, this problem was first sent as a highball boulder. Take many pads. Crux is at a reasonable height, but that slab just keeps on going....
FA Steve Moss

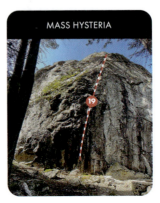

78 | McLELLAN

Shane C. and Harvey on *Romancing the Stone* (V5).

BURGLED BURGERS

☐ **20. BURGLED BURGERS V0**
Warm-up boulder across from *Ask Carlos*.
FA George Hughbanks

ASK CARLOS

☐ **21. ASK CARLOS V5** ★
Start crouched on the slabby flake and use both arêtes to help bump you up and over to the right side face!
FA Shane Collins

THE SWOOP

☐ **22. THE SWOOP V1**
Starting on the low horn, climb the lip from right to left. The likelihood you'll fall into the pit is low.

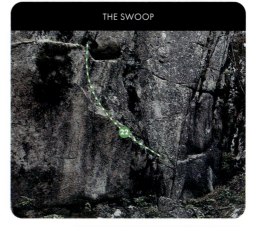

SPOKANE BOULDERING | 79

Cam F. on *Always Climb Up* (V4).

SCARLETT JOHANSSON

☐ 23. ALWAYS CLIMB UP V4 ★★
Climb up thin holds to a high committing finish. A little sharp but proud... plus it'll look great on your insta. #climbingbrandambassador
FA Alex Rice

☐ 24. ALEX ARÊTE PROJECT
Climb the arête right of *Always Climb Up*. Landing looks a little blocky.

☐ 25. SCARLETT JOHANSSON V5 ★★★
From a stand start move up through sidepulls to good edges and an excellent finish. Ultra classic.
FA Alex Rice

80 | McLELLAN

BABY ARÊTE

☐ 26. DRIVE V4
Crimp up the short face.

☐ 27. BABY ARÊTE V2 ★
Climb the thin arête from a low start.

KITTY CAT WALL

☐ 28. SCATTY CAT V4
This wall is under the left side of The Sunshine Wall at the entrance to The Hood. Use some good holds on the slabby corner to make your way to the tall finish.
FA George Hughbanks

☐ 29. SLEEPY COUGAR PROJECT
This line has some thin crimps.

WELCOME TO THE HOOD

☐ 30. ROMAINE V3 ★ ★ ★
Starting matched on the corner shelf, climb up the arête to big gap between good holds at the 2/3 point. Commiting and classic.
FA Arden Pete

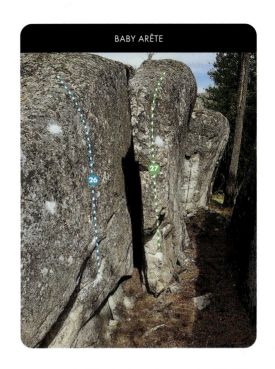

BABY ARÊTE

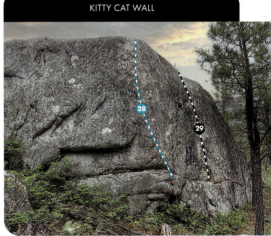

KITTY CAT WALL

ROMAINE

SPOKANE BOULDERING | 81

WELCOME TO THE HOOD (CONT)

☐ 31. LEFT EXIT V1
Commence with a low match on a shelf made from a broken rock. Move left to follow the crack up and left.
FA Arden Pete

☐ 32. HOOD TUFF V5
Start perched on the small boulder with hands matched on a good incut rail. Move up to slopers using the crack system with the left. Stay on the face as much as you can then go straight up.
FA Arden Pete

☐ 33. WELCOME TO THE HOOD PROJECT
Start matched on the big bulge in the center of the rock and make moves through a blank face hugging the arête. Looks doable, but hard.

☐ 34. CALION RONDE V4 ★
Start right hand in a seam with a small notch for your finger and your left hand pinched in the same seam below. Bust up and left and head straight up on good rounded holds.
FA Arden Pete

☐ 35. SOL ALCANCE V2
Start laying back in the far right crack with your right hand and your left hand in the adjacent left seam. Make one move up to a sloper and then press the top-out.
FA Arden Pete

Jeni C. on Sunshine Wall.

☐ 36. LAZY LAYBACK V4
Start in the right hand slopey seam with your foot on a left-leaning sloping rail in a layback position. Trend up and continue laybacking until you reach jugs at the top of the bulge. A wild ride.
FA Arden Pete

☐ 37. BELINDA'S BURRITO V2 ★
Sit start very low on the corner with good opposing sidepulls. Make a few moves up to a crack system on your right and then up.
FA Arden Pete

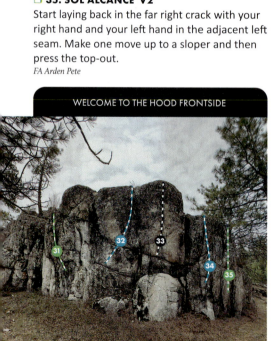
WELCOME TO THE HOOD FRONTSIDE

WELCOME TO THE HOOD OTHERSIDE

82 | McLELLAN

SUNSHINE WALL

☐ 38. GREEN SPOTTED MONSTER V0
On the left side of the tall rock, start on a chest-high jug and follow edges and good holds to an easy top.

☐ 39. CAM'S SUNSHINE V4
Start standing on the good edge and follow the vertical fracture using crumbly small holds.
FA Cameron Freiburghaus

☐ 40. SUNSHINE LEFT V3 ★★
Start matched on the head-high shelf with bad feet and go straight up.

☐ 41. SUNSHINE V2 ★★★
Start matched head-high on the left-hand shelf and traverse right into to the mega-jug. Juggy moves lead up to the corner. A bit reachy.

☐ 42. SUNNY D V2 ★★★
Same start as *Sunshine*, but after the first few moves climb up to a behemoth hold. Really fun! To complete *Sunny's Double D*, dyno rightward to the jug on *Sunshine* and then lunge all the way up and left to the next mega-jug.

☐ 43. SUNSHINE RIGHT V1 ★★
With a low start in the seam on the far right, follow the good juggy break in the rock out left.

Nate L. on *Sunny D* (V2).

SPOKANE BOULDERING | 83

THE COMMONS

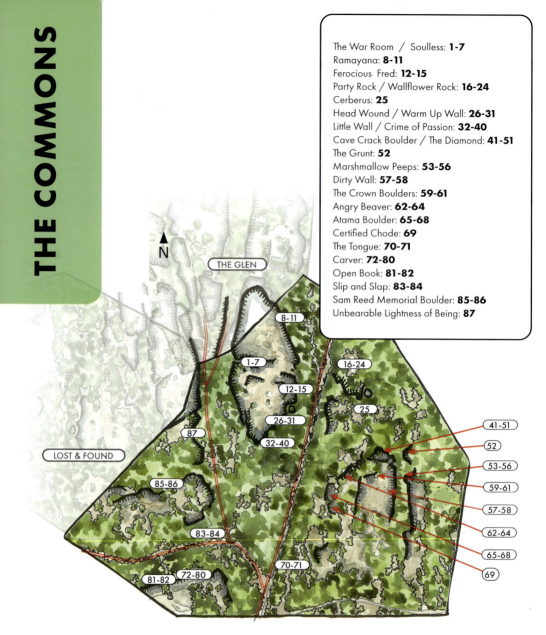

The War Room / Soulless: **1-7**
Ramayana: **8-11**
Ferocious Fred: **12-15**
Party Rock / Wallflower Rock: **16-24**
Cerberus: **25**
Head Wound / Warm Up Wall: **26-31**
Little Wall / Crime of Passion: **32-40**
Cave Crack Boulder / The Diamond: **41-51**
The Grunt: **52**
Marshmallow Peeps: **53-56**
Dirty Wall: **57-58**
The Crown Boulders: **59-61**
Angry Beaver: **62-64**
Atama Boulder: **65-68**
Certified Chode: **69**
The Tongue: **70-71**
Carver: **72-80**
Open Book: **81-82**
Slip and Slap: **83-84**
Sam Reed Memorial Boulder: **85-86**
Unbearable Lightness of Being: **87**

THE COMMONS

From the lower parking lot, take an uphill and rocky left up an old service road. Drive carefully (this road has claimed at least 4 5 cars at the time of writing) for about 0.4 mile passing a deeply rutted section with a C-shaped detour on the right. The Commons is littered with rocks on both sides. It's a common misconception that the moniker is a tribute to the rapper dubbed Common.

Aaron B. on *Soul In Hand* (V8).

THE WAR ROOM

☐ 1. EGG TOPIC V3
Starting on the face just left of *The War Room*, climb the right side of the arête.
FA George Hughbanks

☐ 2. THE WAR ROOM V4 ★★
Sit start with fun moves.

☐ 3. BATTLE CRY V2 ★
The problem on the right.

SOULLESS

☐ 4. SOUL SLINGER V2 ★
Move up and left with a press into the slab.

☐ 5. SOUL IN HAND V8 ★★
Sit start with a left-hand crimp and right hand pinch on the arête. Bust up to a pinch, a drive by, and a heady top-out.

☐ 6. SOULSTICE V3 ★★
Stand start on a good left sidepull and a right pinch. Climb straight up with fun movement to a highish top-out.

☐ 7. SOUL SHINE V4 ★
Sit start in compression with a sloper on the right-hand arête. Bust a move.

THE WAR ROOM

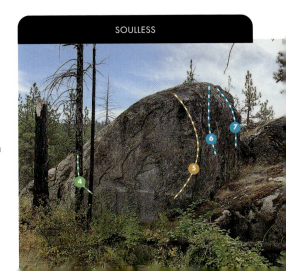

SOULLESS

RAMAYANA

☐ 8. HANUMAN V2 ★★
Start matched at the chest-high crack, move up and right with a pinch next to the seam, and then trend up and left following the slanting and slopey edges.

☐ 9. VISHNU V2
Start matched on a good jug on the corner with high feet perched on the edge, trend left towards the crack and follow all the way up.

☐ 10. BALASANA V1
Start with your hands on head-height slopers and use all the incut edges and blocky seams to ascend.

☐ 11. RAMA V3
Start with your left hand on a small head-high crimp and your right hand at about chest height. Make delicate moves using some small crimps, a gaston, and possibly a mono pocket to trend up the crack shape.

BEAR DEAD BLOWS

☐ 12. BEAR DEAD BLOWS V6 ★
This mini sport route has been bouldered before...but we wouldn't recommend it. (Nate bailed from the lip, lol. NO SEND)
FA Steve Moss

FEROCIOUS FRED WALL

☐ 13. FEROCIOUS FRED V8 ★★★
Start sitting on the left side of the face with a left-hand pinch and right hand in the crack. Progress to a right hand sidepull and swing up to the lip. Classic.
FA Bryan Franklin

☐ 14. FAT FINGERED FRED V10 ★
Start on the far right on the face. Traverse left along the seam and finish as for *Ferocious*.
FA Steve Moss

☐ 15. SAINTLY SAM V2 ★
Start on the chest-high holds and climb the corner. Use those heels, yo. This climb was orginially done as a V4 sit-down start, which is highly recommended.

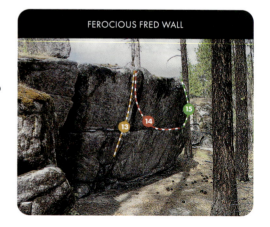

86 | McLELLAN

PARTY ROCK / WALLFLOWER

PARTY ROCK (TRIANGLE) / WALLFLOWER FRONTSIDE

☐ 16. PARTY ANIMAL V1 ★
Starting low on the left, traverse the good rail up the lip of the boulder.
FA Helma Beckey

☐ 17. THE TRIANGLE V4 ★
Start matched on the crimp rail in the center of the face and climb straight up. Drop-knee anyone?
FA Helma Beckey

☐ 18. PARTY ROCK V3 ★★
Bust right from matched on the crimp. Powerful and fun.
FA Helma Beckey

☐ 19. WALLFLOWER SURF V1 ★★
Hop up to the left end of the lip and traverse right to a mantel right of *Elysium*.

☐ 20. ELYSIUM V2 ★★
From a head-high edge, climb up balancy moves to an easy mantel. Lotta fun.

☐ 21. WHAT THE KIDS WANT V5 ★★
Start as for *Elysium*, traverse right on the thinning seam, then bust right into the incut rail and finish it off with a press onto the slab and more climbing.
FA Nate Lynch

☐ 22. WALLFLOWER V0 ★★
From a start on waist-high incuts find your way up great holds to the highest point.

☐ 23. AIN'T NO PARTY (LIKE MY GRANDMA'S TEA PARTY) V2 ★★
With the trees to your back climb the decent holds up the tall bulge.

☐ 24. EBB AND FLOW V9 ★★
Start sitting matched on the obvious jug. Hit the fingerlock, bust out right into compression and grovel over. Have fun and don't forget...taping is cheating.
FA Steve Moss

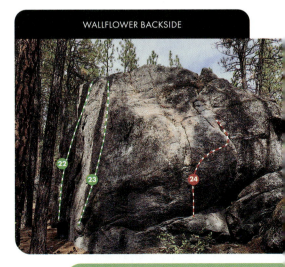

WALLFLOWER BACKSIDE

SPOKANE BOULDERING | 87

Jaleena J. on *Wallflower* (V0). Photo by Ben Boldt

CERBERUS

☐ **25. CERBERUS V3**
Behind the Wallflower rock. Climb the left arête, finagling yourself into the overhang for extra steeze.

HEAD WOUND CAVE

☐ **26. CONCUSSION V8 ★**
Start in the deepest corner of the cave. Go straight to the lip, and then traverse the lip right to the arête. Grade unconfirmed.

☐ **27. HEAD WOUND CAVE V4 ★ ★**
Start in the deepest corner of the cave. Traverse out the crack into a vertical encounter with the arête. Pumpy for pebble wrestlers.

☐ **28. SNITCHES GET STITCHES V3 ★**
Starting on the low detached jug, climb up the hanging face on edges, as with the finish of *Head Wound Cave*.

WARM-UP WALL

☐ **29. WARM UP WALL (5.9 FACE) V1**
Various easy problems on the chunky slabby wall. Do whatever you'd like. The far right corner holds a fun layback crack.

Nate L. on *Snitches Get Stitches* (V3) in the Headwound Cave.

HEAD WOUND CAVE

☐ **30. LAYBACK DIHEDRAL V0 ★**
Do what you can inside of the crack and try your best. You've got this, friend. You're doing great and your hair is fantastic.

☐ **31. GOLDEN RATIO V4 ★**
Start on a high right hand sidepull, climb through fun moves to a high top-out that we haven't done yet because it was wet. We weren't scared.

WARM-UP WALL

SPOKANE BOULDERING | 89

LITTLE WALL (MANTEL WALL)

☐ **32. BUILDING BLOCKS V1** ★
Start matched on the sloping block on the left side of the short wall. Climb up and mantel. Also an option for a beginner's mantel to the left. Honestly, many options and variations are available here—go crazy.

☐ **33. FURTHER EDUCATION V3** ★
Traverse right on the lip to mantel at *Call to Arms*.

☐ **34. CALL TO ARMS V7** ★
Start with double underclings at waist height on the left end of the wall. Pinch the arête and fire for the lip out left. Traverse a move left and mantel.
FA Steve Moss

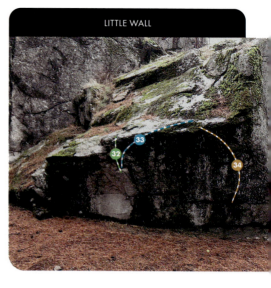

CRIME OF PASSION

☐ **35. 5.8 DIHEDRAL V0** ★
Climb the crack in the dihedral on the far left side of the tall face. Good fun.

☐ **36. CRIME OF PASSION V9** ★★
Start matched on a head-height crimp rail. Climb straight up using small holds into a right-facing crimp rail before committing (or not committing) to the blocky jug high on the face.
FA Nate Lynch

Arden P. on *Crime of Passion* (V9).

90 | McLELLAN

Steve M. on Mr. Wenzel (V9).

☐ 37. FORBIDDEN BUCKET V7 ★
Start about 12 feet right of *Crime of Passion* on small chest-high crimps. Climb through a triangular pinch and then left, following a seam to the blocky jug. Unrepeated and unconfirmed...but we'd guess it's hard.
FA Arden Pete

☐ 38. INSOLENCE V8 ★
Start matched on a high crimp right of *CoP*. Climb right through a thin hold, a triangular pinch, and into *T.E.N.O.F.*
FA Steve Moss

☐ 39. THE EVOLVING NATURE OF FLAKES V4 ★★
Start on the far right of the face, just up the slab, on decent edges. Climb trending left on crimps to the sloping edge and over the top with good holds.
FA Arden Pete

☐ 40. AIN'T NO FOOLIN' AROUND V4
Start at *Evolving Nature of Flakes* but climb up and right over the sloping landing. Yikes.
FA Arden Pete

Mike V. on *The Evolving Nature of Flakes* (V4). Photo by Sari L.

SPOKANE BOULDERING | 91

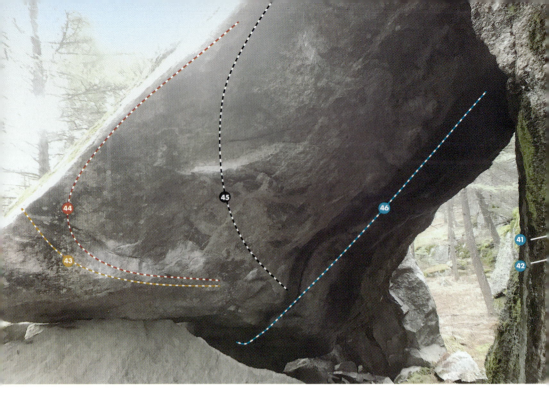

CAVE CRACK BOULDERS

☐ 41. RELIGIOUS GUILT V4 ★
Start low left, climb the wall under *Mr. Wenzel* up and right.

☐ 42. LOVELY LITTLE LIES V4 ★
Climb the short corner on the face below the apex of *Mr. Wenzel*. Start sitting from a jug.

☐ 43. EASY OUT V6 ★
Start as for *Mr. Wenzel*, but mantel as soon as you reach the lip.
FA Nate Lynch

☐ 44. MR. WENZEL V9 ★★★
Start at the overhang on the edge of the slab with a good left-hand crimp, and your right hand far out on a lonely sloping crimp. Climb left to the lip then up to a heady rock-over at the apex of the roof. Very Good.
FA Nate Lynch

☐ 45. MALICIOUS MISCHIEF PROJECT
It appears possible to start a few moves right of *Mr. Wenzel* in the crack...but instead of following the low line, bust up to the sloping shelf in a huge span and finish at the apex. We'd love to see this one go...

☐ 46. CAVE CRACK (BEST CRACK IN SPOKANE) V5 ★
Climb the hand crack in the roof from a stand start. Top out using the boulder behind you. Classic.
FA Helma Beckey

☐ 47. THE RHINO V4
A rock that you wish had more climbing options, but alas anything under the roof will be forever a bridesmaid, never a bride. The start on the southeast side with a right hand on the lowest part of the horn and a left-hand under the roof and a smeared foot provides a tough "fall-in" move, and a chill cruise to the top.

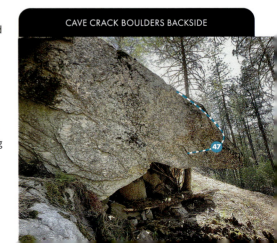

CAVE CRACK BOULDERS BACKSIDE

92 | McLELLAN

Shane C. on *The Rhino* (V4).

DIAMOND SLAB

☐ **48. FROM THE STEEP SIDE V2** (NOT PICTURED)
Begin as for *Bait and Switch* but head left.
FA Helma Beckey

☐ **49. BAIT AND SWITCH V7** ★★★
Starting on a good flat edge, climb right through the corridor just around the corner and then up. Technical, tensiony, and terrific.
FA Steve Moss

☐ **50. DIAMOND SLAB V7** ★★
Climb the center of the slab eventually reaching the left arête. Alternatively, try to climb the slab with no arêtes to the apex...good luck!
FA Helma Beckey

DIAMOND SLAB

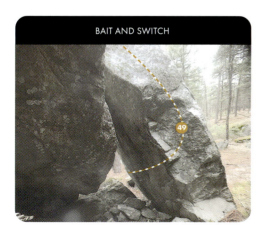

BAIT AND SWITCH

☐ **51. DIAMOND EASY V2** ★
Climb the slab using the right arête.
FA Helma Beckey

SPOKANE BOULDERING | 93

THE GRUNT (NOT PICTURED)

☐ 52. THE GRUNT V4
Big, dirty, and all by itself. Just like the moon. Unconfirmed—maybe harder.
FA George Hughbanks

MARSHMALLOW PEEPS

☐ 53. SEA FOAM V1
From a right hand edge and left-hand sidepull, pull up, press and slap.
FA George Hughbanks

☐ 54. CANDY FLOSS V2
With a right hand pinch under the prow and feet on the slab, pull yourself through the overhang.
FA George Hughbanks

☐ 55. MARSHMALLOW PEEPS V2 ★
Climb straight up from the big jug.
FA George Hughbanks

☐ 56. EARS V0 ★★★
From the right side of the rounded bulge, climb up and left with big moves and holds. Really good!
FA George Hughbanks

MARSHMALLOW PEEPS FRONTSIDE

MARSHMALLOW PEEPS BACKSIDE

DIRTY WALL

☐ 57. CRESCENT MOON V2
Start on the left side of the loose crescent towards the large middle rounded edge and pull up and over the blank bulge.

☐ 58. LA FIERA V2
Use the flat rail start to make your way to squeezing seams up and left. Start out further right and add a grade for "La Dura Fiera."

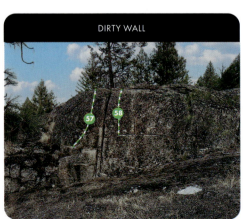
DIRTY WALL

94 | McLELLAN

THE CROWN

☐ **59. THE CROWN V2** ★★
From left-facing jugs move up through big blocky jugs, topping out at the apex. Good fun.

☐ **60. THE JESTER V2**
Not technically on the Crown boulder but just below it. Start on the left side on the half-basketball shaped hold. Move up the blocks to the top using the good round edges on the sides. **VAR:** Traverse into *The Stir* or *The Symbol* for some extra grades.

☐ **61. THE STIR V3** ★
Start low (lower) in the flake under the bulge. Move up the next flake system and after the large jug stay to the right on the face. **VAR:** Traverse into either problem from the left or right.

☐ **62. THE SYMBOL V3** ★
Start with your back to the tree with a right hand on a crimp at stomach height and an awkward undercling near your thigh for your left hand. Move right on edges and head right and up on crimps, though you could go straight up. **VAR:** you can probably guess, huh?

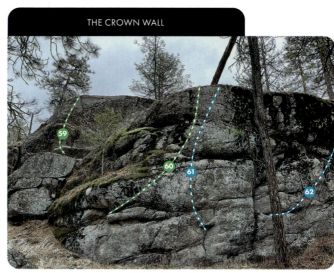

THE CROWN WALL

ANGRY BEAVER

☐ **63. LOUNGE LIZARD V1**
Start on the left side of the wall with chest-high holds and climb straight up.
FA George Hughbanks

☐ **64. CALM COYOTE V1** ★
On the right side, start low in the horizontal seam and trend up and right following the higher-angled seam.
FA George Hughbanks

☐ **65. ANGRY BEAVER V1**
Same start as #64 but straight up.
FA George Hughbanks

ANGRY BEAVER

SPOKANE BOULDERING | 95

ATAMA BOULDER

☐ 66. ARBITRARY AGRESSION V6 ★
Sit under the overhang on the left side of the face with a poor left-hand hold in the roof and a right hand crimp around the corner. Proceed up the side of the overhang on thin crimps, mantling into the notch above. A bit painful at first, but neat nonetheless.

☐ 67. GOLDFISH V1
Start standing. Climb up small holds to the horizontal crack and drop. Venturing to the top on fragile crimps clocks in around V6 for the adventurous. Could clean up well...

☐ 68. ATAMA NO AMENONUHOKO V8 ★ ★
Start standing at the high undercling. Move left to a seam, up through small crimps, and back right to a jug pinch on the right side of the spearhead-shaped dihedral. Commit for the lip.
FA Steve Moss

☐ 69. MOSHI MOSHI V5 ★
From the start hold of *Atama*, move right using small round crimps, stab a foot on the right hand slab, and bump until you can bump no more. Lunge for the jug pinch and ignore the butterflies at the top.
FA Shane Collins

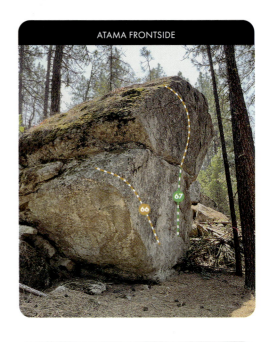

ATAMA FRONTSIDE

ATAMA BACKSIDE

Chad R. on *Angry Beaver* (V1). Photo by George Hughbanks

Nate L. on *Atama* (V8).

CERTIFIED CHODE

☐ **70. CERTIFIED CHODE V3** ★
A very small boulder to the right if looking at Atama. Start at the bottom of the arête with two good opposing crimps on the corner. Follow the arête up. You can use the seam to the left if you'd like, they are about the same. Choose your own adventure!

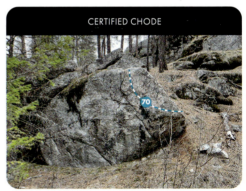

THE TONGUE

☐ **71. UNDERNEATH PROJECT**
From the grainy shelf under the roof, levitate yourself past a barely-there sidepull crimp and around the lip. We don't think this will go.

☐ **72. JUMP START PROJECT**
Seems like this feature could be climbed by jumping to the suspended lip and mantling or traversing to the right.

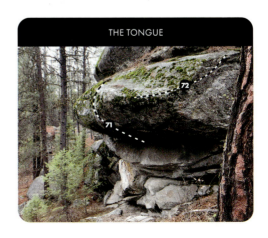

SPOKANE BOULDERING | 97

CARVER BOULDER

☐ **73. SOMETHING TO SAY V5 ★★★**
Sitting, grab a left-hand crimp with the right hand on a jug on the arête. Climb the path of least resistance. It's a bit harder to find than you'd think....Classic.
FA Cam Freiburghaus

☐ **74. MY BOY MAZLO V7 ★**
Start as for #73. Stay on the right side of the small face using the right arête and a big move to the lip. Somewhat contrived.
FA Shane Collins

☐ **75. SERRATED V10 ★**
Start on the undercling as for *Carver Low*. Move left to the arête, then right into the second hold on *Carver*. Grade unconfirmed.
FA Chris Covillo

☐ **76. CARVER LOW V8 ★★**
Start sitting matched on the undercling on the left side of the face. Climb into *Carver*.
FA Chris Covillo

☐ **77. CARVER V7 ★★★**
Start matched on the blocky jugs in the center of the overhung face. Make a few large moves on perfect full-pad edges. Classic.
FA Cam Freiburghaus

Cam F. on Something to Say (V5).

☐ 78. CARVER EXTENSION V8 ★★
Start sitting, match on the sloping feature as far right as possible, traverse left along the feature into the beginning of *Carver*. If there is a rock in your butt, you're starting at the right place.
FA Shane Collins

☐ 79. CASPER V2 ★
Start as for *Carver Extension*, climb to the low lip with a tricky quasi-press.

☐ 80. LOWDOWNER V2 ★★ (NOT PICTURED)
Start from a crouch on the wall opposite *Carver*. Climb fun blocky holds trending left to a slopey lip. Drop here or soldier on.

☐ 81. HIDDEN PROJECT
On the wall opposite *Carver* also lies a crimpy project.

OPEN BOOK

☐ 82. CORNER V1
Stem up the dirty corner.

☐ 83. OPEN BOOK V2 ★★
From a high left crimp and a right hand low on the arête, make big moves up good holds. Very good.

Cam F. on Carver (V7).

SLIP AND SLAP

☐ 84. SLIP AND SLAP V4 ★
Ascend the left side of the face, traversing crimps left, then up.

☐ 85. FAST FASHION V5 ★★
From a sit start on the left-facing jug rail, climb up and right implementing a neat pocket on this very sequential problem.

OPEN BOOK

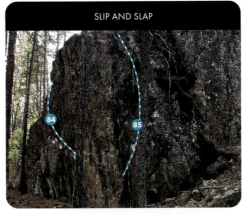

SLIP AND SLAP

SPOKANE BOULDERING | 99

SAM REED MEMORIAL

☐ 86. SAM REED V3
Follow the seam to the top. This rarely gets climbed and is very loose—be careful. Many other possibilities exist.

☐ 87. THE BACKSIDE V5 ★
On the backside of Sam Reed, start as deep in the small cave as you can and make a handful of fun moves out right to the arête. Use the face to help you to the top. Look at you go!

ENBEARABLE LIGHTNESS OF BEING

☐ 88. UNBEARABLE LIGHTNESS OF BEING V5 ★★
Climb the left side of the tall bulge from a stand start. Good edges give way to crimps higher up. Good movement and heady.
FA Brett Jesson

SAM REED MEMORIAL FRONTSIDE

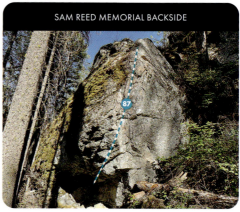

SAM REED MEMORIAL BACKSIDE

UNBEARABLE LIGHTNESS OF BEING

Mollie A. on *Unbearable Lightness of Being* (V5)

Arden P. on *The Molar Center* (V4).

LOST & FOUND

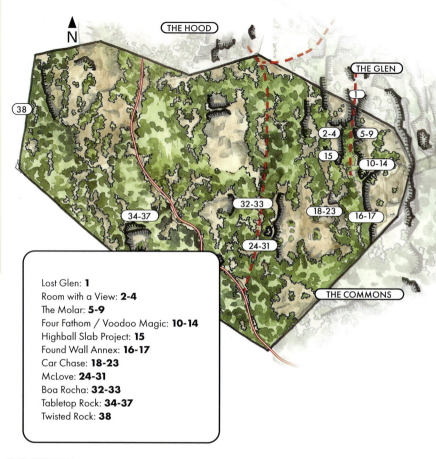

Lost Glen: **1**
Room with a View: **2-4**
The Molar: **5-9**
Four Fathom / Voodoo Magic: **10-14**
Highball Slab Project: **15**
Found Wall Annex: **16-17**
Car Chase: **18-23**
McLove: **24-31**
Boa Rocha: **32-33**
Tabletop Rock: **34-37**
Twisted Rock: **38**

LOST & FOUND

As the southwestern-most clump of boulders in the main area, the Lost & Found area holds a good selection of lines that are typically the first to dry after a rainy Northwesty day. With easy access from The Glen, The Hood, and The Commons this is a must-hit in your McLellan circuit. Holding classics like *VooDoo Magic*, *McLove Handles* and *The Molar* all within a stones throw, this open area is a favorite.

LOST GLEN

☐ 1. LOST GLEN V2
When taking the corridor through The Molar and Room with a View to get to The Glen, you'll pass this problem on the rock wall on your right after you squeeze yourself up. Start matched on a head-high hold and make your way up to the vertical seams.

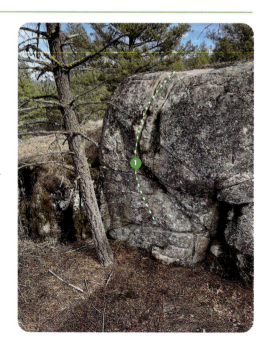

102 | MCLELLAN

ROOM WITH A VIEW

☐ **2. MANDIBLE MANTEL V0 ★ ★ ★**
Mantel onto the starting jug, reach for the lip and mantel all over again.

☐ **3. BABY TOOTH V1**
Start low on the corner, making a couple little moves right and up. Small and pleasant.

☐ **4. ROOM WITH A VIEW V4 ★**
Starting low, slap up grainy holds with ongoing tension.
FA Shane Collins

ROOM WITH A VIEW

TOOTH FAIRY (NOT PICTURED)

☐ **5. TOOTH FAIRY V1**
This is the small rock with a few options opposite The Molar. Use this fella to warm up or have fun on however you'd like.

THE MOLAR

☐ **6. THE MOLAR HUG V1 ★**
On the back side of The Molar, hug the two sides and up you go!

☐ **7. THE MOLAR LEFT V2 ★**
Starting from high right hand sidepull and a lower left-hand sidepull, climb up and left topping out at the arête.

☐ **8. THE MOLAR CENTER V4 ★**
With the same start as the left, climb nearly straight up using an interesting left-hand ear hold.

☐ **9. THE MOLAR RIGHT V4 ★ ★ ★**
A perplexing start finishes pretty high in four memorable moves. Reach high from under the roof to get matched on the starting edge. Grab a left-hand undercling and then move steadily into the right-facing edge—moves so good you'll dream about them. Can be started lower for a lot more difficulty.
FA Fred Beckey

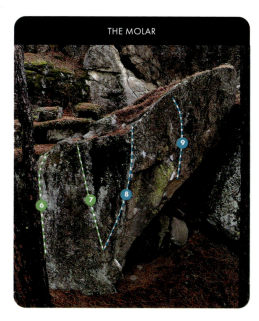
THE MOLAR

Ally C. on *The Molar Right* (V4)
Photo by Jon Jonckers

FOUR FATHOM

☐ **10. BLUE WATER V3** ★
Climb the shortest part of this tall wall.

☐ **11. 4 FATHOM WALL V?** ★
The mossy tall face..

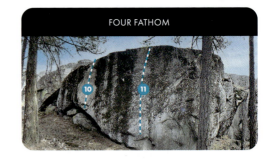

VOODOO MAGIC

☐ **12. EATING AT THE Y V7** ★
Climb the angled sloping seam. Harder than it looks.
FA Arden Pete

☐ **13. VOODOO MAGIC V4** ★ ★ ★
Start standing with a high left-hand sidepull and right hand in the crack. Move to good left-hand holds and then transition left onto the face for some excellent (hard) moves to the top—objectively not a V4. Classic!

☐ **14. BLACK MAGIC V7**
Start as for *Voodoo Magic*. Climb the overhang all the way to the top without using the wall to your right...too much.
FA Shane Collins

☐ **15. HIGHBALL SLAB PROJECT** (NOT PICTURED)
Around the corner from *Voodoo*, climb the BIG west facing slab on flat crimps to a left-trending rail. Don't fall. Seriously don't. Shane doesn't think it'll go. That's all the motivation Nate needs.

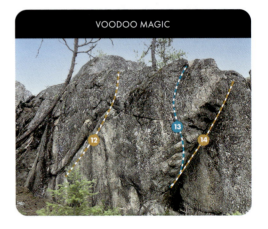

Nate L. on Voodoo Magic (V4)

FOUND WALL ANNEX

☐ **16. HOTSTOPPER HUCK V3**
From a crouched start with a decent left hand and a flat right hand hold, squeeze the low skinny part of the rock, position yourself with the good incut right hand undercling and the larger left-hand jug, and make two fun moves to the upper part of the bulge and top straight up.

☐ **17. CALDER'S ARÊTE V3**
Start on the the low horn feature on the slabby arête.

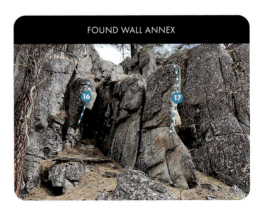

Jeremy C. on *Voodoo Magic* (V4).

CAR CHASE

☐ 18. AGGRAVATED ASSAULT V2
Start around the left-hand corner with your left hand following a good seam and your right hand using a couple small edges to balance yourself up.
FA John Calder

☐ 19. CAR CHASE V1
Hug the arête with your left hand on a broken block around the arête and right hand on a good jug. With a high foot, bop your way to a good left-hand jug and shimmy up.
FA John Calder

☐ 20. HIP WADERS V1
The leftmost of the three phallic skinny pillars. Start standing on the low bulge and make awkward moves to the top.
FA John Calder

☐ 21. MAROON NISSAN V1
Start crouched on the horn shaped feature in the middle of three pillars, follow the pinch rail up to an easy finish. Full value if you only use the pinch.
FA John Calder

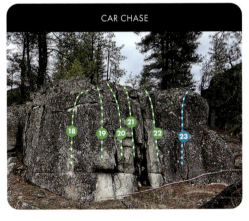

☐ 22. PILFERERS V2
The rightmost penis-looking pillar and the hardest of the three. Starts sitting on the good shelf and uses some slappy compression moves to top out.
FA John Calder

☐ 23. REASONABLE FORCE V3
Starting low on the top of a good flake, use the next couple of good holds to help you maneuver to a sloping hold on the arête and a blank top.
FA John Calder

SPOKANE BOULDERING | 105

McLOVE

☐ 24. WHIPLASH V3
From a sit start squeezing the corner with a bad right hand, make a desperate launch for the lip above.
FA Shane Collins

☐ 25. FUN AND DONE V1 ★★
Make a big move from the pair of jugs, then move right on good holds to a simple top-out.

☐ 26. EARLY ONSET GERIATRIC V6 ★
Start on two crimps on the corner (right of the *Fun and Done* jugs). Make a big move to a sloping edge and up through crimps into the finish of *Fun and Done*. Don't break a hip.
FA Nate Lynch

☐ 27. CENTER LINE PROJECT
Climb the thin face over the jumbled landing.

☐ 28. HIPS DON'T LIE PROJECT
From a low hold on the left-facing rail, move up through a balancy sequence.

☐ 29. McLOVE HANDLES V3 ★★★
Climb the slightly overhung triangle face of the small boulder. Begin as low as your wingspan will allow. Great intro to compression climbing.

WHISKEY FOR ONE

☐ 30. WHISKEY FOR ONE V4 ★★
Move from the low incuts into another crimp and bust to the rail of *Tequila* to finish.
FA Nate Lynch

☐ 31. TEQUILA FOR TWO V3 ★★
Start matched on the rightmost jug. Follow the rail left on interesting holds and balancy moves to the lip.
FA Nate Lynch

MCLOVE

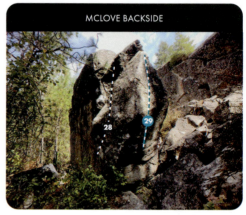

MCLOVE BACKSIDE

WHISKEY FOR ONE

Shane C. on Whiskey for One (V4).

BOA ROCHA

☐ 32. DELICATE SLAB V4
On the far left corner of Boa Rocha, this fussy little effer only exists to cause pain. Start matched on the small, clean, credit-card crimp and stab your feet on the flat, featureless, slabby face. Make two or three tic-taky moves with insecurity for the top. Small but hard.

☐ 33. BOA ROCHA V3
The center line on the face. Start on opposing chest-high sidepulls, move to the atari-shaped feature up and to the left, only to balance your way to good jugs on the far right for a high top-out. Good rock.

George H. on *Delicate Slab* (V4). Photo by Chad Ramsey

TABLETOP ROCK

☐ **34. PUMPKIN WAFFLE V0**
On the arête down from *Baby Fett*, use good, stomach-height holds on the arête and climb up.

☐ **35. COFFEE AT BOOTS V1**
Just to the right of *Pumpkin Waffle*, climb the seam.

☐ **36. RITTER RUN V2**
Find the fridge-shaped cut in Tabletop Rock on the southeast side. Start on the edge and use the dihedral to get it up...heh.

☐ **37. BABY FETT V7** ★
Start underclinged in the low seam, using the obvious small left-hand crimp and some tight footwork. Bust to the sloping edge.
FA Steve Moss

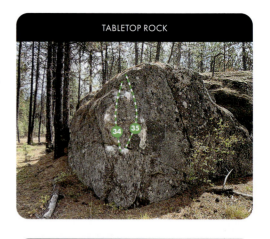

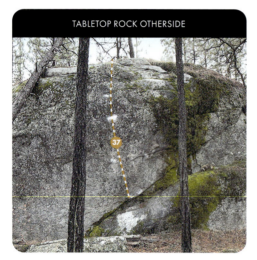

Steve M. on *Baby Fett* (V7).

108 | MCLELLAN

TWISTED ROCK

☐ 38. TWISTED PULL V3 ★
Start on two flat chest-high crimps and pull through to the right-facing seam on the face. Take that seam up and right.
FA Shane Collins

REMOTE ROCKS

☐ 1. JAWS V12 ★★
Start low on the left arête, climb up the arête into a tricky section at the lip and what looks to be the mantel of a lifetime.

☐ 2. POGO POWER V9 ★★
Start matched high in the sloping pod, move left to a good undercling, levitate to the lip and mantel. Simple. A few very small holds below could turn this into Spokanes hardest problem.
FA Nate Lynch

Nate L. on Pogo Power (V9).

Chad R. on *Inguinal Fortitude* (V3). Photo by George Hughbanks

Fern Gullies Parking

FERN GULLIES

KAMIAKIN

☐ **1. KAMIAKIN V5** ★
Climb the tall face left of the arête.
FA Steve Moss

☐ **2. QUALCHAN'S ARÊTE V6** ★
Climb the tall soaring arête.
FA Alex Nikolayev

INGUINAL FORTITUDE

☐ **3. BREANNE'S SIT DOWN CRACK PROBLEM V2**
Sit down. Climb the crack.
FA Breanne

☐ **4. V0 AND SONS V0** ★

☐ **5. INGUINAL FORTITUDE V3**
Stand start left of the overhang, move right and up.
FA George Hughbanks

☐ **6. STEPFORD V2** ★

MASTHEAD BOULDER

☐ **7. BARNACLES V5**
Start as for *Stowaway*, but climb straight up on the less appealing stone.
FA Nate Lynch

☐ **8. STOWAWAY V7** ★
Start sitting with a left-hand sidepull and right hand sloping edge on the arête. Climb up and right using a big gaston and a throw to a jug out right. Unique.
FA Nate Lynch

☐ **9. WAHEELA V8** ★★★
Start sitting as for *Stowaway*, but move into the overhang with your left hand on the arête, climbing the entire length of the overhang for a full-value problem. Excellent stone.
FA Drew Schick

☐ **10. MASTHEAD PROJECT** ★★
Climb the gorgeous overhang on small holds matched on the crimp.

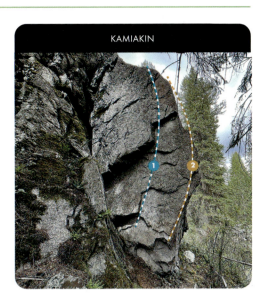

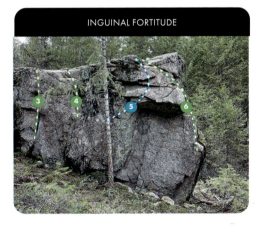

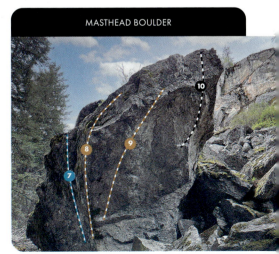

Nate L. on Masthead Project

THE FUNK (NOT PICTURED)

☐ **11. THE FUNK V2** ★
From a sit, climb the short southeast corner of the boulder just up the hill west of *Masthead*.
FA Nate Lynch

☐ **12. GYM SOCKS V2**
Climb up the edges on the south face just around the corner from *The Funk*. Stand start.

FELACIO

☐ **13. FELACIO V6** ★
A one-mover on the obvious hanging prow partway up the talus field. Start matched on the south face of the boulder. Pop to the lip.
FA Alex Nikolayev

FELACIO

Shane C. on Fekky (V5)

112 | MCLELLAN

FREDDIE MERCURY

☐ 14. BOHEMIAN RHAPSODY V4 ★★★
The Freddie Mercury Boulder is high on the talus field past *Felacio*. Start standing with opposing holds and tech your way up in compression. Grade unconfirmed.
FA Steve Moss

☐ 15. FREDDIE MERCURY PROJECT ★★
Sit start with the right-facing incut rail. Move left into *Bohemian Rhapsody* and core up!

☐ 16. KILLER QUEEN V9 ★
Start low on right-facing incuts, move up right into the seam and beyond. Hard.
FA Alex Nikolayev

FEKKY

☐ 17. FEKKY V5 ★★
Start low in compression. Climb up the overhang avoiding the wall to the left.
FA Shane Collins

☐ 18. WAY TOO MUCH V2 ★
Climb the dihedral juts right of *Fekky*.

☐ 19. CRESCENT PROJECT
Start from the head-height angled rail, move left to the arête and up using a high heel.

THE ANVIL (NOT PICTURED)

☐ 20. THE ANVIL V3 ★★
Start sitting matched in the crack, move left toward the point, over a worsening landing. Awkwardly mantel.
FA Shane Collins

FREDDIE MERCURY

FEKKY

Nate L. Crescent Project

Alex C. on *Johnny is a G* (V6).

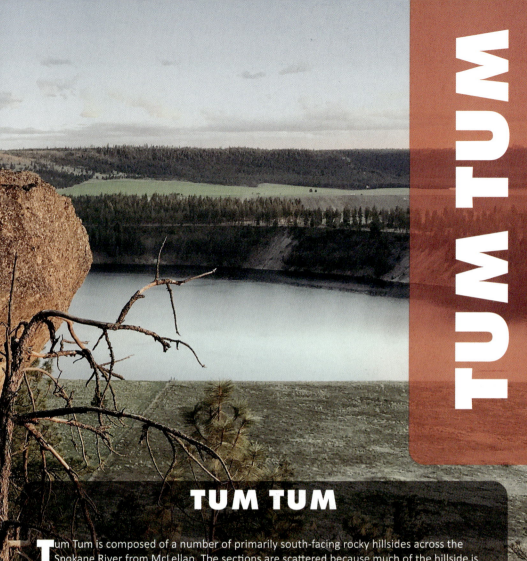

TUM TUM

Tum Tum is composed of a number of primarily south-facing rocky hillsides across the Spokane River from McLellan. The sections are scattered because much of the hillside is privately owned and not climber-accessible. In the past decades these scattered bands were commonly referred to as First Canyon, Second Canyon, and Third Canyon. Unfortunately, the order and starting point for "First" Canyon differed per friend group and whether Mercury was in retrograde.

In this guide, we're explicitly re-classifying each jumble of rock to avoid any future miscommunications. If, for example, you're meeting your buddy out there but due to unrealized alternate definitions of "First Canyon" you're left waiting for like 45 minutes in the blazing sun without water, crash pads, or chalk (because your friend said that he would bring some for you) and when you decide to explore some of the rocks near the road while you wait, you get assaulted by an uncompromising rattlesnake that deflates your untenable wilderness-outdoorsy-guy ego and bound you to a car ride home without any climbing on your only Saturday off...Matt...but I digress.

We'll start going through this area from east to west starting with the closest to Spokane and moving outward.

TUM TUM

Looking at the Lower West End hillside from the parking lot. This steep and rocky terrain is indicative of the greater Tum Tum area.

DRIVING DIRECTIONS

From Spokane: From the south, take N Maple St, W Northwest Blvd, or N Driscoll Blvd to WA-291 or heading from the north take 9 Mile Rd/W Francis Ave to meet WA-291. From where Francis turns into the highway, the pullout for the hairpin boulders are found 20.5 miles down on the right. Parking for the Lower East is just before the hairpin.

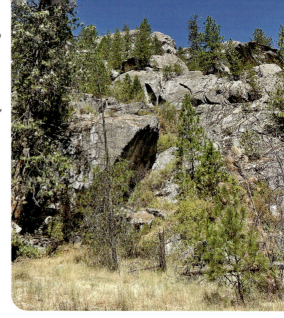

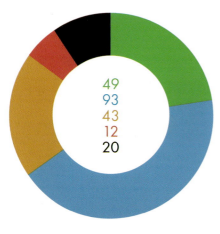

49
93
43
12
20

The pullout for the Corona Boulders is close to two miles down at 22.1 miles from the start of the highway. The Craiglandia parking lot is about another two miles down at 24.6 miles from the start of the highway. West End Parking is the next right at the 25 mile mark, with Corkscrew Canyon Road being the next right after that.

From HWY 2/Reardan, WA:
You can leave HWY 2 at Reardan, WA and take WA-231 down to the Spokane River for 14.3 miles and then at the dam, take a right on WA-291 for five miles to hit the West End

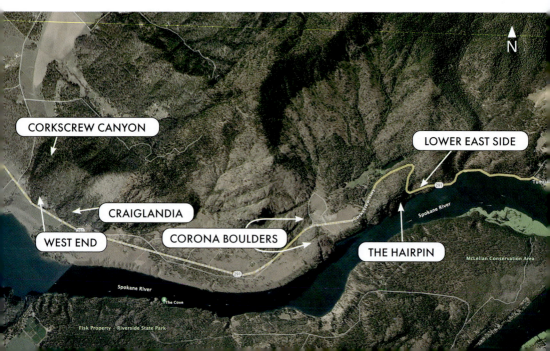

LOWER EAST SIDE

This small area is the first encountered when coming from Spokane. With a handful of moderately-graded lines, this spot is just off Highway 291 before you start making your way uphill to the hairpin turn going up to the other areas.

THE FIST

☐ 1. FISTICUFFS V3 ★ ★
Start matched on a slopey edge on the arête. Make moves up the corner and top out trending left. Harder than it looks, but great fun.
FA Matt Duddy

☐ 2. JAMETURE NIGHT V7 ★
Start with a right hand in the slopey crack and left hand in the pocket. Move up and left into the finish of *Fisticuffs* or into a thrutchy jamming finish.
FA Dave Shepard

☐ 3. FINGERCUFFS V3
Sit start hugging both sides of the opposing holds in the cracks, compress up and trend straight up.
FA George Hughbanks

ICE PRINCESS

☐ 4. GRAPE APE V2 ★
Start on the left side of the wall with your left hand on the left-pointing nose feature and right hand chest-high sidepull. Follow nice holds straight up.
FA George Hughbanks

☐ 5. ICE PRINCESS V3 ★
Starting with a left hand in the obvious neck-high notch and the right hand on the good edge down to the right. Moves up and left using great incuts and blocks to gain the lip. There is a variation to the right.
FA George Hughbanks

THE FIST

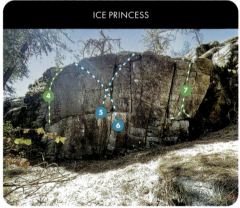

ICE PRINCESS

☐ 6. BRAVE BULL V4 ★
With a left hand on the slopey seam under the right side of *Ice Princess* and the left hand on a small sidepull on the face. Leave the scrunchy start, making some gaston moves left and up to a ledgey top.
FA George Hughbanks

☐ 7. THREE-TOED SLOTH V2 ★
Starting in a very low crouch, hugging both sides of the block, manage your way up to the block in the top middle of the face, and top out with the help of the large seam.
FA George Hughbanks

SPOKANE BOULDERING | 117

THE HAIRPIN

Overlooking Lake Spokane, The Hairpin area is a short walk from the roadside parking located (you guessed it) between the two hairpins corners on Highway 291. Most of the problems are located on a gently overhanging cliff band. The area offers a range of moderate to hard problems.

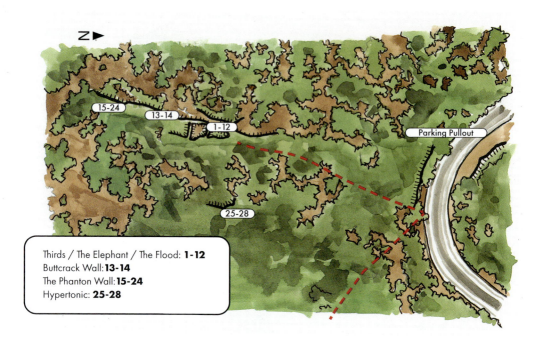

Thirds / The Elephant / The Flood: **1-12**
Buttcrack Wall: **13-14**
The Phantom Wall: **15-24**
Hypertonic: **25-28**

THE HAIRPIN

THIRDS

☐ 1. PENCIL NECK GHOST V1
Sit start with a left-hand edge and right hand pinch on the coner. Move to good holds and trend right.

☐ 2. DING DONG DARLING V3
Start standing with widely-spaced, blocky, right-facing sidepulls. Move up and left to good shelves on the slab. Lower start involving the pocket? Go get it.

☐ 3. DOCTOR WAS THE MOTHER V3 ★
Sit start on opposing holds. Power up.
FA Travis Wenzel

118 | TUM TUM

Melissa M. on The Flood (V3)
Photo by Serra B.

ELEPHANT

☐ 4. NATE'S LOVELY ELEPHANT V5 ★
Start sitting with your left hand on the arête, and right hand on a tiny nubbin in the overhang. More fun than at first glance.
FA Shane Collins

☐ 5. HYPER DARK V0
Start on the corner of the boulder opposite *Mark of the Beast* and traverse up and left, topping out at the notch.

SPOKANE BOULDERING | 119

THE FLOOD

☐ **6. SHORT ROOF V4** ★
Start sitting with both hands in the crack in the back of the low roof. Climb out (no dabbing) and pull a weird mantel.
FA Nate Lynch

☐ **7. MARK OF THE BEAST V10** ★★
Start on the evil-eye jug. Climb left and up through a small right hand sidepull to the crack, before navigating the roof and an exposed mantel.
FA Steve Moss

☐ **8. SON OF THE BEAST V8** ★★
Start on the evil-eye jug. Dyno up and right to the crack. Finish it off. Grade unconfirmed.
FA Cam Freiburghaus

THE FLOOD BACKSIDE

☐ **9. THE COVENANT V6** ★★
Commence from a left hand at head height and a right hand undercling. Involves a pop to a hard-to-find sweet spot and overhead pinch. Fun.
FA Nick Tansy

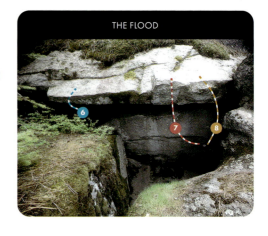
THE FLOOD

☐ **10. THE FLOOD V3** ★★★
Traverse the rail from a low stand start into a cruxy mantel involving devilish slopers.
FA Nick Tansy

☐ **11. THE BETRAYAL V5** ★★
Sit-down start using the large flake-like feature on the shelf. Move up to a crimp then right to the sloper. Cruxy mantel.
FA Nate Lynch

THE FLOOD BACKSIDE

Alex N. on *The Fool* (V5).

☐ 12. THE SACRIFICE V6 ★ ★
Start sitting matched on the low shelf. Make the big reach for a crimp to the right and then conjure your way to the sloper above. Tricky in it's simplicity, and possibly sandbagged...
FA Steve Moss

☐ 13. THE FOOL V5 ★
Sit start matched on the crimp above the low shelf. Move up crimps to the sloper rail and finish.
FA Nate Lynch

☐ 14. THE DANCE V1 ★ ★
Sit start on the obvious jug, move up good incuts into hidden holds, then boogie your way left, standing on the sloping rail to top out.

BUTT CRACK WALL

☐ 15. BILLY'S BUTT CRACK V3 ★
Climb the crack in the orange face starting from a big undercling.

☐ 16. HAPPY TRAIL V1 ★
Climb the slabby wall on decent holds.

BUTT CRACK WALL

SPOKANE BOULDERING | 121

Melissa M. on *Billy's Butt Crack* (V3)
Photo by Serra B.

PHANTOM WALL

☐ 17. PHANTOM V4 ★★
Starting on the flat jug at the back of the overhang, move up blocky holds to an engaging mantel.

☐ 18. STOKING THE FIRE V6 ★
Commence from a right hand edge and left-hand sidepull. Climb up and left into a real-deal top-out.

☐ 19. PHANTOM UNMASKED V2 ★★
Start low with a left-hand sidepull and a right hand edge avoiding the detached blocks at the base. Climb up sidepulls into a thinner finish. Excellent.
FA George Hughbanks

☐ 20. MECHANICAL BULL V4 ★★
From a left hand in the sloping slot at head-height and a right hand undercling, boulder up fun holds on the overhung face.
FA Nate Lynch

☐ 21. BACKSTAGE RODEO V7 ★
Start as for *Mechanical Bull* but traverse right into the finish of *Flaky Little Friends*.
FA Matt Duddy

☐ 22. FLAKY LITTLE FRIENDS V8 ★
Power up to victory after starting with your left hand on an obvious head-height crimp and right hand low sidepull.
FA Alex Nikolayev

PHANTOM WALL

122 | TUM TUM

☐ 23. LOCK IN A SOCK V9 ★★
Start matched on a high undercling, climb right and up into left-hand sidepulls and a right hand arête. The holds are a bit toothy, but the movement is excellent. Harder if shorter.
FA Nate Lynch

☐ 24. RBG V2 ★★
Stand start from a left-hand sidepull slot and right hand rounded edge. Move past the giant pinch into easier climbing in the dihedral above. Sit start from low edges in slots for a fun V4 variation.
FA George Hughbanks

☐ 25. MILLENNIAL V3 ★
Start on left-facing holds in the crack. Move left and up on holds in the many seams.
FA George Hughbanks

☐ 26. BULGY ARÊTE PROJECT ★
Climb the bulgy arête that thins higher up.

PHANTOM WALL RIGHT

Cam F. on *Phantom* (V4)

Alex N. on *Flaky Little Friends* (V8). Photo by Serra B.

SPOKANE BOULDERING | 123

HYPERTONIC

☐ **27. THE SOLUTE V3** ★
From high edges climb right on more beautiful edges.

☐ **28. DISSOLUTION PROJECT** (NOT PICTURED)
Project on thin crimps just around the corner from *Hypotonic*.

☐ **29. HYPOTONIC V5**
Climb the arête on wrong-facing rails.
FA Chris Covillo

☐ **30. HYPERTONIC V6** ★
Traverse the lip left over a blocky landing.
FA Chris Covillo

HYPERTONIC FRONTSIDE

HYPERTONIC BACKSIDE

Melissa M. on *Hypotonic* (V5).
Photo by Serra B.

Nate Lynch on *Lock in a Sock* (V9).

CORONA BOULDERS

The Corona Boulders area contains a few scattered problems on both north and south sides of the highway. For the area just west of the Quarry, we have included the known boulders on public property. Unfortunately, some historic climbs on the north side of the road are on private property and are not listed in this guide.

MARGE SIMPSON

☐ **1. MARGE'S ARÊTE V1**

☐ **2. MARGE'S DIRTY BAG V3**

☐ **3. MARGE'S DIRTY CLIPPERS V3**
Best moves at the top are just like Marge's hair—a bit taller than is necessary.

☐ **4. MARGE'S UNCOMFORTABLE BUNCH V3**

☐ **5. MARGE SIMPSON V5 ★★**
Climb the 3D feature up to the right end of the rock.

HOUSEWIFE

☐ **6. HOUSEWIFE V4 ★★**
Climb the left end of the overhang using the left arête.
FA Shane Collins

☐ **7. ANALOG WOMAN (IN A DIGITAL WORLD) V6 ★**
Start with a low crimp, move to the (small) crimps above and toss for the lip. Fun stuff?
FA Nate Lynch

MARGE SIMPSON LEFT

MARGE SIMPSON RIGHT

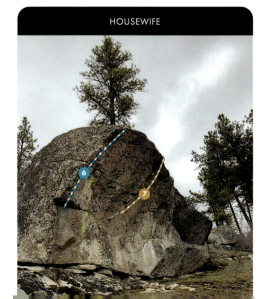
HOUSEWIFE

SPOKANE BOULDERING | 125

CRAIGLANDIA

About 100 yards east of The West End lies a bumpy parking field that hides a climber-manufactured dirtbag hangout area, that is hereby dubbed Craiglandia as a small thank you to Craig Anderson—the owner of the property who graciously allows the community to inelegantly clamber about his land, to fumble their opprobrious bodies on the steep hillside's Bunyanesque boulders. We thank you, Craig. And we promise to never damage the property, leave garbage, be obnoxious, or sue you when we get hurt.

SIGN TO AGREE HERE:_____

Also, be sure to ALWAYS close the climbing rope "gate" behind you when entering or exiting Craiglandia.

Sweet Cheeks: **1-2**
Little Flatiron / Nevermind / The Cloud: **3-13**
Supafly: **14-15**
The Feedlot: **16-20**
Crumbled: **21-22**
The Boss: **23-24**
Tidbit: **25**
The Dam: **26**
Black Pedal Betty: **27**
Dorm Fridge: **28-31**
The Rook: **32**
Dead Dog Boulder: **33-43**
Statue of Liberty: **44-45**
Campfire Kids: **46-47**
Scrumptious: **48**
BOGO / Public Enemy: **49-52**
Log On It: **53**
Club G Spot: **54**
The Elitist: **55-56**

CRAIGLANDIA

SWEET CHEEKS

☐ 1. LONELY ONLY PROJECT
Appears there is potential on this vertical face. Looks like some fun squeezing on the left.

☐ 2. SWEET CHEEKS V0 ★★★
Climb the tall right side of the face on rails.
FA George Hughbanks

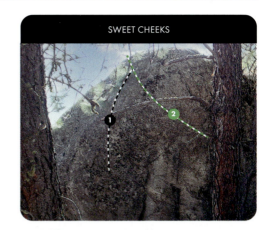

LITTLE FLATIRON

☐ 3. WRINKLE RESISTANT V1 ★★
From a sit-start "jug," move up the arête on fun holds. Rock over with hands at the apex.

☐ 4. LITTLE FLATIRON V3 ★
Starting lower on the center of the overhung wall, move up incuts to a big move for the lip.

☐ 5. IRON ON V2 ★
Start as for *Little Flatiron*, but traverse to the right arête for a less burly finish.

Rylee E. on *Little Flatiron* (V3).

Daniel M. on *Cumulus* (V1).

NEVERMIND

☐ 6. NEVERMIND V4 ★★
Start low on opposing sidepulls. Finagle your way up and right. Tricky and engaging.

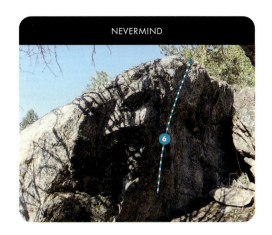

THE CLOUD

☐ 7. MAMMATUS PROJECT
This dominating rippled wall does not yet have a line. It appears that a problem could begin near the center and exit out left.

☐ 8. NIMBOSTRATUS PROJECT
Potentially, there's a line on the right side of the boulder traversing crimps to the apex with the slab to your back.

☐ 9. STRATUS V0
Climb the left end of the short overhanging wall on good holds from a sit start.

☐ 10. CIRRUS V1 ★★
Start as for *Stratus* but follow the seams right under the small tree.

☐ 11. CUMULUS V1 ★
Starting from the good jug, climb up the overhang on fun holds to an engaging mantel.

☐ 12. CONTRAILS V5 ★★
Starting from the same jug as *Cumulus*, climb right along obvious holds and bigger moves to the slopey lip hold. Classic!

☐ 13. NOCTILUCENT V7 ★
Sit start matched on the calcified edge. Move up more edges/slots.
FA Nate Lynch

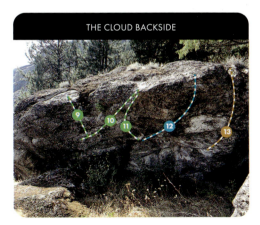

SPOKANE BOULDERING | 129

Kelly B. on *Supafly* (V4).

SUPAFLY

☐ **14. SUPAFLY V4 ★★★**
Start on the slab, move into the overhang, and make a committing lunge for a right-facing jug. Top out immediately left of the apex. Unique and fun movemement—let it fly!

☐ **15. PASSABLY FLY V5 ★**
Start crouched on the left arête. Move up the overhanging arête into toothy bulges.

SUPAFLY

Daniel M. on *Grass Fed* (V4).

130 | TUM TUM

Nate B. on *The Way of the Cookie* (V7).

FEEDLOT

☐ 16. HAY'S IN THE BARN V2 ★★
Climb the tall slab. There are reportedly better holds higher up. We cannot confirm or deny.

☐ 17. GRASS FED V4 ★★
From a stand start on the best section of the horizontal rail, move up and right through incuts, and rock onto the slab above. Can feel a bit balancy near the top.

☐ 18. THE FEEDLOT V5 ★★★
Start as for *Grass Fed*, but continue farther right into a big driveby to the slotted jug. Continue up the crack to a rock-over. Can be started even lower left for more challenge.

☐ 19. SILAGE V8 ★
Start matched on the undercling. You did it? Good work. Now move up and right—difficult no matter the method—into better holds and move right to the top. It also appears possible to take this start more directly up, or possibly left, into *Feedlot*. Get it, get it, get it.

☐ 20. COW MASSEUSE V3 ★
Start on low holds below the finish of *Silage*. Move up and right to top.

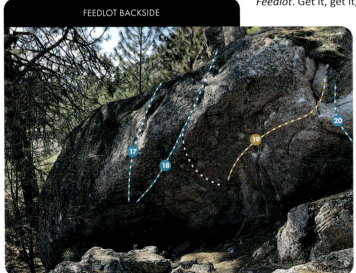

SPOKANE BOULDERING | 131

CRUMBLED

☐ **21. ROOF TRAVERSE V3** (NOT PICTURED)
Traverse the hanging roof lip from left to right. Top out.

☐ **22. THE WAY OF THE COOKIE V7** ★
Stand start from a pair of blocky holds. Move up and right through somewhat tricky and crumbly moves. Fun movement on less-than-stellar rock.

THE BOSS

☐ **23. THE ASSISTANT V4**
Climb the detached block. Unconfirmed.

☐ **24. WHO'S THE BOSS? V8** ★★
Start low with a right hand crimp near the lip and a left hand under on the blocky hold. Traverse left into the sloper and mantel—a test of perseverance. Or brute force. Your choice.

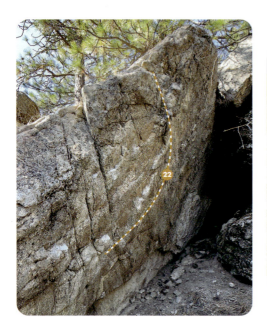

Rylee E. on *Tidbit* (V3).

132 | TUM TUM

TIDBIT

☐ **25. TIDBIT V3** ★★
Start sitting with a low left-hand sloper and a better right hand. Move up the short prow. Fun!

THE DAM

☐ **26. THE DAM V4**
Start sitting with crimps, bump into the flexing jug (careful!) and up the lip to the left. A V3 variation tops out straight up in the notch.

BACK PEDAL BETTY (NOT PICTURED)

☐ **27. BACK PEDAL BETTY V5** ★★
Seen just downhill from *The Barber* and *Topiary*. Start with a low left-hand crimp and higher right hand sidepull. Climb to the apex. A lower right hand undercling boosts it at least a grade.

DORM FRIDGE

☐ **28. THE BARBER V4** ★ (NOT PICTURED)
On the SE river-facing side of the Dorm Fridge Boulder start with a left-hand undercling and right hand sidepull. Slap up and keep going.

☐ **29. TOPIARY V3** ★ (NOT PICTURED)
Between *The Barber* and *Dorm Fridge* on the vertical east-facing wall, climb the left-facing rib from an odd sit start.

☐ **30. DORM FRIDGE V4** ★
Climb the lip starting low left right on the face and jugs above.

☐ **31. KEGERATOR PROJECT**
Climb from a sit in the overhang on small holds into *Dorm Fridge*. Quite difficult.

TIDBIT

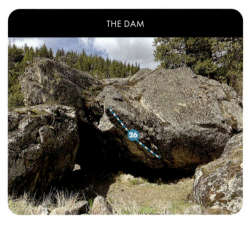
THE DAM

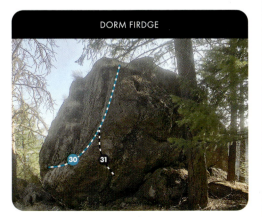
DORM FIRDGE

Brett J. on *Who's the Boss?* (V8)
Photo by Serra B.

SPOKANE BOULDERING | 133

THE ROOK

☐ 32. THE ROOK V3
Climb from left to right, then back on lip. Awkward?

DEAD DOG BOULDER

☐ 33. CAMPBELL'S SOUP V7 ★
Match on the undercling. Crank for a send. More rewarding than one would think.
FA Alex Campbell

☐ 34. NUMBERS GAME V3
Supposedly there is a moderate problem here…

☐ 35. GOODIE TWO SHOES V4 ★★
Start sitting with a left hand in the seam and right hand on the neat arête pinch. Move up in compression to the lip and a tricky mantel. Top gets a bit dirty.

☐ 36. SAY GOODBYE TO YOUR GOOD SIDE V6 ★★
Same start as for *Goodie Two Shoes*, but climb right around the corner into *The Appostate*. Powerful and while a little scrunchy, it is still quite good.

☐ 37. THE APOSTATE V4 ★★
Sit-down start on the landing rock (not in the hole) with your left hand on the arête pinch and right hand on the sidepull. Compress to the lip and traverse right to top out.

☐ 38. TROLL TOLL V8 ★
Start on a left-hand sloping sidepull and opposing right hand edge. Move up on a previously V6+ dyno—a broken hold has drastically altered the beta. Sandbagged?
FA Alex Campbell

☐ 39. THE LEGEND OF RED O'KELLY V5 ★★★
Start sitting matched on the obvious jug. Crank to incuts and through a techy sequence to a sloper above. Move left to gain a jug and rock up to victory. Ultra classic.

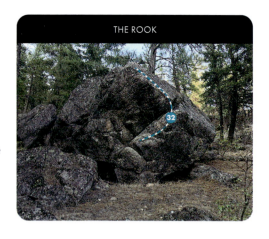
THE ROOK

DEAD DOG BOULDER LEFT

Alex C. on *Troll Toll* (V8).

134 | TUM TUM

40. DEAD DOG V4 ★★
Stand start from a pair of incuts, ascend into the large flake then up incut crimps to a high finish. Classic. Variations: Start low to the right on incut edges just to the side of the orange jug and bust into the start holds of *Dead Dog*, fighting the barn-door for *Doggone* (V6). Make the opening moves of *TLORK* and then traverse incuts right into the flake for *Red Dog* (V5).

41. PIANO MAN PROJECT ★★
Starting on the orange lichen jug, move up and left into comfy flat and rounded crimps, finishing as for *Dead Dog*. Could use some brushing, but will likely clean up into a classic testpiece.

42. VOW OF SILENCE V6 ★
Starting from the same orange jug, climb up and trend right into a high finish.

43. PRECIOUS DAYS OF ETERNITY V3 ★★
Climb the tall overhanging face from a stand start on good holds. Starting from the orange jug start for *Forever Silent*.

Chelsea M. on *The Legend of Red O'Kelly* (V5)
Photo by Serra B.

DEAD DOG BOULDER FRONTSIDE

SPOKANE BOULDERING | 135

STATUE OF LIBERTY

☐ **44. TRAVERSE PROJECT**
Traverse from edges on the left side of the rock into the finish of *Statue of Liberty*. A bit exfoliating on the forearms.

☐ **45. STATUE OF LIBERTY V7 ★ ★**
Jump to a smooth left-hand edge and high right hand barely-there sloper. Get a foot on and bust to the lip. It's not over until you're standing on the top. Can also be climbed from a lower and very sharp right hand sidepull, eliminating the need to jump. If your pad stack and height sum up to more than 6'6" you're doing it wrong.
FA Johnny G

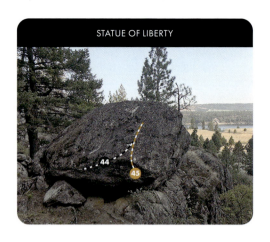
STATUE OF LIBERTY

CAMPFIRE KIDS

☐ **46. CAMPFIRE KIDS V3 ★**
Starting on opposing edges, climb up the left arête with the crux near the lip.
FA George Hughbanks

☐ **47. FELIX IGNIS V4 ★**
Start on the two farthest right, right-facing edges. With some tricky footwork move right into the undercling, establish on the flake, then bust back left into the finish of *Campfire Kids*.
FA George Hughbanks

CAMPFIRE KIDS

SCRUMPTIOUS

SCRUMPTIOUS

☐ **48. SCRUMPTIOUS V6 ★ ★**
From a stand on the slab, make a big move (dyno?) to the bucket rail just out of reach in the overhang. Bust out via heel hooks then move through crimps to the jugs on the bridge of the nose. From there take it up the slab to the left, or take the big drop for less glory.

Daniel M. on Goodie Two Shoes (V4).

Drew S. on Mythical Beast (V12)

BOGO

☐ **49. FIVE FINGERED DISCOUNT V2 ★★**
Start standing with good incuts. Follow the crack/rail left until a big rock-up is required to top out. Fun.

☐ **50. BUY ONE, GET ONE V6 ★★**
Start sitting on crimps just below the start of the previous problem. Climb more or less straight up implementing a right hand gaston. Fun.

☐ **51. THE SHRUB V8 ★**
A difficult struggle with the bulge from a sit start on the rail. Follow the thinning seam.

BOGO

PUBLIC ENEMY

☐ **52. PUBLIC ENEMY V3**
Climb the thin face on uncomfortable holds...or maybe don't.

HIGH BOULDERS

Nate L. on Buy One, Get One (V6).

CLUB G SPOT

☐ **53. CLUB G SPOT V1**
Climb the lip from right to left.

THE ELITIST

☐ **54. THE ELITIST (AKA MYTHICAL BEAST) V12 ★★★**
Start on opposing incut crimps at the bottom of the overhang. Climb the rounded prow on crimps and slopes. Doesn't let up until you're standing on top. THE Classic Johnny G. testpiece.

☐ **55. ANYTHING GOES V3 ★** (NOT PICTURED)
Start matched on the obvious left-facing jug. Climb.

CLUB G SPOT

PUBLIC ENEMY

THE ELITIST

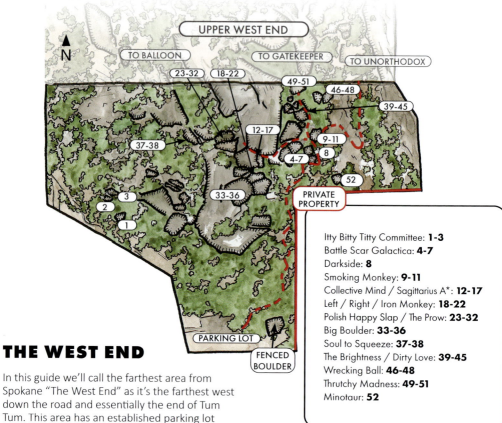

Itty Bitty Titty Committee: **1-3**
Battle Scar Galactica: **4-7**
Darkside: **8**
Smoking Monkey: **9-11**
Collective Mind / Sagittarius A*: **12-17**
Left / Right / Iron Monkey: **18-22**
Polish Happy Slap / The Prow: **23-32**
Big Boulder: **33-36**
Soul to Squeeze: **37-38**
The Brightness / Dirty Love: **39-45**
Wrecking Ball: **46-48**
Thrutchy Madness: **49-51**
Minotaur: **52**

THE WEST END

In this guide we'll call the farthest area from Spokane "The West End" as it's the farthest west down the road and essentially the end of Tum Tum. This area has an established parking lot (Discover Pass necessary) with two fenced-off boulders protecting Native American paintings. I feel like we shouldn't have to mention this, but don't jump these fences or try to climb these boulders. Seriously.

LOWER WEST END

ITTY BITTY TITTY COMMITTEE

☐ 1. ITTY BITTY TITTY COMMITTEE V6
Start on underclings, finish on jugs. Unconfirmed —could be easier.

140 | TUM TUM

JET BLACK

☐ **2. JET BLACK V2** ★
Start standing with the scooped edge. Think you can sit it? Add a few grades.
FA George Hughbanks

☐ **3. RAL 9005 V3** ★
Start sitting on the short arête. Bingo Bango Ha-ta-ta, and you're done.
FA George Hughbanks

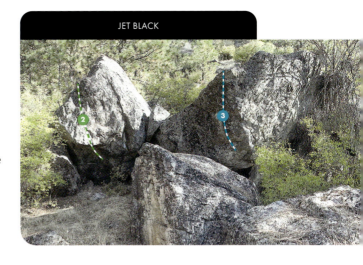

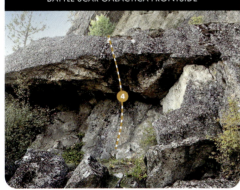

BATTLE SCAR GALACTICA

☐ **4. BATTLE SCAR GALACTICA V6** ★★
Climb the slab into crack on the large overhanging block above.

☐ **5. HARDER STUFF PROJECT**
A couple possible short lines in the aspens.

☐ **6. THE PLAN V0** ★
Climb the short corner on good ledges.

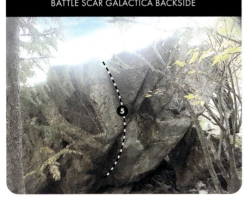

SPOKANE BOULDERING | 141

BEARS, BEETS, BATTLESTAR GALACTICA

☐ **7. BEARS, BEETS, BATTLESTAR GALACTICA V3**
Climb thin crimps from a matched edge start.

DARKSIDE

☐ **8. DARKSIDE V3** ★
Climb grainy holds left, use the arête, and then commit for the lip. Alternate harder variation starts lower on the left arête.
FA George Hughbanks

Megan H. on *Darkside* (V3). Photo by Serra B.

142 | TUM TUM

SMOKING MONKEY

☐ **9. SURF DU BLOCK V3** ★
Start with a low sit start on the lip. Climb fun lip holds all the way to the apex to top.
FA George Hughbanks

☐ **10. SMOKING MONKEY V11** ★
Start sitting very low with a double undercling. Use magic of some sort to gain a sloping edge and crimps in the steep dihedral. Tricky with unique movement.

☐ **11. TURD IN THE PUNCHBOWL V6**
From a high stand start on two small holds, bust to the lip. That's it. Batteries not included.

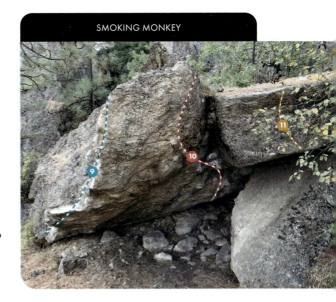

COLLECTIVE MIND

☐ **12. ORCA V4** ★ (NOT PICTURED)
From a low start traverse right on the lip, rocking over where it meets *Collective Mind*.

☐ **13. COLLECTIVE MIND V8** ★★★
Start on the smooth jug at the arête. Traverse left into to techy moves around the bulge, into crimps and then the lip. Rock over.

☐ **14. THINK TANK V0** ★ (NOT PICTURED)
Climb the arête straight up from the jug start of *Collective Mind*.

Alex N. on Smoking Monkey (V11).

SPOKANE BOULDERING | 143

Steve M. on *Sagittarius A** (V9).
Photo by Angus M.

SAGITTARIUS A*

☐ **15. SAGITTARIUS A* V9 ★★**
Sit start on a left-hand sidepull and a right hand gaston on the bulge. Move up the bulge to the good lip. Bring all the tension you can muster and try not to fall into the hole...
FA Dimitri Kalashnikov

☐ **16. EVENT HORIZON V2 ★★** (NOT PICTURED)
Tall face opposite *Think Tank*. Fun climbing on solid holds and a committing final move. Be mindful of what happens if you come back down the fast way.

☐ **17. PISTOL WHIP PROJECT**
Low start on a right hand undercling and a low left-hand. Slap through some slopers and get that FA. Simple.
FA [insert your name here]

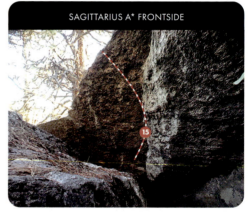
SAGITTARIUS A* FRONTSIDE

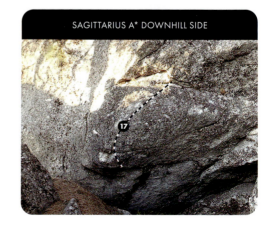
SAGITTARIUS A* DOWNHILL SIDE

144 | TUM TUM

LEFT-RIGHT

☐ **18. LEFT V2**
Start low on jugs, move up and right on blocky holds to a cruxy top-out.

☐ **19. RIGHT V2**
Cimb the left-facing, right-trending rail. (wait... what?)

IRON MONKEY

☐ **20. IRON MONKEY V4**
Climb the small triangular block from a sit with a left-hand nubbin and a right hand sharp sloper. Not worth the calories.

☐ **21. HOWLING MONKEY V1 ★**
Climb the tall arête from a stand.

☐ **22. THE PIT V1 ★★** (NOT PICTURED)
Just above and south of *Iron Monkey* is a fun little one mover. Start from the jug flake and move to the lip. Oh, and don't fall into the hole.

POLISH HAPPY SLAP

☐ **23. SLAP HAPPY V3 ★**
Sit start matched on a low edge, go up and slap for the edge. If I say anything else this description will be longer than the problem.

☐ **24. RUSSIAN HAPPY SLAP V6 ★**
Start as for Slap Happy, traverse low into the start of *PHS*.

☐ **25. POLISH HAPPY SLAP V4 ★★**
Sit start matched on the large sloping shelf. Bust way up to an edge above and an engaging mantel. Fun.

LEFT-RIGHT

IRON MONKEY

Johnny G. on *Event Horizon* (V2).

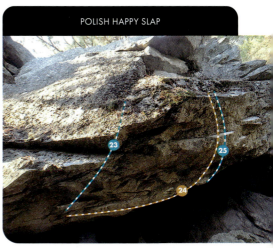
POLISH HAPPY SLAP

Tony C. on *The Prow* (V6).

HEALING POWER

THE PROW

☐ 26. HEALING POWER V10 ★★
Sit start matched on the rail, move up and right, flex your shoulders, your glutes, and every other muscle in your body. Send. Good rock, unique movement. Small but classic. Commonly just climbed to the shelf, as it's difficult to descend from the apex of the rock.

☐ 27. THE PROW V6 ★★★
Start matched on the sloping edge under the prow. Steep with unique moves and a pretty setting. Mantel onto the small ledge above head height. Climb all the way to the top for the thrilling send (or don't, safety is cool too).

☐ 28. THE PROW LOW PROJECT
Start sitting low under the prow and make power moves on small holds to put this longstanding project to rest.

☐ 29. CAVE 1 PROJECT
Enough holds exist in the deepest section of the cave for a line to come together.

☐ 30. POPE OF MOPE V6
Start on the detached shelf and climb out the friable overhang.

☐ 31. FLASH IN THE PAN V6
Reportedly this climbs out the short overhang left of *Lounge Chair*.

☐ 32. LOUNGE CHAIR V4
Start on the detached shelf and climb out the friable overhang.

THE PROW

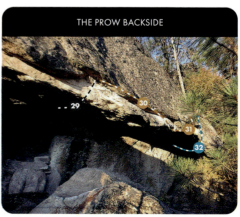

THE PROW BACKSIDE

146 | TUM TUM

BIG BOULDER

☐ **33. THE FOUR V5** ★
Sit start matched on the undercling/sidepull into a tricky mantel onto the slab and take it to the top.

☐ **34. FAT BOY SLIM PROJECT** ★
A classic V10 traverse until holds broke. Might still go from the start of *Johnny*....

☐ **35. JOHNNY IS A G V6** ★★
Start on the head-height, right hand, rounded crimp and a left hand on a sharp crimp. Move up incuts into a big move for the flat jug below the lip. Simple and classic...just don't pee your pants, we are fairly certain you won't fall of the edge.

☐ **36. POTENTIAL PROJECT**
While a bit crumbly, a motivated climber with a high fear threshhold could put up a line that follows the seam to the finishing jug of *Johnny*.

SOUL TO SQUEEZE

☐ **37. SOUL TO SQUEEZE V9** ★
Start standing with bad holds on each side of the rock and a high left heel. Make hard compression moves up through some pinches to an undercling under the lip. Force your way to sharp holds to top.

☐ **38. SOUL TO SQUEEZE SIT V11** ★
Sit start for a much harder proposition.

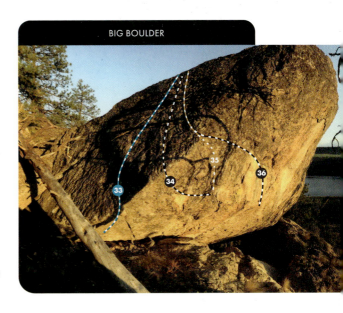

Steve M. on *Soul to Squeeze* (V9).

SPOKANE BOULDERING | 147

Kelly J. on *The Brightness* (V7).
Photo by Serra B.

THE BRIGHTNESS

☐ 39. MAN ON THE MOON V0
Climb the slab to a tall finish. Also the cleanest downclimb, so keep that in mind.

☐ 40. STARING AT THE SUN V2
Climb the tall arête from a stand start.

☐ 41. SPEED OF LIGHT V5 ★
Traverse the tall face R to L from obvious edges into *Staring at the Sun* and top out. Starting all the way right adds a grade or two.

☐ 42. THE BRIGHTNESS V7
Climb the center of the tall face over the poor landing. Likely needs some cleaning.

THE BRIGHTNESS

MOUSE HOUSE

MOUSE HOUSE

☐ 43. MOUSE HOUSE V3 ★
Sit start matched on the left-hand lip. Pop right and compress up. Tiny but good.

Melissa M. on *Wrecking Ball* (V9).
Photo by Serra B.

148 | TUM TUM

CENTENARIAN

☐ **44. CENTENARIAN V3** ★
Sit start matched on the obvious pinch. Climb up fun holds to the apex of the boulder. A detached block is on for feet.

DIRTY LOVE

☐ **45. DIRTY LOVE V2**
Climb the curving crack from a low start.

WRECKING BALL

☐ **46. EXCUSES AND EXFOLIATION V5**
(NOT PICTURED)
Sit start just under the lip outside the corridor from the finish of *Bulldozer*. Move up and traverse the lip from right to left. A bit unpleasant on the forearms.

☐ **47. BULLDOZER V8** ★ ★
Sit start from a jagged left-hand edge and right hand crimp. Finish as for *Wreckng Ball*.

☐ **48. WRECKING BALL V9** ★ ★
Starting from the obvious jug, climb left on jagged incut crimps into a sequential crux and tenuous move to the lip. A classic of the area, and oh, so crimpy.

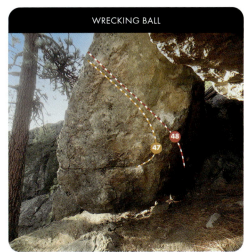

Russell H. on *Thrutchy Madness* (V4)

THRUTCHY MADNESS

☐ 49. EXIT LEFT V2 ★
Climb the left arête. *Thrutchy Madness* can exit here for a slightly easier variation.

☐ 50. THRUTCHY MADNESS V4 ★★★
Start sitting matched low on the rail. Move left on slopey holds to a good incut then rock up to edges and the lip. It may be worth checking out the top, as the good holds can be hard to see.

☐ 51. THRUTCHY CRAPNESS V6 ★
Start as for *Madness*, but climb more or less straight up on crimps. Tough and better than its name implies.

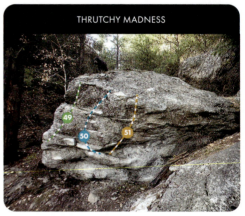

THRUTCHY MADNESS

THE MINOTAUR

☐ 52. THE MINOTAUR V10
A reportedly hard problem that we haven't tried. Likely starts low somewhere and ends high somewhere.

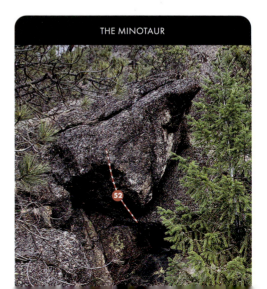

THE MINOTAUR

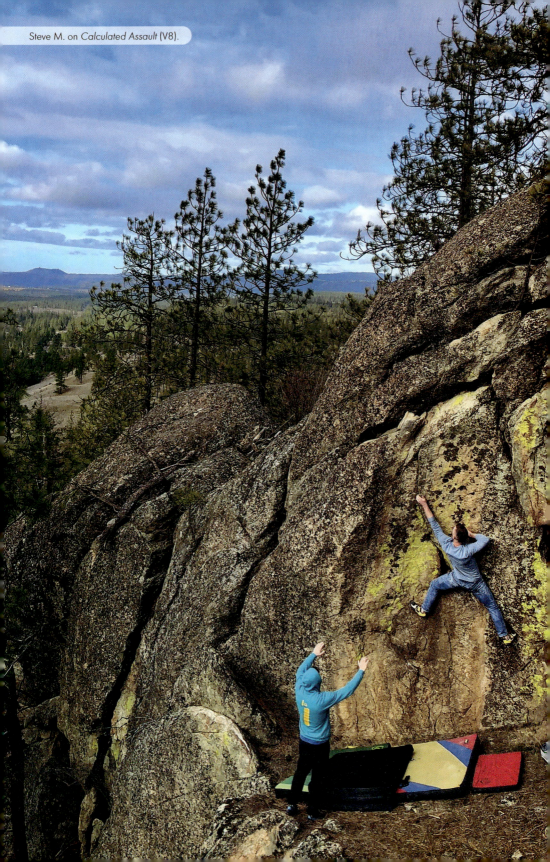
Steve M. on *Calculated Assault* (V8).

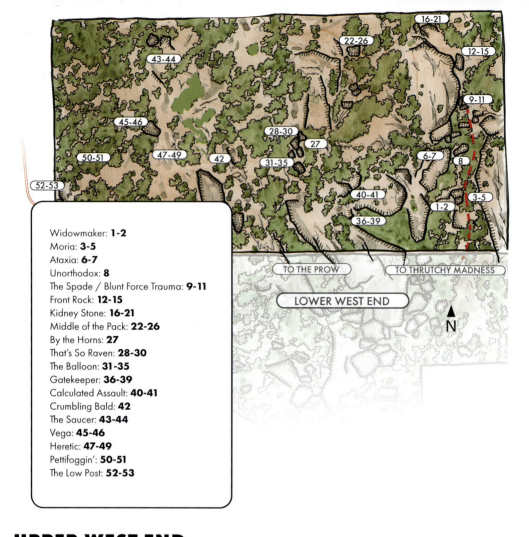

Widowmaker: **1-2**
Moria: **3-5**
Ataxia: **6-7**
Unorthodox: **8**
The Spade / Blunt Force Trauma: **9-11**
Front Rock: **12-15**
Kidney Stone: **16-21**
Middle of the Pack: **22-26**
By the Horns: **27**
That's So Raven: **28-30**
The Balloon: **31-35**
Gatekeeper: **36-39**
Calculated Assault: **40-41**
Crumbling Bald: **42**
The Saucer: **43-44**
Vega: **45-46**
Heretic: **47-49**
Pettifoggin': **50-51**
The Low Post: **52-53**

UPPER WEST END

WIDOWMAKER

☐ 1. WIDOWMAKER V5 ★★★
Stand start form obvious edges. Commiting move to the lip. Instant Classic.
FA Matt Duddy, Nick Tansy

☐ 2. RIGHT FACE OF WIDOW PROJECT
Potential up the thin face right of *Widowmaker*.

MORLA

☐ 3. SUSPENDED V5
Start low in the big crack in the boulder. Follow it up.
FA Matt Duddy

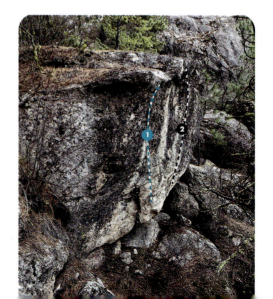

152 | TUM TUM

Steve M. on *Widowmaker* (V5).
Photo by Cam F.

☐ 4. GMORK V3
Start low on the incut rail. Move up and left.

☐ 5. MORLA V3 ★
Start low on the incut rail. Move up and right on rounded holds.
FA Nick Tansy

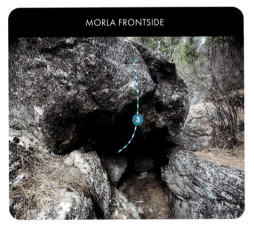
MORLA FRONTSIDE

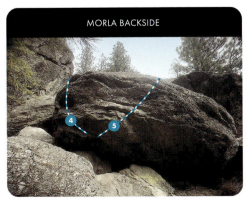
MORLA BACKSIDE

Steve M. on *Ataxia* (V7).

SPOKANE BOULDERING | 153

ATAXIA

☐ 6. ATAXIA V7 ★★
Start low matched on the obvious Jug. Climb techy or powerful...or both. Definitely worth your time.
FA Bryan Franklin, Nick Tansy

☐ 7. ATAXIA EXTENSION V9
Climb *Ataxia* and then, from the first hold on the lip, move right before going up to a nice chicken head. Bring the tension.
FA Bryan Franklin

UNORTHODOX

☐ 8. UNORTHODOX V6 ★★
Match on the flat hold in the overhang, bust up left, hold the swing, and climb the vert wall to finish.

THE SPADE

☐ 9. ACES HIGH V8 ★★
Start sitting on opposing rounded edges. Move up and right into a left-facing sidepull and the nipple hold shared with *The Spade*. Then follow the crack left, or bust for the lip where able. Very good.

☐ 10. THE SPADE V10 ★★
Start low on undercling crimps. Move left to the nipple hold finishing as for *Aces*. A lower, harder and yet undone sit start seems plausible.

Cam F. on Aces High (V8)

BLUNT FORCE TRAUMA

☐ **11. BLUNT FORCE TRAUMA PROJECT** ★★
Sit start with a grainy left-hand and a smooth right hand pinch on the arête. Climb up the funky dihedral/arête with all the tricks you've got. Steve M. shed some blood to get the landing climbable, so put in some effort, okay?

FONT ROCK

☐ **12. MODERN NO. 20 V1** ★
Start standing matched on the high edge. Simple, but the landing could be better.

☐ **13. HAETTENSCHWEILER V3** ★
Start low on the left-facing incuts. Climb straight up through flakes.

☐ **14. CLARKSON V4** ★★
Start as for *Haetten* but move rightward along the seam into *Proxima Nova*. Fun.

☐ **15. PROXIMA NOVA V3** ★★★
Start from the head-high flake and make big moves between comfy holds. Or do it as a dyno to the lip...

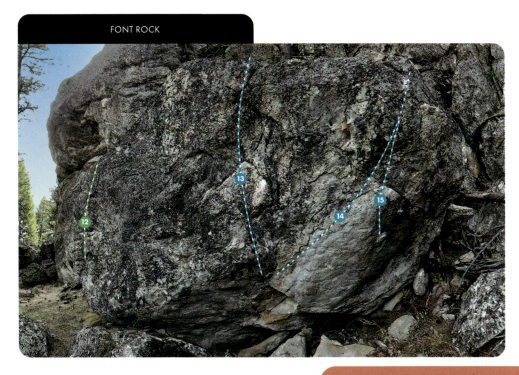

SPOKANE BOULDERING | 155

KIDNEY STONE

☐ 16. KIDNEY STONE TRAVERSE V5
Start low on the bread loaves from a sit and traverse topping at *Redbull*.

☐ 17. 24/7 REDBULL V3
Sit start from jugs. Move right up the rail while somehow not dabbing.

☐ 18. URETHRAL EUPHORIA V5 ★
Sit start from a crimp edge, move up to crimps and lunge for the lip!

☐ 19. EW V4
Sit start, crank into toothy underclings. Feels like a worse version of *Passing the Stone*....

☐ 20. PASSING THE STONE V6
Sit start, move right to the grainy gaston, and then crank into the toothy underclings. Yikes!

☐ 21. BLOODY PISS V7 ★
Sit start matched on a crimp edge, move up through small flexing crimps. Not particularly a classic, but you better get it before the crimps say farewell to this world.

KIDNEY STONE LEFT SIDE

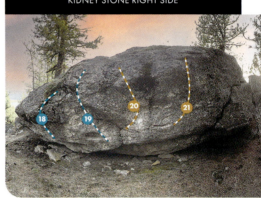

KIDNEY STONE RIGHT SIDE

MIDDLE OF THE PACK

☐ 22. COMEBACK KID V2 ★
Start sitting under the short corner. Climb mostly friendly holds up the overhang. This one may need a little love with a wire brush.

☐ 23. STICK IN THE SPOKES V2 ★★
Start on the right-facing edges, climb up more decent holds.

☐ 24. BREAKAWAY V3 ★
Start sitting on left-hand edge and right hand split hold. Move up through edges traversing left to a good hold at the lip.

☐ 25. MIDDLE OF THE PACK V8 ★
Start as for *Breakaway*, but climb straight up to decent holds at the lip. Use crimps on the way there or don't.

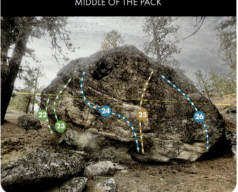

MIDDLE OF THE PACK

☐ 26. DO IT ALONE V3 ★
Low start on crimps, bust to the jug then climb left into the finish holds on *Middle of the Pack*. Mantel isn't the most simple.

156 | TUM TUM

Nate L. on *Urethral Euphoria* (V5).

BY THE HORNS

☐ 27. BY THE HORNS V8 ★
Start standing with a low left-hand pinch/sidepull/undercling right hand pinch. Move up the bulge with tricky moves. Sit Start anyone? Grade unconfirmed.

THAT'S SO RAVEN

☐ 28. THE LAWMAN V3 ★★
Start on a pair of chest high holds. Bust to a right hand edge and up the corner and keep it together for the mantel.

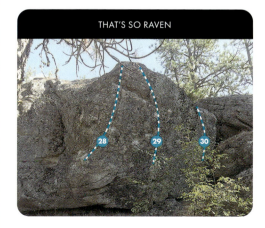

☐ 29. THAT'S SO RAVEN V4 ★
Climb the center crimpy face.

☐ 30. THE FUTURE V3 ★
Start on chest high opposing crimps. Move up and right finishing at the shortest point of the face.

SPOKANE BOULDERING | 157

THE BALLOON

❏ 31. BALLOON ANIMALS V4 ★★
Start low with a right hand on the big incut and left-hand on the jug just around the arête. Make a couple moves into a big crank to a right hand sidepull and an exit out left over the jug. Classic movement, bit of a stepped landing. Starting from *Helium Huffer* and traversing into this is fun and adds a grade.

❏ 32. HELIUM HUFFER V7 ★
Start matched on the incut flake, crank up right to some micro crimps and on to better holds above. Not a great fall zone

❏ 33. THE AERONAUT PROJECT ★
Start on the jugs above the sloping rock, make big moves to jugs below the lip. Possibly...

❏ 34. LATEX PROJECT
Climb the corner from a stand start up the cracks. It doesn't look inspiring, but is likely tough.

❏ 35. CELLOPHANE PROJECT
Climb the bulgy low corner. You know, once you clean it.

Tucker R. on The Lawman (V3).

THE BALLOON

GATEKEEPER

☐ **36. GATEKEEPER PROJECT**
Sit start match on the right-facing incut, move up widely spread small holds while not dabbing...

☐ **37. THE GATEKEEPER V5** ★★★
Sit start on the big flat ledge. Climb up through the downward facing sidepull. Just a little tricky, and a lot of fun. Classic steep problem.

☐ **38. FANNIE LIKES 2 DANCE V5** ★★
Start as for *Gatekeeper*, but go right along the crimps and edges in the seam and to the juggy lip. Good for short and tall alike.

☐ **39. THE BOUNCER V3** ★
Start low on the right hand arête in compression and slap up. Good climbing with an exposed fall and one uncomfortable hold.

CALCULATED ASSAULT

☐ **40. CALCULATED ASSAULT V8** ★★
Sit start matched on the obvious low jug. Move through good holds into thinner territory in the crack above. Technical movement on great rock. Careful on the extended top-out, it's a bit loose. Most people won't fault you for a drop from the lip.

☐ **41. EASY THING V1**
We didn't actually climb anything on the uphill side of this boulder but it looks like it could be easy and fun after some brushing. Wait, you thought we would do ALL the work?

CRUMBLING BALD

☐ **42. CRUMBLING BALD V1**
Just down the hill from *The Balloon*, start on the far right of this diminutive boulder. Climb up and left.

GATEKEEPER

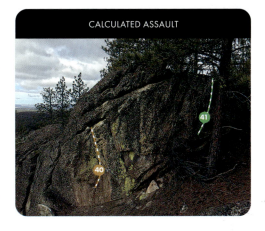

CALCULATED ASSAULT

CRUMBLING BALD

SPOKANE BOULDERING | 159

THE SAUCER

☐ 43. THE SAUCER V2
Start with a left-hand incut and right hand grainy sloper. Climb to the very high and heady lip.

☐ 44. THE VERY SMALL PLATE V2
Start on the two obvious holds. Move to the lip and right to top. We would recommend you don't pass up this rare opportunity to toe hook the lip from the start.

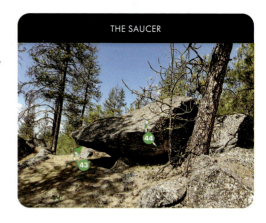

VEGA

☐ 45. VEGA V4
From the white crystaly granite in the lower left side of the large boulder, start with your left-hand in a good slot on a budge and the right hand crimp next to it. Using whatever bad feet you find push up to the next slot in the overhang. Continue right over the dirty bulge using very cool nuggets to help get you up.

☐ 46. VEGA PROJECT

HERETIC

☐ 47. HERETIC V5
Using the blunt undercling to help prop your feet up, make your way to good holds high on the left corner using some hidden crimps deeeeeep in the crack. A little weird.

☐ 48. PROJECT
Start on the right side of the boulder, using the crescent-moon shaped hold to jettison yourself to a bad seam.

☐ 49. SLIPPERY SLOPED V2 (NOT PICTURED)
Behind and above *Heretic*.

160 | TUM TUM

PETTIFOGGIN'

☐ **50. PETTIFOGGIN' V3**
Start at the far right of the mouth feature and traverse left to the arête using great holds to climb up the blocky finish.

☐ **51. SCRUM THINK V0** (NOT PICTURED)
On the back side of Pettifoggin' - a couple of fun moves on good holds!

THE LOW POST

☐ **52. NO SUCH THING AS A FISH V1**
Follow the right-facing lay back seam up and enjoy the air under your toes!

☐ **53. THE LOW POST V2**
Tall. Bring pads.

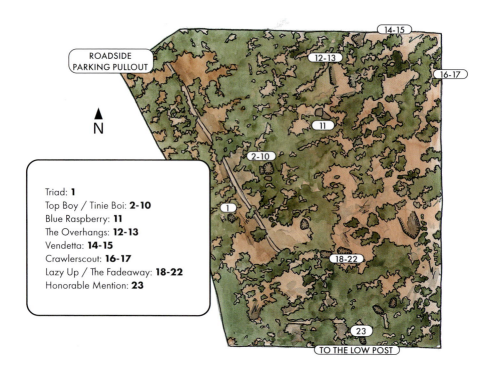

Triad: **1**
Top Boy / Tinie Boi: **2-10**
Blue Raspberry: **11**
The Overhangs: **12-13**
Vendetta: **14-15**
Crawlerscout: **16-17**
Lazy Up / The Fadeaway: **18-22**
Honorable Mention: **23**

CORKSCREW CANYON

This is a small area just past The West End that holds a few scattered problems. You can access this area through the back side of The West End or by parking up Corkscrew Canyon Road about 0.3 miles.

TRIAD (NOT PICTURED)

☐ 1. TRIAD V1
Start sitting under the small triangular overhand on the road-facing side of the boulder. Make a few slaps.

TOP BOY

☐ 2. MADE IN THE MANOR V1 ★★★
From the neck high edge, move up into the crack, follow it trending left to its terminus, hit the lip, mantel. Simple and classic.

☐ 3. FESTER SKANK V3 ★★
Start sitting left-hand sidepull, right hand in the low seam. Tic tak your hands and feet up through knobs and crimps to escape the small overhang to a simple top-out. If it feels sandbagged, you're doing it wrong...

TOP BOY EAST SIDE

162 | TUM TUM

☐ 4. OFF THE WALL V2 ★
Start sitting on the corner matches in the seam. Move up good holds to the arête and then into the good right-facing slots left of the arête. Mantel in the corner, can be a bit tricky.

☐ 5. TOP BOY V5 ★★★
Start on flat holds at right end of the rail in the center of the boulder. Make fun moves up and left on (mostly) good holds into a commiting lunge for the lip at the left arête. Instant classic

☐ 6. THE ROADMAN V2 ★★
Start as for *Top Boy* but move up and right on big holds up and around the right arête.

☐ 7. POP THE CORK V7
Start crouched left-hand undercling, right hand crimp, slap to a slopey hold and power up to better holds above. Punchy.

☐ 8. THE CORKSCREW ROOF PROJECT
Start low in the cave, move through gnarly compression moves to a rough transistion to the headwall. This one will be very hard.

TINIE BOI (NOT PICTURED)

☐ 9. GET GOLD WITHOUT DIGGING HOLES V1
This is little boulder sits directly up the hill from Top Boy and holds two little lines that are totally worth a burn. Start this line on the left overhung side as a sit start and use incut crimps to the lip.

☐ 10. SINK LIKE A STONE V1
Start sitting on a low crimp rail and make moves left through interesting features to top out.

BLUE RASPBERRY

☐ 11. BLUE RASPBERRY AND OTHER LIES V4 ★
Start sitting on the obvious jug, climb the overhang to jugs leftward on the lip. Not the prettiest rock, but fun movement.

Nate L. on *Top Boy* (V5).

TOP BOY NORTH SIDE

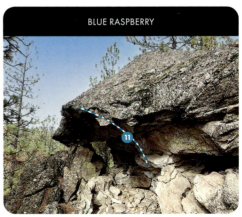
BLUE RASPBERRY

SPOKANE BOULDERING | 163

THE OVERHANGS (NOT PICTURED)

☐ **12. OVERHANG 1 PROJECT**

☐ **13. OVERHANG 2 PROJECT**

VENDETTA (NOT PICTURED)

☐ **14. THE VENDETTA PROJECT**
Start all the way low and left in the notch and follow the bottom part of the "V" right to the finish. More overhung than it looks.

CRAWLERSCOUT (NOT PICTURED)

☐ **15. CRAWLERSCOUT   V1**
Not a solid, but the views are nice.

☐ **16. BABY SCOUT   V1**
The similar slab just above *Crawlerscout*.

LAY UP (NOT PICTURED)

☐ **17. LAY UP   V6**
The far left side of the boulder, start matched on the crescent moon log hold and press up using crimps to top. If you get your butt off the ground you did the hard part.

☐ **18. STEP BACK THREE   V4**
Cram your heel in the broken bottom of the center face and use a high left-hand crimp with a lower and worse right hand crimp to get going. You have plenty of bad options for crimps here but make your way right to a sharp flat edge and top out. You can also keep traversing on the face for a few moves into the project's top out for an added grade or 3.

☐ **19. PROJECT**
The middle of this wall could go as a hard climb.

FADE AWAY

☐ **20. FADE AWAY LEFT   V2**
Starting matched on a low crimp on the slab, make your way using the arête up and into a good, sharp jumbled jug and gain the lip. A little chossy.

☐ **21. FADE AWAY RIGHT   V2**
Start matched on the low arête and move up to neat slopey features. Pull high feet up and top out. This could be given another grade because of the headiness of the fading-away landing underneath you if you want, but the moves aren't that bad.

FADE AWAY

164 | TUM TUM

FUN CLIMBING FOR ALL AGES & ABILITY LEVELS

233 E LYONS AVE. SPOKANE, WA
509-822-7604
BLOCYARDGYM.COM
@BLOCYARDGYM

ROCKS OF SHARON

Matt D. on *Sunset Traverse* (V7).

ROCKS OF SHARON

Sharon Stone: **1-4**
Pornos and Porcupines: **5**
Heartbreaker: **6-11**
Robin Hood: **12-15**

When flying into Spokane from the, south the views from the left side of the plane looking west are well...a little flat and—let's just be honest—kinda boring. However, a window seat on the opposite side presents a different vista. Flying over the Palouse, the view looks like an ocean of waving green crops and rolling hills that turn steeper and more prominent. One of the biggest surprises is the jutting bulge of the aptly named Big Rock—the centerpiece of The Rocks of Sharon in the Dishman Hills Conservation Area. While it may first seem out of place, it is truly a beacon for what lies to the north.

Rocks of Sharon is not just a bouldering area: it serves for a casual hike and dog-walk. It's a sport or trad climber's moist dream (let's not get too hyperbolic here) with great routes up, down, and around these faces. And notably, the only local place you can force a multi-pitch climb—and that's actually awesome.

The collection of boulders is quite small—just a handful—but each line offers something different and exciting. From the committing swing on *Windstorm* to the delicate movements of *The Archer*, there's a bit of everything jammed into this handful. Often overlooked because of the mile-long uphill approach and the small quantity of problems, the best way to describe the bouldering would be, "Worth it." Is it a destination? Absolutely not. The best climbing spot in the area? Nope. But if you decide to go there and get a few problems in, it will be worth the long hike and the sharp, sharpy-sharp—like really, ouch. (The other author would like to note here that they really aren't sharper than the bulk of Spokane rock... for better or worse). The views at 3400 feet inspire awkward date hikes and basic instagram posts. There's nice scenery to take in while strapping your shoes and chalking up. When the sun is about to fall behind the radio towers to the west, the sky shows off hues of colors so vivid you'd swear the universe had turned the saturation levels up to high. We honestly could go on, but we're about to write more in this intro than in the boulder descriptions themselves

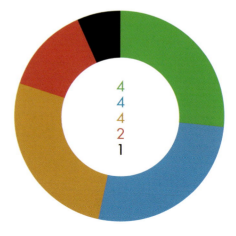

GETTING THERE:
From Spokane, travel south on S Palouse Highway six miles past 57th Street, turn right on S Stevens Creek Road and follow to the parking lot at 2.2 miles.

168 | ROCKS OF SHARON

Charlie L on The Family Stone (V1)

ROCKS OF SHARON

SHARON STONE

☐ **1. SHARON STONE V2 ★★**
Start standing, do some pressing. Send.

☐ **2. THE FAMILY STONE V1 ★**
Stand start, move right and then up.

☐ **3. THE SWORD IN THE STONE V1 ★**
Start low in the good right-facing seam.

☐ **4. STONE COLD STEVE AUSTIN V0 ★★**
Climb in the corner on nice holds.

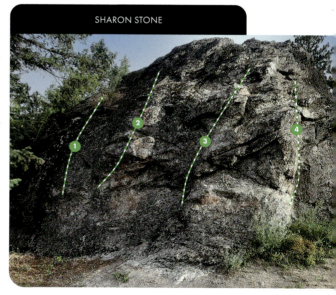

FADE AWAY

Jeremy C. on Windstorm (V6)
Photo by Serra Barron

PORNOS & PORCUPINES (NOT PICTURED)

☐ 5. PORNOS AND PORCUPINES V4 ★
Start sitting (more like laying) at the lower left side of a small cave on the north side of Chronic Rookie rock. Ascend decent holds to the lip, avoiding butt dragging. A little on the powerful side. Quills are a real danger—one of the authors got one in the butt while climbing this.
FA Nate Lynch

HEARTBREAKER

To get to Heartbreaker coming from the Steven's Creek Trailhead, follow the main single track trail all the way to the to Sharon Stone boulder, taking the eastbound trail that follows the base of Big Rock. Continue up the next two switchbacks and veer right at the third along the east side of the prominent rock. Heartbreaker is on the overlook to your right and Archer is below you to the left.

☐ 6. WINDSTORM V6 ★★
Sit start matched on the low jug rail. A big move up then right sets up big moves to and off a lone left-hand crimp in the roof. Be ready for an engaging mantel.
FA Nate Lynch

☐ 7. LOVE TAKER V11 ★★
Start as for *Windstorm*. Follow the traversing holds for *Sunset* to a pair of flat jugs. From here move through a set of tricky small underclings to gain the prow and finish as for *Heartbreaker*. Still unrepeated and grade unconfirmed. Could also be done as a stand start from the flat jugs.
FA Nate Lynch

170 | ROCKS OF SHARON

Rachel S. on *Sunset Traverse* (V7).
Photo by Serra B.

☐ 8. SUNSET TRAVERSE V7 ★★
Sit start as for *Windstorm*, traverse right on holds just under where the roof steepens. Climb into *Category Five* and finish.

☐ 9. HEART OF THE STORM V7 ★★★
Sit start with the low jug and right-facing slot edge. Move left backwards along *Sunset Traverse*, and out the roof as for *Windstorm*. Great holds, movement and setting. Classic.
FA Cam Freiburghaus

☐ 10. HEARTBREAKER V9 ★★★
Start as for *Category Five*, but immediately after its crux, climb left into compression on the prow with the same finishing sequence as *Love Taker*.
FA Nate Lynch, Shane Collins

☐ 11. CATEGORY FIVE V4 ★★
Sit start the same as for *Heart of the Storm*, but climb straight up the overhang into the the large crack and follow good but dusty holds left to the point of the roof to top out. Starting all the way on the right side of the boulder in the seam makes for a great warm-up climb

RACING STRIPES
(NOT PICTURED)

☐ 12. RACING STRIPES PROJECT ★
Sit start with underclings and feet facing toward open space above the slab. Move south on decent holds while trying not to launch your meat into space in the event of a fall.

Nate L. on *Love Taker* (V11).
Photo by Serra B.

Nate L. on the Racing Stripes Project

THE ARCHER

THE ARCHER

☐ 13. THE ARCHER V8 ★
Sit start from the obvious low hueco. Move up through crimps and a difficult snag down low into a sequential high section and a big commiting move to a bucket over the rounded lip. This one is no slouch. The crux hold is a bit hollow, otherwise would have more stars.
FA Nate Lynch

☐ 14. LITTLE JOHN V5 ★★
Sit start in the obvious low hueco. Climb right on crimps and slopers with a tricky sequence and crux lunge for a sharp finger bucket at 9 feet. From there proceed up good holds and knobs to a high top-out.
FA Nate Lynch

☐ 15. WILL SCARLET V4 ★
Sit start on low crimps. Can be climbed as a dyno or via a slightly harder, thin, technical sequence. Top out as for *Little John*.
FA Nate Lynch

172 | ROCKS OF SHARON

Nate Lynch on *The Archer* (V8).

Nate L. on *Heartbreaker* (V9).

Serra B. on *Dirk Diggler* (V5).
Photo by Serra B.

MINNEHAHA

174 | MINNEHAHA

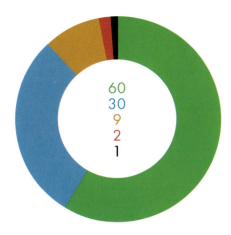

MINNEHAHA

When you think of a small, wooded, riverside park on a rocky hillside overlooking the city, what comes to mind? The swaying of towering pine trees? The feeling of being in the wild when you're 5 minutes away from your car? Is it following faint paths into clearings that each give you a sense of déjà vu? Is it a glimpse of a flowing river through the piney canopy as would inspire an artist's brush?

Whatever bliss you've imagined, add a decrepit parking lot, a splash of graffiti, and the occasional transient camp. Welcome to John H. Shields Park.

The City of Spokane bought this 26 acre area on the southern side of Beacon Hill in 1986, naming the park for the previous owner of the land. His widow sold the property to Spokane County Parks instead of an interested developer. This area previously went by its Native American Souix name of Minnehaha, which means curling water—a reference to the Spokane river.

In prior guidebooks and on internet posts, three names are used interchangeably: Minnehaha (climbers), Beacon Hill (mountain bikers), and John Shields Park (others). For the sake of consistency and with no direspect to Shields, we're using the Beacon Hill moniker for the large hillside above the lower rocks, and Minnehaha for the lower area near the parking lot. In this book, the only further mention of John H. Shields (erroneously, confusingly, and erratically also listed as John C. Shields in several situations) will be on the sign in the parking lot once you show up.

Being so close to everything urban, it's easy to see why Minnehaha and Beacon Hill have become beloved among mountain bikers, hikers and rock climbers. The rock is featured, to say the least. Almost any problem can be climbed several ways on the many incut edges, large shapes, and cracks.

Naysayers will use these reasons to hurl negative opinions about the climbing in this area. These include:
"Everything there is contrived."
"The rocks are not that big."
"It's sharp and slick."
"I don't like traversing every problem."

So let's hit on each of those statements: Yes, there are a lot of traverses here, most of the rocks have seams that flow both vertically and horizontally offering many options and the ability to seriously work on your endurance. Yes, you have a lot of options on how to climb things. Not everything needs tape to guide you where to go. You can just get to the top however you want.

And yes, some of the rocks are diminutive—this is fantastic for climbers with kids or just those who are psyched on climbing rocks that aren't very tall. The ability to go play on actual rock with the whole family is a very special thing. With an urban crag like Minnehaha, it

SPOKANE BOULDERING | 175

Dan T. on *Smokey's Traverse* (V6).

is also a great chance to instill stewardship in young people or new climbers. See it as a chance to help clean up places like this, create memories, and instill an appreciation for nature. Minnehaha is a place we make better and restore to that picturesque version we imagined previously…and also get some climbs in along the way.

That said, this area has served to be a training ground for top alpinists, big wall climbers preparing themselves for Yosemite, and, in the case of a young Johnny Goicoechea, the place to head every day after school to train footwork, technique, and the ability to climb slick texture in preparation for the boulders in Fontainebleau (it worked).

Being the closest and most popular climbing spot in the Spokane Area, Minnehaha is well documented. These boulders have confirmed ascents that date back to the 50s and have been lined out and published in both local guidebooks: Bob Loomis' 1983 *A Guide to Rock Climbing in the Spokane Area,* and in greater detail in Marty Bland's *Inland Northwest Rockclimbs* (2001). Those guidebooks are authoritative guides for Minnehaha and have each and every variation listed. We're going to skip a portion of them and only identify the main lines on each rock. Grab a copy of those guidebooks for more information.

Enjoy.

TO GET TO MINNEHAHA FROM I-90:

Take exit 282 for Hamilton, headed north.

After 0.7 mile on Hamilton take a right onto Mission Ave.

After 0.3 mile, take a left onto E. Upriver.

Continue 3.5 miles and the parking will be on your left.

MINNEHAHA PARK

Warmup Rock: **1-5**
Novice Rock: **6-13**
Fingertip Rock / Finger Ripper / Lichen Traverse Area: **14-30**
Hallway Boulders / Ape Rock / Cornflake / Tarantula Traverse: **31-46**
Morning Cooler Wall: **47-52**
Don Quixote Face / Moss Rock / Secondary Face: **53-58**
Smokey's Traverse: **59-61**
Lower Beacon Hill / Crystal Rock / Barn Door / Upper Bench: **62-78**
Painted Boulder / The Cult Clearing: **79-88**
The Head and the Heart: **89-90**
The Diamond Boulders: **91-96**
Hurtful Boulder: **97-98**
Johnny's Area: **99-101**
Mother Lover: **102**
The Cliff Band: **103**
The Far Side: **104-107**
Upper Area: **108**

SPOKANE BOULDERING | 177

MINNEHAHA PARK

WARMUP ROCK

☐ **1. MAGINOT LINE V3** ★
Commence on the far left side, crouched above the thorn bushes where the head-height seam starts to trail upward. Traverse right and stay low until you can move up and right using the crack with a crescent hold. A variant takes the upper seam.

☐ **2. THE MINNE WARMUP V1**
Start on the crescent hold in the crack and follow the right-side crack.

☐ **3. BATTLE OF THE BULGE V3**
Starting in the large juggy crack with your back to the tree, make a few moves to crimps out right and go up.

☐ **4. FOLLOW THE LEADER V4**
Start on low bad crimps above the drilled out hole and painfully climb straight up.

☐ **5. CHILL V0** (NOT PICTURED)
The dirty arête on the right side. Zero stars.

Shane C. on Maginot Line (V3)

178 | MINNEHAHA

NOVICE ROCK

☐ 6. REGULAR LEFT V1
The far left side of Novice Rock is more of a scramble than a climb.

☐ 7. REGULAR V1
The most vertical (still slabby) portion on Novice Rock. Use great holds to a large ledge and twerk your way up.

☐ 8. LEANING BOOK V1
Start about 10 feet left of the cleft in the middle. Go straight up using the ledges to scramble up. There are about 12 variations on this side of the rock, so choose your own adventure.

☐ 9. THE CLEFT V1
Starting in the deepest part of the cut-out feature of the face known as the cleft, shimmey and stem your way up however you want. Again, a billion lines exist, so have fun with it. Many variations start to the right.

☐ 10. SLAPPING THE NIP V2
Begin on a head-high good edge and make a move to the blunt corner. If you'd like to top it out, that's cool. Or you can just walk off right.

☐ 11. HIDDEN CRACK V1
Up right and behind Novice Rock is a graffiti-filled face with a really awesome pinch feature on it. On the rock directly to your left is an easy and fun crack. Not so hidden.

☐ 12. QUASIMODO V2 ★
This is the climb with the awesome pinch. Start crouched low with hands on the crimp seam above the drilled bolt hole and climb up through the awesome pinch and top out right. Fun!

☐ 13. MIKE'S CLIMB V1
To the right of *Quasimodo*, climb up the arête-y blocks. Just okay.

SPOKANE BOULDERING | 179

FINGERTIP ROCK

☐ 14. TINA'S TIPS V2
Start on the middle slanting edge and follow it up to a large horn. Continue up and right following another seam.

☐ 15. FINGERTIP TRAVERSE V2
Start far right and low. Traverse left to the end of the first seam, go up to the next, and follow that left all the way to the walk-off slope.

FINGER RIPPER CRACK (NOT PICTURED)

☐ 16. FINGER RIPPER CRACK V0
The small crack system on *Finger Ripper*.

☐ 17. FINGER RIPPER V1
The rock just west of the *Don Quixote* face, offers many lines—all of them are pretty easy. Go crazy, Tiger.

LICHEN TRAVERSE AREA

☐ 18. DIRK DIGGLER V5 ★ (NOT PICTURED)
Start by hugging either side of the hanging block, pressing your foot on the detached block in front of you. Use the left face and the sharp, terrible incut crimp in the overhang to gain the jug and fumble your feet up.

☐ 19. ROYAL ARCH V2
Begin on the left side of the traverse. Instead of traversing right, head up and left. Start a couple feet to the left on small crimps to add a couple grades.

☐ 20. TWO HANDS AND TWO HOLDS V7
With a left-hand undercling, bust up to a small right hand crimp and left gaston. Finish via a big move to the rail. Start a couple inches to the right on good holds for a much easier variation.

☐ 21. THE TRAVERSE V1 ★★
Start on the far right on a good edge. Climb up and left to a good seam that fractures the wall into a V-shaped finish. Drop here or go back. You can start this problem from the left side (start of *Royal Arch*) or the right side. For good measure, do both.

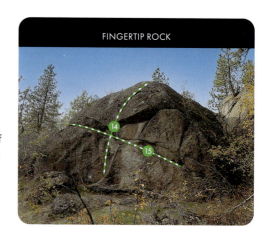

☐ 22. THE CUT V2
Start smushed, matching on a chest-high flat crimp and follow the vertical seam for two moves to the good jug. Go up.

☐ 23. LICHEN ME MUCHO V1
Start on the low triangle feature to the right of the large slanted crack. Move up to the seam and then left up the dirty crack.

☐ 24. TRY A LITTLE TENDERNESS V2
Start on the large bulge and work your way up and right to a dicey finish.

☐ 25. PROMETHEUS + VAR V2 (NOT PICTURED)
This is just downhill a few feet from this rock. Ascend the right side from the rail.

180 | MINNEHAHA

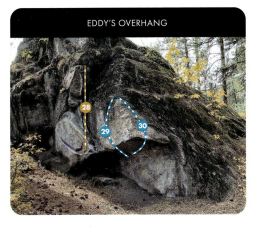

EDDY'S OVERHANG

Cierra G. on *Eddie's Overhang* (V3)
Photo by Serra B.

EDDIE'S OVERHANG

☐ **26. 90s GLOW V0** (NOT PICTURED)
The left side of the wall on which *Eddy's Overhang* ends holds a few different lines you can play on—in typical Minnehaha fashion, choosing your own adventure. A couple hard lines have been pieced together, as well.

☐ **27. NO TOP V6** (NOT PICTURED)
Start on low crimps and jump to a slopey rail. It doesn't top out—womp, womp.

☐ **28. NO FLAKE V6**
An eliminate left of the massive arrow feature that calls the tip of the arrow out of bounds. Using the arrow deducts a couple grades.

☐ **29. EDDIE'S FACE V4**
Starting with a left-hand squared-out undercling and the right hand in a good slot next to it, move to a far left crimp on the face and then hold tight to gain a right hand to finish up.

☐ **30. EDDIE'S OVERHANG V3** ★★
Start in a great undercling on the right side of the rock and make moves to the right corner to slap and follow up.

THE HALLWAY BOULDER

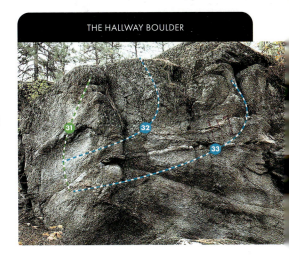

THE HALLWAY BOULDER

☐ **31. MASON'S MUSCLE V2**
Start on the low right-slanting ledge and crank directly up to next ledge and directly to the top after.

☐ **32. MASON'S MUSCLE VARIATION V3**
Same start as *Muscle* but traverse right until you can top out through the V shaped crack.

☐ **33. PAUL'S CLIMB V3**
Great climb, A+.

SPOKANE BOULDERING | 181

Breanna on Masan's Muscle (V2). Photo by Chad Ramsey

APE ROCK

☐ **34. DECEPTION STRETCH V3**
Start matched low on the left-facing sidepull edge and balance your way to the good middle jug and hidden dish crimps after. Head right after the jug for a little easier variation.

☐ **35. MONKEY DIRECT V4 ★**
Start very low with a right hand in a sharp incut and the left-hand painfully in the low crack on the arête. Move to great holds and then make a fun, long slap to the slopey top. Excellent.

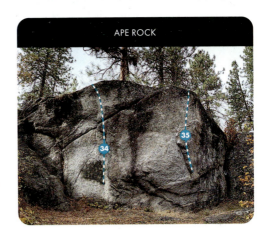

CORNFLAKE

☐ **36. CORNFLAKE TRAVERSE V3 ★**
On the far left side of the wall, start with smeary feet and good undercling holds. Traverse right and up to insecure-feeling flakes and buldging jugs.

☐ **37. CHRIS' CLIMB V2**
Start on the fin-shaped hold in the middle of the face and move up and right on bad holds with worse feet. It's extremely possible this hasn't been climbed after an important flake broke in 2016.

☐ **38. STEPPIN' OUT V4**
Climb left of the arête and right of the good holds and climb straight up. Hard for the grade.

☐ **39. THE CORNER V0**
Start matched on the huge flat corner ledge, go up.

☐ **40. THE SLAB V2** (NOT PICTURED)
Spokane's own "*Hesitater.*" Start on the large low bulge and move up to an okay rail near the crack on the left. Jump.

SPOKANE BOULDERING | 183

TARANTULA TRAVERSE

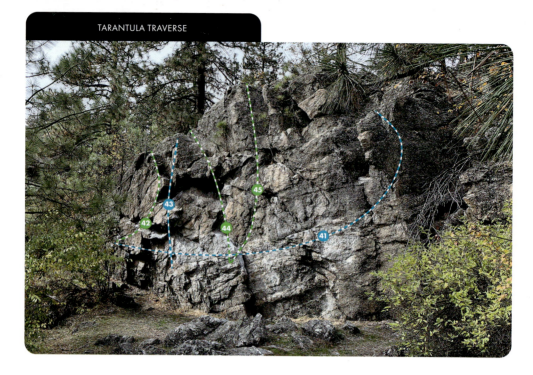

TARANTULA TRAVERSE

☐ **41. TARANTULA TRAVERSE V3** ★★
Start matched on the obvious right-facing flakey jugs on the left and make a move to the incut cornered hold. Continue moving right and staying low through a cruxy move from the large middle jug to the small crimps with no feet, continue right even more until you reach the far corner. Follow the column up and finish.

☐ **42. DAVE'S PROBLEM V2**
Start as for the traverse but go up to the right–slanting seam and follow to the large square–shaped block to finish up.

☐ **43. TURK'S GREASE V3**
Starting with a chest high right hand undercling in a small flake and a lower left undercling, move up hugging the big blocks above you.

☐ **44. TARANTULA DIRECT V0**
Start in the huge, obvious, white center jug and go up.

☐ **45. TARANTULA RIGHT V1**
Start in the huge, obvious, white jug and instead of following left, leave the good holds for the crimps and go up right.

☐ **46. TARANTULA TURD V0** (NOT PICTURED)
The small, lifeless checkered clump of granite between Tarantula and Cornflake. Climb this one however you want.

Stacia L. on *Tarantula Traverse* (V3). Photo by Jaleena Jacobs

184 | MINNEHAHA

MORNING COOLER WALL

Alex N. on *Flying Saucer* (V6). Photo by Serra B.

☐ 47. SLAB PROBLEM V4
The detached block left of the tree. Start with a left-hand undercling crimp and a right hand head-high crimp and climb straight up.

☐ 48. THE SHEPHERD'S WAY V2
Start on a head-high slopey ledge and climb left and up on not great feet.

☐ 49. SCARRED GROUND + VAR V2
Start right of *Shephard's Way* and go straight up. You can make this as easy or hard as you'd like.

☐ 50. FLYING SAUCER V6
Identify the thin crescent-shaped hold in the middle of the rock, good. Now find a chest high right hand and head-high left hand for bad start holds and make your way to the saucer. Then continue hard climbing up.

☐ 51. OLD SCHOOL ACHILLES V4
With a head-high slopey right hand and a left slopey sidepull on the vertical rail, climb up into the ledgey overhang and finish up the good left edges.

☐ 52. THE MORNING ARÊTE V2
Start on the right hand feature using good low holds in the crack of the arête and follow up.

MORNING COOLER WALL

SPOKANE BOULDERING | 185

Dane C. on Smokey's Traverse (V6).

MOSS ROCK

☐ 55. WOW, AMAZING V3
Start on the far left crimp and good right hand incut and traverse all the way right into *Mesmerized*.

☐ 56. DAD'S 50! V3
Start matched in the right hand side jug under the crack and make a move up to a great jug on the face. Move left and follow the pillar up.

☐ 57. MESMERIZED V4 ★★
Same start as Dad's 50 but go straight up.

SECONDARY FACE

☐ 58. EAST COASTER TRAVERSE V7 / V3
Start far left on a good flake with smeary feet on graffiti. Traverse all the way right and walk-off.

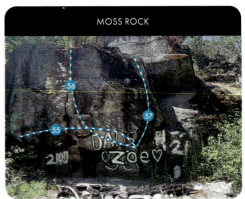

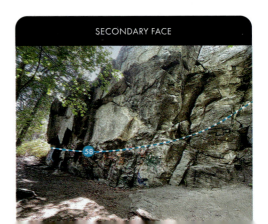

186 | MINNEHAHA

SMOKEY'S TRAVERSE

SMOKEY'S TRAVERSE

☐ **59. SMOKEY'S TRAVERSE V6** ★★★
Starting on the left-most sloping edge on the far right side of the rock, make a couple of moves to get you on better holds just above the lip. Using good holds and consistently using your right heel to take some weight off, head all the way left to a good midway sloper and gain back some energy to get you through the cruxy shark-tooth crimp and tiring finish. One of the best problems in the Spokane area.

☐ **60. SMOKEY'S LOW V8**
Same climb as *Smokey's* just start lower and farther right on a worse sloping ledge.

☐ **61. HUGE GEORGEBANKS V2** (NOT PICTURED)
The small rock that serves as the base for Smokey's—many variations all fun!

LOWER BEACON HILL (NOT PICTURED)

☐ **62. SKYLINE V1**
A painted boulder just up the trail from *Cholo*, still behind *John's Problem*. Start on small crimps in the middle of the face, making moves out to the slanting arête on the right without the help of the feet from the detached blocks on the right. Again, you can go left and straight up, too. Lots of unspectacular options here.

☐ **63. CHOLO V2**
Once *John's Problem* is topped up you'll see *Cholo* pretty nicely in front if you. A very skinny refrigerator shaped block. Start matched low in the crack on the right and press your feet on the opposing block to gain the lip. More fun than it looks.

☐ **64. SCREE V3**
Sitting by itself just east of John Roskelley's Crystal Rock on the hillside is blankish vertical face. Start on small head-high crimps on the face and use a few good edges to follow the face up.

SPOKANE BOULDERING | 187

LOWER BEACON HILL

CRYSTAL ROCK

☐ **65. CRYSTAL CRACK V0**
Climb the crack!

☐ **66. JOHN'S LAYBACK V2**
Starting very crouched and matching on a low flat edge on the left side of the rock, make a move up to an incut seam on the right and follow the blunt arête to a good top.

☐ **67. TINY EIGER V2**
Start low and matched in the obvious white mouth in the middle of the rock and climb inside the scooped rock.

☐ **68. TINY EIGER RIGHT V2**
Same start but move right and follow the right side of the scoop up on white granite clumps.

☐ **69. ROSKELLEY WARMUP V1**
Follow the dirty seam up and take the lip up and left to the top.

BARN-DOOR ROCK

☐ **70. WHITE BIRD V2**
Start at the tip of the large jug on the left and follow up and left with great ledgey holds the whole way. Take the jug haul to the left for a V0.

☐ **71. BIRDS AREN'T REAL V2**
Start in the thorn bush. lol just kidding...kinda. Start standing on the ledge above the thorn bush and climb the crack up and left. There are a ton of options here and you can come up with about 5 variations to this problem.

☐ **72. BARN-DOOR CHIMNEY V0**
The right-most chimney on the face, straight forward.

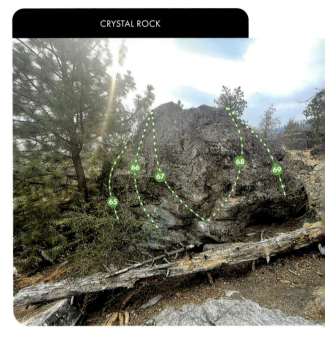

Nate L on *Infinity Traverse* (V6).

UPPER BENCH

☐ **73. FRICTION BOULDER V0**
(NOT PICTURED)
Three variations on this little guy. Left, Center and Right. All the same difficulty and name so we're consolidating into one.

☐ **74. KNIFE-EDGE CRACK V2**
Start matched in the belly-high notch in the crack and follow the crack up for two moves.

☐ **75. UPPER BENCH V0**
Start on the obvious ledge and climb the ledges to the left and up.

☐ **76. THE PILLAR V1**
Start low on the left block at the bottom of the pillar. Climb just the pillar.

☐ **77. RIP SAW V2**
Directly to the right of the pillar use the head-high right-slanting crimp rail as your start and climb up just slightly right staying away from the arête.

☐ **78. THE INFINITY TRAVERSE V6 ★**
A few feet down and east of Rip Saw, start as low as possible on the far right under the boulder and make thuggish moves up to incut crimps. Follow the crimps right to the corner for the top.

UPPER BENCH

SPOKANE BOULDERING | 189

BEACON HILL

PAINTED BOULDER

The Painted Boulder is the largest free standing boulder in the park and very hard to miss while exploring the area. This massive rock can be used as a great point of reference to help find your way around. From the trail passing on the SW side of the boulder, taking the left fork options will take you close to Girl's Best Friend, right at the first fork will get you close to Revolution, and full commitment to the right forks steeply behind the boulder will take you through to the Cult Clearing. Additionally, you can climb this boulder too! While the tall faces on the rock should be done with a rope (the photo below is not a recommendation), the backside of the boulder has many edges, jugs, and crimps to play on with a few lines that can be made up including a fun line on the right hand-side in the back of the cave. If you're looking for a hard line, check out the adjacent rock on the north side of Painted Boulder with the tall arête to try the DUI Project

☐ 79. MISFIT ANGEL V5
Starting in the overhang roof ledge use small crimps and the rock in front of you for feet make your way to the flake jug and jug seam up to the top. Dirty? Maybe hard? This is directly below Painted Boulder.

☐ 80. PAINTED BOULDER
There aren't really "boulder problems" on this massive rock, just a bunch of neat things to kinda play on without a rope. That being said, we don't recommend soloing this big guy as the top-out is a little bulgy and not the spot you want to be stuck. Once found in this "stuck" position like one of the authors, you may be forced to use a bolt as a pocket while you're falling which will, in some way or another, rip your damn finger open. Mostly we are including this in the book as a marker to help navigate through the Beacon Hill area. Lost? Find this rock. It's big, you can do it.

Shane C. on the *Painted Boulder*.
Photo by Chad Ramsey

THE CULT CLEARING

☐ **81. BLOCKADE V1** (NOT PICTURED)
Start on the right hand arête in the low cut out rock and use fun holds to gain the top via the right arête. Watch out for ivy. This is the first rock by the circle pit.

☐ **82. NISE 1 V1**
Start matched on the right slanting rail. Make fun moves up to the ledges to top out. Many variations.

☐ **83. NISE V2**
Start with the good undercling and head left and up with real smeary feet and go up delicate slab staying right of *Nise 1*.

☐ **84. YOUT V2**
Start matched in the low undercling then move to the jugs on the face and top out straight up. Small. Very small.

☐ **85. UNDER YOUT V2**
Start the same as *Yout* but stay under the roof traversing left to the far leftside lip.

☐ **86. MOUTH V3**
With a low left-hand sidpull and a crimp on the face near your head, make your way up using great holds to the mouth (be sure to check the mouth before your start climbing). Hug the detached Boulder above it to the top.

☐ **87. THE REVIVAL V1** (NOT PICTURED)
Sit start with your hands low in the seam behind the left side underclings, using the detached rocks in front of you make your way up the seam to the middle ledge. Take the middle crack up to the top. Everything to the left of you is poison ivy but this climb is VERY good.

☐ **88. THE REVIVAL RIGHT V3** (NOT PICTURED)
Begin matched on a good broken jug on the right hand arête over a scary fall and with a right heel pull yourself up the arête. Make sure you have a spotter. There's a thread on the internet that calls this problem a V10 and we're pretty sure that's a mistake but we'll let you decide.

THE CULT CLEARING FRONTSIDE

THE CULT CLEARING BACKSIDE

THE CULT CLEARING OTHERSIDE

SPOKANE BOULDERING | 191

FLOODED/HEAD & THE HEART

☐ 89. FLOODED V2
Start on the far right side of the undercling edge, make a move up, and trend left.

☐ 90. THE HEAD AND THE HEART V6 ★★
Start with a high right hand in the open mouth of the crack and your left on a flakey crimp on the face. Make a couple tough pulls, reach the horn at the lip, and then slowly parse out the delicate top.

THE DIAMOND BOULDERS

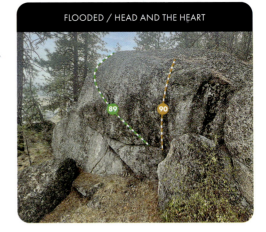

FLOODED / HEAD AND THE HEART

☐ 91. BUMBLES V1
On the left-side corner, with a rock as your seat, start as low as you can and make your way up (you have a lot of options).

☐ 92. ANAHATA V5
Start sitting under the small overhang with your let hand on a crimp around the left side corner and your right hand in a good slot. Make a few thuggish pushes and then pull the lip, lol.

☐ 93. FOR SCORE V4
The small detached block directly to the right of *Anahata*. This was a completely different problem until the entire column broke from the center and hundreds of pounds of granite nearly smushed a human body into the ground.

☐ 94. GIRL'S BEST FRIEND V9 ★★
Start crouched, hugging the bottom edges of the diamond-shaped chockstone and make a hard stick to the crimp in the center of the face. Another big move to a good hold on the right side of the block will get you to the hefty top. Use your feet on the rocks to either side of the diamond to make it a few grades easier. We wouldn't recommend that, though.

☐ 95. THE BARN V4
Start with underclings near your chest on incut holds on the left side of the bulgey rock and make your way up and over.

☐ 96. TUMMY RUBBER V3
Start on the slopey edge under the budge and rub your little tummy all over the spicy and gritty rock.

Nate L. on *Girl's Best Friend* (V9).

Shane C. on *The Head and the Heart* (V6).
Photo by George Hughbanks

THE DIAMOND BOULDERS

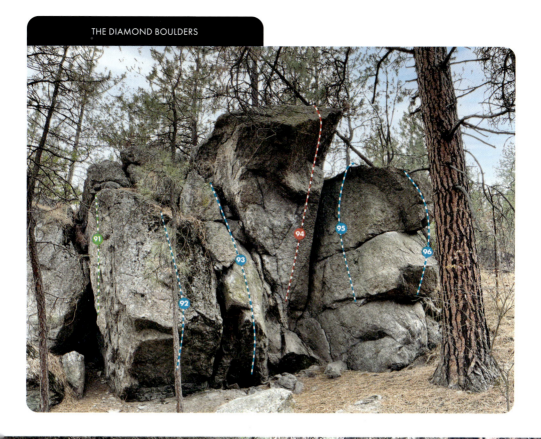

Mollie A. on *Tummy Rubber* (V3)

HURTFUL BOULDER (NOT PICTURED)

☐ 97. THREESOME V3
Starting on the left side of the overhung face, use a low right hand sidepull and high left pinch to establish on the arête, then make two moves on very painful holds. Follow the right crack to top.

☐ 98. FIVE IS A CROWD V5
On the low far left side sits a slanting shifted chockstone. Start with a left hand on the left arête and a right hand on an edge just under its lip. Awkwardly contort up the arête to its top-out (before the top-out to *Threesome*).

JOHNNY'S AREA

Johnny's Area still has a bunch of potential to explore—you can test your footwork on *Revolution* or check out the rambunctiously wild dyno over ivy to the right and uphill from the same boulder. Or head down and east to the flat meadow for the cutest short little triangle-shaped rock with a few lines on it.

☐ 99. THE APPROACH V2 (NOT PICTURED)
Just down and to the left of *Revolution* sits a small and short crack—follow it up and left. The easiest V2 in the park and possibly the world.

☐ 100. REVOLUTION V10
Johnny's first hard problem in Minne. Start low on underclings and compression climb out the bulge. Grade is unconfirmed and likely stout. Can be climbed from a stand for roughly V8.

☐ 101. SPHERICAL CANON V4
Start low and right follow the slanted ledge into the incut sidepulls on the face using the featureless slab face and the arête to perch into a gap between two rocks as your top-out.

MOTHER LOVER

☐ 102. MOTHER LOVER V6 ★★★
On the low left arête, start matched with a high heel and make a few thuggy moves on the left arête to eventually gain the face to assist with the top-out. Watch out for posion ivy to the right.

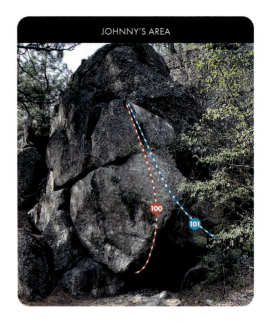

JOHNNY'S AREA

MOTHER LOVER

THE CLIFF BAND (NOT PICTURED)

☐ 103. THE CLIFF BAND
The Cliff Band (aka Oppression Ledge) is a long stretch of bolted short routes that can be bouldered. Several lines are available all along the band, so play around and have fun!

UPPER BEACON HILL

THE FARSIDE ROCK

☐ **104. REBELS V2**
Start as low as you can in the crescent-shaped jug at your knees. Move left and up using sweet pinches and underclings to a foot-lacking top-out.

☐ **105. HEATWAVE V2**
Same start and finish as *Rebels*. From the start, head right on a good seam and work a nose-like feature to get over to the top (or topout straight up from the nose for a variation).

☐ **106. SUM OF ALL SIDES PROJECT**
Start on the slab using undercling crimps and move up the right-leaning arête. Once able, trend left on a horizontal seam and up to a tall finish. For a variation, start a little farther left and go straight up, or for another variation, follow the arête up.

☐ **107. YEAR OF REGRETS V1** (NOT PICTURED)
On the far right side, make your way up a slab into the dirty dihedral thing.

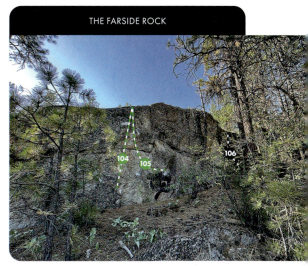
THE FARSIDE ROCK

UPPER AREA (NOT PICTURED)

☐ **108. UPPER BEACON AREA**
You can find the Upper Area just up and left from The Farside Rock—there's a large cluster of small rocks along the powerlines with little known about them. This is a great playground for some exploration and carefree climbs.

Nate L. on *Revolution* (V10).

SPOKANE BOULDERING | 195

POST FALLS

Shane Collins on *Another Dam Problem* (V4).

POST FALLS BOULDERS

The limited quantity of bouldering at Post Falls shouldn't deter visitors. The problems are enjoyable and unique, and encompass the spectrum of difficulty. Located in Q'Emiln Park, the boulders are easily accessed by a short downhill walk. Most are just downcanyon from a spillway that releases water when flow exceeds what is neccessary to generate power. As such, during rainy times of year and spring snowmelt, the climbing is inaccessible.

GETTING THERE
Take exit 5 off I-90 and go south on Spokane St. for 0.8 miles. Turn right on W Parkway Drive into the parking lot.

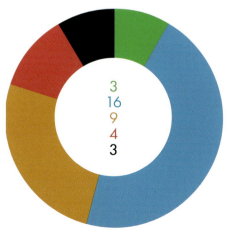

3
16
9
4
3

196 | POST FALLS

POST FALLS

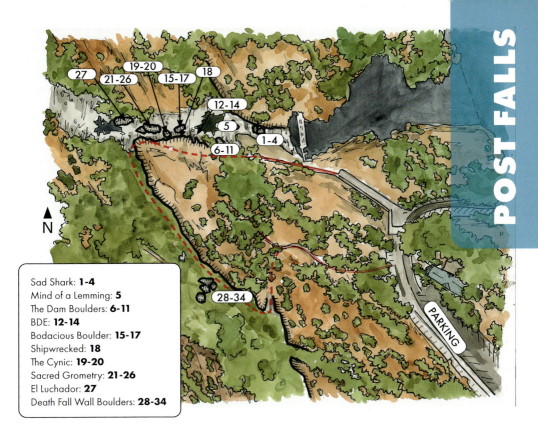

Sad Shark: **1-4**
Mind of a Lemming: **5**
The Dam Boulders: **6-11**
BDE: **12-14**
Bodacious Boulder: **15-17**
Shipwrecked: **18**
The Cynic: **19-20**
Sacred Grometry: **21-26**
El Luchador: **27**
Death Fall Wall Boulders: **28-34**

SPILLWAY

SAD SHARK

☐ **1. KUNG FURY V6** ★
Involves a large dyno. That's just about all we know. Classic beef.
FA Angus Meredith

☐ **2. CONTRIVANCE OF THE MIND V4** ★
From the right hand lone jagged crimp and left-hand incut above, climb leftward with tricky movement and a squeeze through the hole.
FA Cam Freiburghaus

☐ **3. SAD SHARK V4** ★★
From the right hand lone jagged crimp and left-hand incut above climb right into a slopey mantel.
FA Nate Lynch

☐ **4. MORE THAN YOU PAID FOR V3** ★
From a sit start at the lip of the low corner pull on and mantel. That's it. Super simple.
FA Cam Freiburghaus

SPOKANE BOULDERING | 197

PLAGIARIZING APOLOGISTS

☐ **5. PLAGIARIZING APOLOGISTS V1**
Stand start from the big rail, go left and up.

DAM BOULDERS

☐ **6. CHASING THE DRAGON V3** ★
Start matched low on the lip for a sit start. Move up and right on a variety of holds and mantel at the apex.

☐ **7. RULE OF THIRDS V1** ★★
From jugs in the center of the overhang make a few big moves up to the apex.

☐ **8. GOLDEN RATIO V0** ★
Climb the right arête.

☐ **9. ANOTHER DAM PROBLEM V4** ★★
Starting with a left-hand edge and right hand sidepull, tech your way up the left arête to a commiting move to the horn.
FA Cam Freiburghaus

☐ **10. DAM STRAIGHT V8** ★
Start sitting matched on the right-facing flake. Move up to the flexy crimp rail (Gentle!) then balance and chuck your way to the horn. Tension, tech, and Toblerone.
FA Nate Lynch

☐ **11. DAM RIGHT V6** ★★
Start as for *Dam Straight*, but move right from the flexy crimp rail with a tricky sequence. Techy and fun. Has a tendency to moss up fast, so bring a brush.
FA Nick Nick Tansy

BDE

☐ 12. BDE SIT PROJECT
More bang for your proverbial buck. Climb from a low sit adding moves into *BDE*.

☐ 13. BIG DICK ENERGY V9 ★★
Start standing with a head-height, left-hand, block pinch and a right hand sidepull jug. Compress out the finger of rock to the jugs at the tip and top out. Potentially stiff for the grade and a bit heady as you finish. The landing is a bit jumbled; we'd recommend 4+ pads and a spotter.
FA Nate Lynch

☐ 14. JUST THE TIP V5 ★
Start matched on the jib just under the end of the phallus. Campus to jugs on the corner and continue up.

BODACIOUS BOULDER

☐ 15. BODACIOUS BOULDER LEFT V3 ★
Start on opposing holds at the corner, move through a good flake to the lip.

☐ 16. BODACIOUS BOULDER V5 ★
From opposing holds, lunge for the lip and finish it off.

☐ 17. HARD MANTEL PROJECT
1-2 simple moves from a stand into what is reportedly a rough mantel...yet to be topped.

Nate Lynch on *BDE* (V9).

BDE

BODACIOUS BOULDER

Alex C. on *The Cynic* (V9).

SPOKANE BOULDERING | 199

SHIPWRECKED

☐ **18. SHIPWRECKED (AKA MATT AND DAVE GO TO JAIL) V5** ★★
From a stand start on the rail, climb blocky holds up the bulge.
FA Matt and Dave

THE CYNIC

☐ **19. THE CYNIC V9** ★
Start matched on the sloping rail at the very back of the small cave. We recommend a copious number of toe hooks and three months of eight-minute-abs to finagle your way to the lip without dabbing. Weird and butt dragging, yet quite fun.
FA Nate Lynch

☐ **20. MERE PESSIMISM V6** ★
The "high" start of *The Cynic*, Start on the obvious jugs at the left end of the crack.

SACRED GEOMETRY

☐ **21. SALIVATE V4** ★★★
Start from the lowest jugs. Climb the hanging prow. Celebrate. Instant classic.

☐ **22. SACRED GEOMETRY PROJECT** ★★★
Climb the thin thin center of the tall face. It's hard not to be inspired and completely shut down by this looming boulder.

☐ **23. PLAYHOUSE V9** ★
Start as for *Roundhouse Low,* but exit left onto jugs. Unconfirmed.
FA Drew Schick

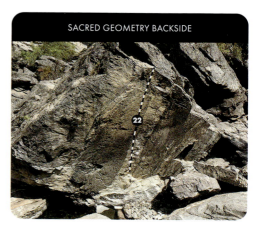

200 | POST FALLS

Matt D. on *Salivate* (V4).
Photo by Angus M.

☐ 24. ROUNDHOUSE V6 ★★
From a sit start climb up and right on hard to see quartz holds.
FA Alex Nikoleyev

☐ 25. ROUNDHOUSE LOW V10 ★★
Start lower making tough moves into *Roundhouse*. Grade Unconfirmed.
FA Drew Schick

☐ 26. REX KWON DO V6 ★★★
Start high with a left-hand edge and right hand bulge. Big moves on smoth blocky holds.
FA Nick Nick Tansy

SACRED GEOMETRY OTHERSIDE

EL LUCHADOR

☐ **27. EL LUCHADOR V6** ★
Climb the center of the face.
FA Angus Meridith

DEATH FALL WALL

LIL' DABBY

☐ **28. LIL' DABBY V5** ★★
Sit start with a left-hand edge, right hand undercling. Move to the arête/lip, climb up and right to the apex to top out on either side of the point. Expect a bit of a slide down the slope if you fall...

MOM'S SPAGHETTI

☐ **29. MOM'S SPAGHETTI V4** ★★
Start on the low left blocks, follow the lip and only ever cook pasta al dente. Sticking to the wall is for climbers, not noodles.

☐ **30. ALFREDO V3** ★ (NOT PICTURED)
Climb the triangular slab to the left of *Mom's Spaghetti*.

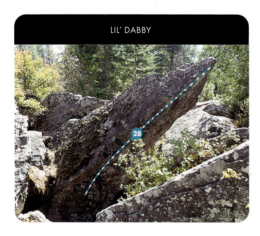

LIL' DABBY

MOM'S SPAGHETTI

DIME IN A DOZEN

☐ **31. DIME IN A DOZEN V3**
Climb out the tiny cave from decent slot holds.

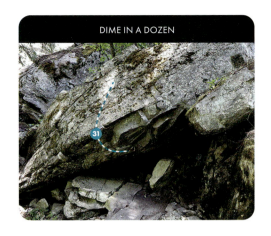

THE HOG

☐ **32. THE HOG V5** ★
Starting siting in the overhang. Move up and right without dabbing on the tree.

☐ **33. BIG DABBY V7** (NOT PICTURED)
For a dose of silly difficulty, start on tiny undercling crimps and bust to the final jug of *The Hog*.

MISTRESS MISERY

☐ **34. MISTRESS MISERY V6** ★
Stand start from left-hand undercling flake and right hand crimp. Tricky footwork, a big slap to gain the lip, and a traverse left on rounded holds leads to the top. Not bad.

SPOKANE BOULDERING | 203

Micha H. on one of the assorted climbs.

FAR OUT

Park in the Post Falls Community Forest lot on W. Riverview Drive and follow the Blue Diamond Trail Loop counter clockwise trending NE. Go down a decent hill and through a few trail intersections while following the Blue Diamond trail markings. The rocks are hidden 50 feet to the left (west) at about 0.9 mile down the trail. GPS in QR library in the index.

EXCAVATOR

☐ 35. EXCAVATOR V3 ★★

Stand start on small chest-high holds. Move to the flat jug above and quest through the overhang. Potential exists for more lines on this section of the wall and surrounding area as of the writing of this book.
FA Micha Haslett

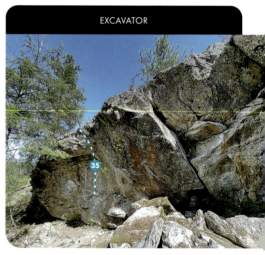
EXCAVATOR

ARE YOU TOPPING OUT?

ARE YOU TOPPING OUT?

☐ 36. ASSORTED CLIMBS V0-6 ★★★

There are a plethora of options on the well-featured and pleasantly overhanging wall. Good rock quality and interesting holds with a head-building top-out if you saunter above the jug rail at the 10 foot level. Couldn't ask for a better place to use as an outside training grounds...assuming you can get past the hike.

Boots
BAKERY & LOUNGE

24 W Main Ave
(509) 703-7223
Open 8-4 daily

Climber Owned & Operated

Mellow, funky cafe/bar offering premade vegan & gluten-free dishes, baked goods, coffee & cocktails.

BANK'S LAKE

Bank's Lake is located just southwest of Grand Coulee in Central Washington. This area is typically dry and sunny during Spokane's wet and wintery months. Just shy of two hours away, it's a great winter destination. The boulder zones are scattered along Highway 155 inside of the Columbia Basin Project near Steamboat Rock—a basalt butte that rises 800 feet above the lake that surrounds it. During the last Ice Age, Steamboat stood as an island in the new bed of the Columbia River where it had been diverted by ice dams. Once the ice dams burst there were massive floods creating the Scablands of Central Washington. Afterwards the Columbia returned to its original course, leaving Steamboat Rock as a prominent feature of the dry Grand Coulee. Lucky for us, some chunks of boulders stayed behind.

DRIVING DIRECTIONS

Follow US-2 W to WA-21 N in Lincoln County for 64.5 miles.

- Follow WA-174 W and WA-155 S to Northrup Rd in Grant County.

- Once you hit Wilbur, turn right onto WA-21 N (signs for WA-174/Republic Grand Coulee Dam) for 32 miles.

- Turn left onto WA-155 S/Grand Coulee Ave.

- Highway Rock's Pullout is 5.7 miles from this left turn.

- The split for Northrup Canyon and Northrup Point comes up at 6.8 miles.

- Northrup Canyon's dirt parking lot near the horse pit is 0.4 miles up the road to the left.

- Northrup Point feeds directly into the large parking area.

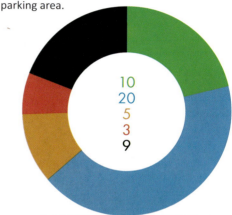

Warm Up Boulder: **1-7**
Knife Dab: **8**
Lousy Lip / Arête Boulder: **9-13**
Snot Rocket: **14**
The Jump: **15**
The Nose: **16**
A Horse with No Name: **17-20**
The Lean: **21**
Elevation: **22-25**
Road Rock: **26-28**
Xeno: **29**
The Perch: **30**

206 | BANK'S LAKE

Bryan C. on *Papa Tortilla* (V8). Photo by Angus M.

BANK'S LAKE

NORTHRUP CANYON

WARM-UP

☐ **1. EAST LIP TRAVERSE V2** ★
Start matched on the lip jug at the southwest corner of the boulder. Traverse the lip right to the next corner and top out.

☐ **2. CENTER LINE V3** ★★
Start on the chest-high edges. Move up to the shelf above, then right to top out. Starting farther down to the left adds a few grades.

☐ **3. CLASSIC CORNER V1** ★★★
Stand start on the obvious hold on the corner. Make fun moves on good holds.

☐ **4. SLAB V2**
Climb the concave slab from a stand start.

☐ **5. CORNER V3** ★★★
Start sitting matched on the seam edges. Tech your way up to big edges above. Classic.

☐ **6. WEIRD CORNER V2** ★
Begin low on the obvious left-facing jug. Make an awkward lunge to smoother climbing above.

☐ **7. OVERHUNG EDGES V1** ★★
Stand start with the large V-shaped jug rail. Climb big edges and mantel. Can be climbed either left or right for relatively the same difficulty. Good intro to heel hooking.

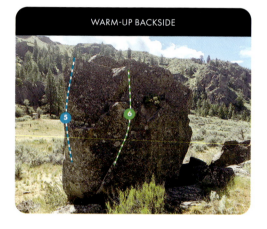

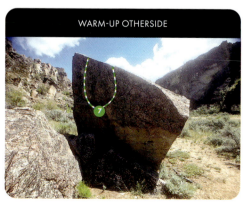

Nate L. on #36 *Slab* (V4)

KNIFE DAB

☐ 8. KNIFE DAB V4
Start on holds. Then move to more holds. Could use a brush. Tough top.

LOUSY LIP

☐ 9. LOUSY LIP V5 ★
Start sitting on the left end of the inviting lip. Traverse right and up with a sequence-dependant crux.

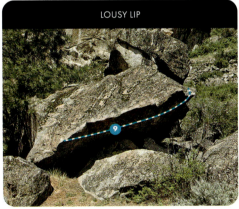

SPOKANE BOULDERING | 209

Nate L. on *East Side Project*.

ARÊTE BOULDER

☐ **10. EAST SIDE PROJECT** ★ ★
Starting just under the bulge, make tough moves up and right, then up the high face.

☐ **11. SUNNY ARÊTE V4** ★ ★ ★
Sit start at the bottom of the soaring arête. Move up edges to better holds near the top. Classic.

☐ **12. SHADY SLAB V4** ★
Start as for *Sunny Arête*, but make a tricky rock right unto the slab a few moves in. Not so classic.

☐ **13. BUCKAROO V10** ★ ★
Starting on good holds in the overhang, make a huge reach, core up, and then move to the low lip. Is quite tough. Could use a little excavation.
FA Drew Schick

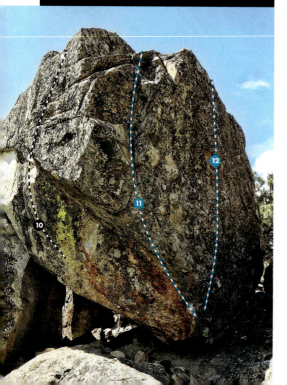
ARÊTE BOULDER FRONTSIDE

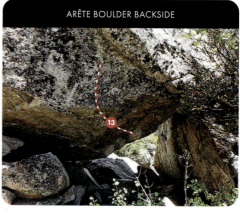
ARÊTE BOULDER BACKSIDE

Steve M. on the *West Side Project*, now *Buckaroo* (V10).

SNOT ROCKET

☐ 14. SNOT ROCKET PROJECT
From a stand start, bust to the sloping hold above, then on to what looks to be a difficult mantel.

THE JUMBLE

☐ 15. THE JUMBLE V3 ★
Stand start on edge at the left arête. Move up and right over a slightly uneven landing.

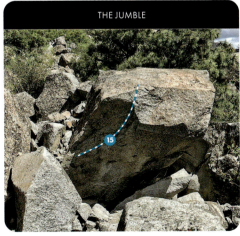

SPOKANE BOULDERING | 211

THE NOSE

☐ **16. THE NOSE V3** ★★★
Starting at the overhang, make a few moves up blocky holds and then rock up, reaching for the slanting crack.

SNAKE PIT

☐ **17. SNAKE PIT PROJECT** ★
Climb the hanging rail over the stepped landing. Looks fun, but needs a bit of protection.

☐ **18. LIP MANTEL V3** ★★ (NOT PICTURED)
Start sitting on the low lip above the top-out of *A Horse with No Name*.

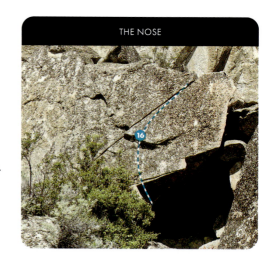
THE NOSE

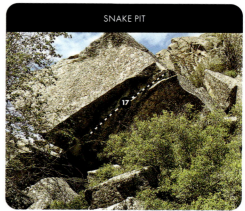
SNAKE PIT

Bryan C. on *Sunny Arête* (V4). Photo by Angus M.

212 | BANK'S LAKE

A HORSE WITH NO NAME

A *Horse with No Name* is located underneath the large Snake Pit Boulder.

Nate L. on *A Horse with No Name* (V10).

☐ 19. A HORSE WITH NO NAME V10 ★★

Start matched on the low rounded crimp. Move up the arête on small holds to a rowdy finish. Technical and a bit reachy.
FA Drew Schick

☐ 20. CRIMP PROJECT

Traverse crimps right into a lunge for the lip. The lip move is V5 on it's own.

A HORSE WITH NO NAME

ELEVATION

☐ 22. ROTATION V3 ★

Traverse the low lip from left to right topping as for *Levitation*.

☐ 23. LEVITATION V9 ★

Bust for the lip from low crimps. Yikes.

☐ 24. MASTICATION PROJECT

Climb the bulge from a low edge. Funky on toothy holds.

☐ 25. ELEVATION V11 ★★

Dyno to the lip from the obvious chest high holds. So big. Yet to see a third ascent...
FA Johnny G.

THE LEAN

☐ 21. THE LEAN V6 ★

Sit start and slap up grainy slopers. Punchy.

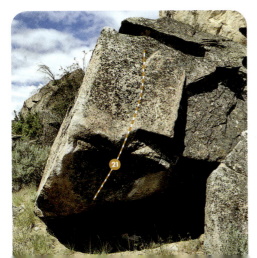

ELEVATION

SPOKANE BOULDERING | 213

ROAD ROCK

☐ 26. ROAD ROCK ROOF V3
Start matched on the jug at the lip. Starting in the low roof on crimps adds a grade, minimum.

☐ 27. ROAD ROCK LIP V4
Start matched on the rounded edge at the lip. Move up.

☐ 28. ROAD ROCK ARÊTE V1
Starting on lower blocky jugs, bust up to more jugs.

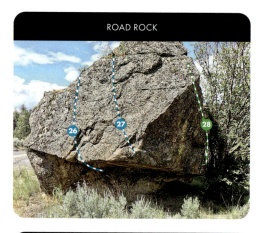

XENO

☐ 29. XENO V3 ★★
This boulder climbs on stone that is very different than the rest. Start low on neat incuts on opposing sides of the small overhung dihedral.

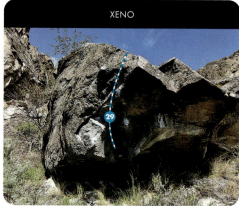

THE PERCH

☐ 30. THE PERCH PROJECT ★★
Start low on good holds in the right-facing rail. Climb the rail into compression as holds diminish in size. Overhangs about 35 degrees.

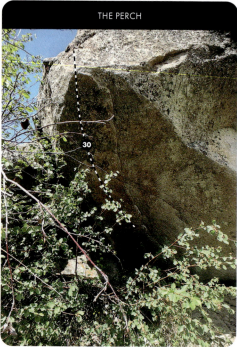

Shane C. on J-Hooks (V5).

214 | BANK'S LAKE

NORTHRUP POINT

LAKEVIEW

☐ 31. JUGS V1
Start on odd holds in the overhang, move to jugs on the lip, traverse right, and top out.

☐ 32. J-HOOKS V5 ★★
Starting on the low sloper and barely-there crimp, traverse right on crimps in the seam, commit to the lip, and summit.

☐ 33. SWEATER PUPPY V6 ★★
Start sitting with your right hand low in the slanting crack and left on the better hold in the horizontal crack. Move diagonally up crimps in the crack to a good slot and pop for the lip. A touch less straightforward than it looks.

☐ 34. FAT NATCHIES V4 ★★
Starting on the obvious large low hold, move up on pleasant holds with some slightly tricky beta. Mantel is a tad cruxy.

☐ 35. FUN BAGS V1 ★
Start standing on large blocks on the arête, move up and rock around to the right side of the arête.

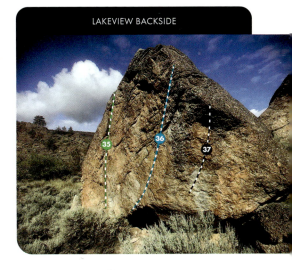

LAKEVIEW BACKSIDE

☐ 36. SLAB V4
Start low on an incut rail just left of the scoop in the wall. Climbs on questionable rock. An easier slab climb is to the left.

☐ 37. LAKEVIEW PROJECT
Starting on the obvious incut patina, climb up thin holds on the slightly steep face. Could use a bit of tidying up.

SPOKANE BOULDERING | 215

HIGHWAY ROCK BOULDERS

216 | BANK'S LAKE

PAPA TORTILLA

☐ **38. BURRITO BABE V4 ★★**
Start matched on the edge in the seam, move up incuts to the lip above. Simple but fun.

☐ **39. TOO MUCH SAUCE TUESDAY V3 ★**
Starting on the obvious jug, climb up and right on mostly good holds while avoiding the dab (crux).

☐ **40. PAPA TORTILLA V8 ★★★**
Stand start on the arête, make balancy moves into true commitment at the top. Classic. (...and by now we all know what "classic" means...be prepped for a battle).
FA Drew Schick

Alex N. on Papa Tortilla (V8)
Photo by Angus M.

PAPA TORTILLA FRONTSIDE

PAPA TORTILLA BACKSIDE

THE QUESADILLA

☐ **41. THE QUESADILLA V7 ★★**
Starting matched on the right arête, move into compression and up, summiting on the right side. Landing needs a few pads.
FA Steve Moss

THE QUESADILLA

SUPERBLOOM AREA

SUPERBLOOM

Superbloom is located 1.4 mi south of Northrup on 155. Park in the oval pullof on the lake side of the Hwy and find the main attraction high on the hill across the Hwy, SSW.

☐ 42. SUPERBLOOM V5 ★★★
Start this wonderful climb from a head-high jug, moving up through crimps, the arête, and edges. Use the righthand seam and left side great flat edge to top it out.
FA Shane Collins

☐ 43. PROJECT
This is a project on the left face of *Superbloom*, deceptively overhanging, until you can get to the tall flat edge.

☐ 44. WHACKOZOID V0
This problem is located immediately under *Superbloom* and is much smaller. It's actually a fun wall to play around on—don't take it too seriously and enjoy the views.
FA Shane Collins

☐ 45. JACK JACK V1
Start sitting on the low slopey rail, move to a couple crimps out right, pop to the right side of the lip, then traverse and walk yourself over left to top.
FA Shane Collins

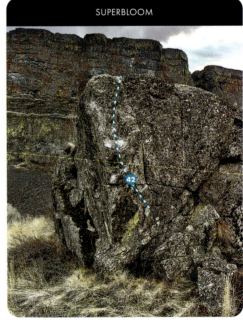

SUPERBLOOM

Myles B. on *Landslide* (V8).

218 | BANK'S LAKE

Megan C. on Beachhouse (V6).

LANDSLIDE

☐ **46. LANDSLIDE V8 ★★**
Sit start matched just under the overhang, then slap up into technical compression.

BEACH HOUSE (NOT PICTURED)

☐ **47. BEACH HOUSE V6 ★★**
Start crouched on edges roughly centered on the face and climb into the dihedral above.

QR LIBRARY

McLELLAN

BABY ARÊTE

CHARLIE'S HAMMOCK

BALD FACED LIAR

CHESSBOARD ROCK

ADMIRAL THRAWN

BOLD SCHOOL

CLASSIC, THE

ANVIL, THE

BULGE, THE

CONSTELLATION BOULDERS

ARDEN'S MIDDLE FINGER

CARVER BOULDER

CORNER STORE

ATAMA BOULDER

CAVE CRACK BOULDERS

CRIME OF PASSION

McLELLAN

CROW'S NEST

FELACIO

HUEVOS RANCHEROS

DIAMOND SLAB

FEROCIOUS FRED WALL

INGUINAL FORTITUDE

EPIC ARÊTE

FUNGUS ROCK

KITTY LITTER

EYEBROWS AND ANUS

HALL OF IMPOSSIBLE

LARRY PETERMAN

FAIRWINDS BACKSIDE

HEAD WOUND CAVE

LIGHTWORK

FEKKY

HIGH TIMES WALL

LITTLE WALL (MANTEL WALL)

SPOKANE BOULDERING | 221

McLELLAN
CONT...

LOW GLEN

PAWS THEN CLAWS

ROMANCING THE STONE

MASTHEAD BOULDER

PENNY DROP

SCAREDLESS IN SPOKANE

NINE MILE BALLS

PIPE DREAM

SCARLETT JOHANSSON

OGRE, THE

PROPAGANDA

SEVEN LOVES YOU

PACK RAT CAVE

PROSTOR'S WALL

SOULLESS

PARTY ROCK (TRIANGLE)

REASONABLE DOUBT

SPACE JAM

McLELLAN

SPARROW FOX

TONGUE, THE

WARM-UP WALL

SUBMARINE BOULDER

TONISHA

WICKED SKENGMAN

SUNSHINE WALL

TREMBLE

TARA'S WALL

UNBEARABLE LIGHTNESS OF BEING

TUM TUM

BIG BOULDER

TENEBROUS

VOODOO MAGIC

FIST, THE

THREE STORY BOULDER

WALLFLOWER

FLOOD, THE

TUM TUM CONT...

ROCK OF SHARON

FONT ROCK

ARCHER, THE

PORNOS AND PORCUPINES

HOUSEWIFE

HEARTBREAKER

SHARON STONE

ICE PRINCESS

POST FALLS

ARE YOU TOPPING OUT?

EXCAVATOR

MARGE SIMPSON

LANDSLIDE

BANK'S LAKE

PHANTOM WALL

BEACH HOUSE

PAPA TORTILLA

THRUTCHY MADNESS

LAKEVIEW

SUPERBLOOM

INDEX BY NAME

SYMBOLS

5.8 Dihedral V0 ★ 90
5.11 World V4 60
7 Little Lies V4 ★ 44
24/7 Redbull V3 156
69 Year Old Traverse, The V8 ★ 51
90s Glow V0 180
99 Problems Project 70
400 Lux 68
400 Lux V1 68

A

Above Trail Head V3 76
Aces High V8 ★★ 154
A Crow Named Carl V3 76
Admiral Thrawn 35
Admiral Thrawn V5 ★★★ 35
Aeronaut Project, The ★ 158
Aggravated Assault V2 105
A Horse with No Name 213
A Horse with No Name V10 ★★ 213
Ain't No Foolin' Around V4 91
Ain't No Party (Like My Grandma's Tea Party) V2 ★★ 87
Alex Arête Project 80

Alfredo V3 ★ 202
All Blue Room V3 50
Always Climb Up V4 ★★ 80
Anahata V5 192
Analog Woman V6 ★ 125
Andre Agassi 67
Andre Agassi V2 ★ 67
Angry Beaver 95
Angry Beaver V1 95
Another Dam Problem V4 ★★ 198
Anvil, The 113
Anvil, The V3 ★★ 113
Anything Goes V3 ★ 139
Ape Rock 183
Apostate, The V4 ★★ 134
Approach, The V2 194
Arbitrary Agression V6 ★ 96
Archer, The 172
Archer, The V8 ★ 172
Arden's Middle Finger 73
Arden's Middle Finger of Fury V6 ★★★ 73
Arête Boulder 210
Arête Potential Project 55
Are You Topping Out? 204
Arrow Edge, The V4 49
Arrow, The V4 49
Ask Carlos 79
Ask Carlos V5 ★ 79
Assistant, The V4 132
Assorted Climbs V0-6 ★★★ 204
A Step Above Project 66
Astronomer, The V2 ★ 77
Atama Boulder 96
Atama No Amenonuhoko V8 ★★ 96
Ataxia Extension V9 154
Ataxia 154
Ataxia V7 ★★ 154

B

Baby Arête 81
Baby Arête V2 ★ 81
Baby Fett V7 ★ 108
Baby Scout V1 164
Baby Tooth V1 103

Back Pedal Betty V5 ★★ 133
Backside, The V5 ★ 100
Backstage Rodeo V7 ★ 122
Bait and Switch V7 ★★★ 93
Balasana V1 86
Bald Faced Liar 60
Bald Faced Liar V7 ★ 60
Balloon Animals V4 ★★ 158
Balloon, The 158
Bank's Lake 207
Barber, The V4 ★ 133
Barnacles V5 111
Barn-Door Chimney V0 188
Barn-Door Rock 188
Barn, The V4 192
Bashy 69
Bashy V5 ★ 69
Battle Cry V2 ★ 85
Battle of the Bulge V3 178
Battle Scar Galactica 141
Battle Scar Galactica V6 ★★ 141
BDE 199
BDE Sit Project 199
Beach House 219
Beach House V6 ★★ 219
Beacon Hill 190
Bear Dead Blows 86
Bears, Beets, Battlestar Galactica 142
Bears, Beets, Battlestar Galactica V3 142
Bebe Steps V1 33
Belinda's Burrito V2 ★ 82
Betrayal, The V5 ★★ 120
Big Boi 36
Big Boi Project, The 36
Big Boulder 147
Big Dabby V7 203
Big Dick Energy V9 ★★ 199
Big Dipper V7 ★★ 77
Birds Aren't Real V2 188
Bitter Bloodclart V8 65
Black Magic V7 104
Black Pedal Betty 133
Blockade V1 191
Bloody Piss V7 ★ 156
Blue Face Wall 35
Blue Raspberry 163

SPOKANE BOULDERING | 225

Blue Raspberry and Other Lies V4 ★ 163

Blue Steel V6 ★ 56

Blue Water V3 ★ 104

Blunt Force Trauma 155

Blunt Force Trauma Project ★★ 155

Boa Rocha 107

Boa Rocha V3 107

Bodacious Boulder 199

Bodacious Boulder Left V3 ★ 199

Bodacious Boulder V5 ★ 199

Bogo 138

Bohemian Rhapsody V4 ★★★ 113

Bohemian Rhapsody Project ★★ 113

Bold School 44

Bold School V3 ★★ 44

Boss, The 132

Bouncer, The V3 ★ 159

Bowling Ball V2 ★ 42

Bowl of Dreams V1 ★ 45

Brave Bull V4 ★ 117

Breakaway V3 ★ 156

Breaking Wind V5 ★ 37

Breanne's Sit Down Crack Problem V2 111

Brightness, The 148

Brightness, The V7 148

Broken Ankles V2 ★★ 48

Buckaroo V10 ★★ 210

Building Blocks V1 ★ 90

Bulge, The 53

Bulgy Arête Project ★ 123

Bulldozer V8 ★★ 149

Bumbles V1 192

Burgled Burgers 79

Burgled Burgers V0 79

Burrito Babe V4 ★★ 217

Butt Crack Wall 121

But Who Cares V3 39

Buy One, Get One V6 ★★ 138

By The Horns 157

By The Horns V8 ★ 157

C

Cakes and Ale (Horseshoe) V4 71

Calculated Assault 159

Calculated Assault V8 ★★ 159

Calder's Arête V3 104

Calion Ronde V4 ★ 82

Call to Arms V7 ★ 90

Calm Coyote V1 ★ 95

Campbell's Soup V7 ★ 134

Campfire Kids 136

Campfire Kids V3 ★ 136

Cam's Sunshine V4 83

Candy Floss V2 94

Can't Knock the Hustle V5 ★ 70

Caprica V3 77

Captain Phasma V1 34

Car Chase 105

Car Chase V1 105

Carver Boulder 98

Carver Extension V8 ★★ 99

Carver Low V8 ★★ 98

Carver V7 ★★★ 98

Casper V2 ★ 99

Cassette Player V1 60

Castle V1 ★ 61

Catching Feelings 66

Catching Feelings V9 ★★★ 66

Category Five V4 ★★ 171

Catnapper V1 64

Cave 1 Project 146

Cave Crack 92

Cave Crack Boulders 92

Cawwwwdiac Arrest V4 76

Cellophane Project 158

Centenarian 149

Centenarian V3 ★ 149

Center Line Project 106

Center Line V3 ★★ 208

Center Slab V2 55

Cerberus 89

Cerberus V3 89

Certified Chode 97

Certified Chode V3 ★ 97

Chapfallen V5 66

Charlie's Banana Hammock V6 ★★ 64

Charlie's Hammock 64

Chasing the Dragon V3 ★ 198

Ched and Choulders 33

Ched Arête, The V3 ★ 33

Cheekbone V6 62

Chessboard Rock 61

Chill V0 178

Chimera 35

Chimera V3 ★ 35

Cholo V2 187

Choulder, The V1 33

Chris' Climb V2 183

Christmas in Key Largo 70

Christmas in Key Largo V3 70

Cirrus V1 ★★ 129

Clarkson V4 ★★ 155

Classic Right Project 54

Classic, The 54

Cleft, The V1 179

Cliff Band, The 194

Cloud, The 129

Club G Spot 139

Club G Spot V1 139

Coffee at Boots V1 108

Collective Mind 143

Collective Mind V8 ★★★ 143

Color Blind V1 56

Comeback Kid V2 ★ 156

Commons, The 84

Concussion V8 ★ 89

Contrails V5 ★★ 129

Contrivance of the Mind V4 ★ 197

Corduroy Summit V0 53

Corkscrew Canyon 162

Corkscrew Roof Project, The 163

Corner Hug V2 ★ 27

Corner Store 42

Corner Store V3 ★★★ 42

Corner, The V0 183

Corner V1 99

Corner V3 ★★★ 208

Cornflake 183

Cornflake Traverse V3 ★ 183

Corona Boulders 125

Covenant, The V6 ★★ 120

Cow Masseuse V3 ★ 131

Craiglandia 126

Crawlerscout 164

Crawlerscout V1 164

Crescent Moon V2 94

Crescent Project 113
Crime of Passion 90
Crime of Passion V9 ★★ 90
Crimp Project 213
Crosswinds V6 ★ 36
Crown, The 95
Crown, The V2 ★★ 95
Crow's Nest 76
Crumbled 132
Crumbling Bald 159
Crumbling Bald V1 159
Crystal Crack V0 188
Crystal Rock 188
CS V1 49
Cube, The 30
Cubicle, The V3 31
Cubic Zirconia V2 30
Cult Clearing, The 191
Cumulus V1 ★ 129
Cut and Run V6 ★★ 63
Cut, The V2 180
Cynic, The 200
Cynic, The V9 ★ 200

D

Dad's 50! V3 186
Dam Boulders 198
Dam Right V6 ★★ 198
Dam Straight V8 ★ 198
Dam, The 133
Dam, The V4 133
Dance, The V1 ★★ 121
Dancing with Myself V6 ★ 50
Darkside 142
Darkside V3 ★ 142
Dave's Gravel 41
Dave's Problem V2 184
Dead Dog Boulder 134
Dead Dog V4 ★★ 135
Deadline (Epic Arête) V9 ★★★ 28
Death Fall Wall 202
Deception Stretch V3 183
Dedos Técnicos 36
Dedos Técnicos V3 ★★★ 36
Deep Blue V1 ★ 62
Degradation V5 ★ 49
Delicate Slab V4 107

Diamond Boulders, The 192
Diamond Easy V2 ★ 93
Diamond Slab 93
Diamond Slab V7 ★★ 93
Dig Dugged V8 ★★★ 37
Dime in a Dozen V3 203
Dime in a Dozen 203
Din, The V3 ★★ 52
Ding Dong Darling V3 118
Dirk Diggler V5 ★ 180
Dirty Love 149
Dirty Love V2 149
Dirty Wall 94
Dissolution Project 124
Doctor was the Mother V3 ★ 118
Do It Alone V3 ★ 156
Dorm Fridge 133
Dorm Fridge V4 ★ 133
Down the Back V1 39
Drive V4 81
DS Store V0 41

E

Early Onset Geriatric V6 ★ 106
Ears V0 ★★★ 94
East Coaster Traverse V7 / V3 186
Eastern Kids V2 ★ 62
East Lip Traverse V2 ★ 208
East Side Project ★★ 210
Easy Out V6 ★ 92
Easy Thing V1 159
Eating at The Y V7 ★ 104
Ebb and Flow V9 ★★ 87
Eddie's Overhang 181
Eddie's Overhang V3 ★★ 181
Eddie's Face V4 181
Edge Takes over for Vinny, The V2 61
Eggs on Plates V1 ★ 33
Egg Topic V3 85
Elephant 119
Elevation 213
Elevation V11 ★★ 213
Elitist, The 139
Elitist (Aka Mythical Beast), The V12 ★★★ 139
El Luchador 202

El Luchador V6 ★ 202
Elysium V2 ★★ 87
Emancipation 30
Emancipation Corner V0 30
Emancipation V1 30
Unbearable Lightness of Being 100
Entrance Boulder 27
Entrance Cruiser V1 27
Entrance Right V1 27
Epic Arête 28
Event Horizon V2 ★★ 144
Evolving Nature of Flakes, The V4 ★★ 91
Ew V4 156
Excavator 204
Excavator V3 ★★ 204
Excuses and Exfoliation V5 149
Exit Left V2 ★ 150
Eyebrows and Anus 29
Eyebrows and Anus V8 ★★ 29

F

Fade Away 164
Fade Away Left V2 164
Fade Away Right V2 164
Fairwinds Frontside 36
Fairwinds V7 ★★★ 36
Falcon Hawk Moon Child V1 ★ 70
Fall of Troy, The V1 67
Fannie Likes 2 Dance V5 ★★ 159
Far Out 204
Farside Rock, The 195
Fast Fashion V5 ★★ 99
Fat Boy Slim Project ★ 147
Fat Fingered Fred V10 ★ 86
Fat Lip V3 62
Fat Natchies V4 ★★ 215
Feedlot 131
Feedlot, The V5 ★★★ 131
Fekky 113
Fekky V5 ★★ 113
Felacio 112
Felacio V6 ★ 112
Felix Ignis V4 ★ 136
Fern Gullies 111

SPOKANE BOULDERING | 227

Ferocious Fred V8 ★★★ 86

Ferocious Fred Wall 86

Fester Skank V3 ★★ 162

Fight or Flight V4 ★ 52

Final Stanza 46

Final Stanza V3 ★ 46

Fingercuffs V3 117

Finger Ripper Crack 180

Finger Ripper Crack V0 180

Finger Ripper V1 180

Fingertip Rock 180

Fingertip Traverse V2 180

Fisticuffs V3 ★★ 117

Fist, The 117

Five Fingered Discount V2 ★★ 138

Five Is a Crowd V5 194

Flaky Little Friends V8 ★ 122

Flash in the Pan V6 146

Flood Backside, The 120

Flooded/Head & The Heart 192

Flooded V2 192

Flood, The 120

Flood, The V3 ★★★ 120

Floozy V2 60

Flushing a Dead Rooster V3 ★★★ 62

Flying Saucer V6 185

Follow the Leader V4 178

Font Rock 155

Fool, The V5 ★ 121

Forbidden Bucket V7 ★ 91

For Score V4 192

Forty Winks V4 ★ 64

Found Wall Annex 104

Four Fathom 104

Four, The V5 ★ 147

Frankline V6 ★★★ 77

Freddie Mercury 113

Friction Boulder V0 189

From the Steep Side V2 93

Full Settings Reset V6 66

Fun and Done V1 ★★ 106

Fun Bags V1 ★ 215

Fungineer V2 60

Fungus among Us V3 60

Fungus Rock 60

Funk, The 112

Funk, The V2 ★ 112

Further Education V3 ★ 90

Future, The V3 ★ 157

G

Galaxy Smear V5 ★ 52

Game 7 48

Game 7 V7 ★ 48

Game Over V1 48

Gatekeeper 159

Gatekeeper Project 159

Gatekeeper, The V5 ★★★ 159

George Cubebanks V2 31

George's Slab 27

George's Slab V1 ★★ 27

Get Gold without Digging Holes V1 163

Get Shorty V1 39

Girl Next Door, The V8 ★★ 66

Girl's Best Friend V9 ★★ 192

Gleaming the Cube V2 ★★ 31

Glen, The 58

Glory Fades V2 78

Gmork V3 153

God Project, The 33

Golden Gate V3 ★★ 56

Golden Ratio V0 ★ 198

Golden Ratio V4 ★ 89

Goldfish V1 96

Goodie Two Shoes V4 ★★ 134

Good Knight V1 61

Grape Ape V2 ★ 117

Grass Fed V4 ★★ 131

Green Crack V1 ★★ 56

Green Spotted Monster V0 83

Grunt, The 94

Grunt, The V4 94

Gym Socks V2 112

H

Haettenschweiler V3 ★ 155

Hairpin, The 118

Halfway Point of Nine Miles Balls, The V1 45

Hall Monitor V8 ★★ 72

Hall of Impossible 72

Hall of Impossible Projects 72

Hallway Boulder, The 181

Hanuman V2 ★★ 86

Happy Trail V1 ★ 121

Harder Stuff Project 141

Hard Knock Life V1 70

Hard Mantel Project 199

Hard-On with a Hacksaw V4 ★★★ 55

Hattrick Swayze V3 ★ 76

Hay's in the Barn V2 ★★ 131

Head and the Heart, The V6 ★★ 192

Headwinds V5 ★★ 37

Head Wound Cave 89

Head Wound Cave V4 ★★ 89

Heartbreaker 170

Heartbreaker V9 ★★★ 171

Heart of the Storm V7 ★★★ 171

Heatwave V2 195

Heeling Power V10 ★★ 146

Helium Huffer V7 ★ 158

Hello Shorty 39

Hello Shorty V2 39

Heretic 160

Heretic V5 160

Hidden Crack V1 179

Hidden Project 99

Hierapolis V3 ★ 72

Highball Slab Project 104

High Times Wall 56

Highway 69 51

Highway 69 Right Side 52

Highway Rock Boulders 216

Hips Don't Lie Project 106

Hip Waders V1 105

Hog, The 203

Hog, The V5 ★ 203

Hood, The 74

Hood Tuff V5 82

Hot and Heavy V5 45

Hot Rod Banana V3 72

Hotstopper Huck V3 104

Housewife 125

Housewife V4 ★★ 125

Howling Monkey V1 ★ 145

Huevos Rancheros 31

Huevos Rancheros V7 ★ 31

Huge Georgebanks V2 187

Hurtful Boulder 194

Hyper Dark V0 119

Hypertonic 124
Hypertonic V6 ★ 124
Hypotonic V5 124

I

Ice Princess 117
Ice Princess V3 ★ 117
Infinity Traverse, The V6 ★ 189
Inguinal Fortitude 111
Inguinal Fortitude V3 111
Insolence V8 ★ 91
Iron Monkey 145
Iron Monkey V4 145
Iron On V2 ★ 127
Itty Bitty Titty Committee 140
Itty Bitty Titty Committee V6 140
Ivy Area 27
Ivy Arête 29
Ivy Arête V1 ★★ 29
Ivy Crest V3 33
Ivy League 33
Ivy League V2 ★★ 33

J

Jack Jack V1 218
Jameture Night V7 ★ 117
Jaws V12 ★★ 109
Jenga V0 ★★ 41
Jester, The V2 95
Jet Black 141
Jet Black V2 ★ 141
J-Hooks V5 ★★ 215
Johnny is a G V6 ★★ 147
Johnny's Area 194
John's Layback V2 188
Jugs V1 215
Jumble, The 211
Jumble, The V3 ★ 211
Jump Start Project 97
Just The Tip V5 ★ 199

K

Kamiakin 111
Kamiakin V5 ★ 111
Kegerator Project 133
Kevin Durant Is Nice V2 38

Kidney Stone 156
Kidney Stone Traverse V5 156
Killer Queen V9 ★ 113
Kitty Cat Wall 81
Kitty Hawk V2 ★ 50
Kitty Litter 50
Kitty Litter V3 50
Knife Dab 209
Knife Dab V4 209
Knife Edge Crack V2 189
Kung Fury V6 ★ 197

L

La Diosa 33
La Diosa V6 ★★★ 33
La Fiera V2 94
Lakeside Boulders 36
Lakeview 215
Lakeview Project 215
Landslide 219
Landslide V8 ★★ 219
Larry Peterman Boulder 41
Larry Peterman Project, The V4
     ★★ 41
Larry's Left Hang V4 ★ 41
Laser Razor V5 ★★ 49
Latex Project 158
Lawman, The V3 ★★ 157
Layback Dihedral V0 ★ 89
Lay Up 164
Lay Up V6 164
Lazy Layback V4 82
Leaning Book V1 179
Lean, The 213
Lean, The V5 ★ 213
Left Exit V1 82
Left-Right 145
Left V2 145
Legend of Red O'Kelly, The V5
     ★★★ 134
Levels V4 ★ 47
Levitation V9 ★ 213
Lichen Me Mucho V1 180
Lichen Traverse Area 180
Lid, The 39
Lid, The V2 ★★ 39
Lightning Bolt 35
Lightning Bolt V2 ★★ 35

Lightwork 67
Lightwork V5 ★★★ 67
Lil' Dabby 202
Lil' Dabby V5 ★★ 202
Lil Lip Left V2 ★ 42
Lip Mantel V3 ★★ 212
Little Bulge Project Left 53
Little Bulge Project Right 53
Little Dipper V6 ★★ 77
Little Flatiron 127
Little Flatiron V3 ★ 127
Little John V5 ★★ 172
Little Wall (Mantel Wall) 90
Lock in a Sock V9 ★★ 123
Lonely Only Project 127
Lost and Found 102
Lost Glen 102
Lost Glen V2 102
Lounge Chair V4 146
Lounge Lizard V1 95
Lousy Lip 209
Lousy Lip V5 ★ 209
Louvre, The 39
Lovely Little Lies V4 ★ 92
Love Taker V11 ★★ 170
Lowdowner V2 ★★ 99
Lower Beacon Hill 188
Lower Beacon Hill 187
Lower East Side 117
Lower West End 140
Low Glen 71
Low Post, The 161
Low Post, The V2 161
Luca Bomb V6 ★★ 46

M

Made in the Manor V1 ★★★
     162
Maginot Line V3 ★ 178
Make It Hot V1 ★ 63
Malicious Mischief Project 92
Mammatus Project 129
Mandible Mantel V0 ★★★ 103
Man on the Moon V0 148
Marge's Arête V1 125
Marge's Dirty Bag V3 125
Marge's Dirty Clippers V3 125
Marge Simpson 125

SPOKANE BOULDERING | 229

Marge Simpson V5 ★★ 125
Marge's Uncomfortable Bunch
   V3 125
Mark of the Beast V10 ★★ 120
Maroon Nissan V1 105
Marshmallow Peeps 94
Marshmallow Peeps V2 ★ 94
Mason's Muscle V2 181
Mason's Muscle Variation V3
   181
Mass Hysteria 78
Mass Hysteria V9 78
Masthead Boulder 111
Masthead Project ★★ 111
Mastication Project 213
Matriarchal Jesting V2 52
McLove 106
McLove Handles V3 ★★★ 106
Mechanical Bull V4 ★★ 122
Mere Pessimism V6 ★ 200
Mesmerized V4 ★★ 186
Middle of the Pack 156
Middle of the Pack V8 ★ 156
Midnight Caller V2 67
Mike's Climb V1 179
Millennial V3 ★ 123
Mind of a Lemming V2 ★ 47
Minnehaha 174
Minnehaha Park 178
Minne Warmup, The V1 178
Minotaur, The 150
Minotaur, The V10 150
Misfit Angel V5 190
Mistress Misery 203
Mistress Misery V6 ★ 203
Moby Lip V5 51
Modern No. 20 V1 ★ 155
Molar Center, The V4 ★ 103
Molar Hug, The V1 ★ 103
Molar Left, The V2 ★ 103
Molar Right, The V4 ★★★ 103
Molar, The 103
Mollie's Run 68
Mollie's Run V1 68
Mom's Spaghetti 202
Mom's Spaghetti V4 ★★ 202
Monkey Direct V4 ★ 183
More Than You Paid For V3 ★
   197

Morla 152
Morla V3 ★ 153
Morning Arête, The V2 185
Morning Cooler Wall 185
Moshi Moshi V5 ★ 96
Moss Rock 186
Mother Lover 194
Mother Lover V6 ★★★ 194
Mouse House 148
Mouse House V3 ★ 148
Mouthful of Lies V3 ★ 71
Mouth V3 191
Mr. Wenzel V9 ★★★ 92
Mr. Who 30
Mr. Who V1 ★★ 30
My Boy Mazlo V7 ★ 98
My Forgotten Man V1 ★ 44

N

Naked Prostor V2 49
Nate's Lovely Elephant V5 ★ 119
Nazca to Gaza 31
Nazca to Gaza V2 31
Neapolitan V3 ★★ 65
Nevermind 129
Nevermind V4 ★★ 129
New American Classic V5 ★★★
   54
New Wave Rookie V10 ★★ 28
Nimbostratus Project 129
Nine Mile Balls 45
Nine Mile Balls V2 ★ 45
Nise 1 V1 191
Nise V2 191
Noctilucent V7 ★ 129
No Flake V6 181
No Lights in the Attic V3 ★ 55
Nonstop Ego Trip V7 ★ 52
Northrup Canyon 208
Northrup Point 215
Nose, The 212
Nose, The V3 ★★★ 212
No Such Thing as a Fish V1 161
No Top V6 181
Novice Rock 179
Numbers Game V3 134

O

Obelidear V0 ★ 43
Ocean Spray V3 ★★★ 30
Off the Wall V2 ★ 163
Ogre, The 62
Ogre, The V4 ★★ 62
Old School Achilles V4 185
Open Book 99
Open Book V2 ★★ 99
Orca V4 ★ 143
Order 66 34
Order 66 Project 34
Overhung Edges V1 ★★ 208

P

Pack Rat Cave Boulders 55
Painted Boulder 190
Papa Tortilla 217
Papa Tortilla V8 ★★★ 217
Paradox in Purple V1 ★★ 51
Party Animal V1 ★ 87
Party Rock (Triangle) / Wallflower
   Frontside 87
Party Rock V3 ★★ 87
Passably Fly V5 ★ 130
Passing the Stone V6 156
Paul's Climb V3 181
Paws then Claws 47
Paws then Claws V2 ★★★ 47
Pencil Neck Ghost V1 118
Penny Drop 66
Perch Project, The ★★ 214
Perch, The 214
Perfect V1 ★★★ 36
Pestiferous Innervations V0 66
Petrov Defense V1 ★★ 61
Pettifoggin' 161
Pettifoggin' V3 161
Phantom Unmasked V2 ★★ 122
Phantom V4 ★★ 122
Phantom Wall 122
Piano Man Project ★★ 135
Pilferers V2 105
Pillar, The V1 189
Pinch Project 51
Pineapple Pizza 51

Pink Wine & Other Vices V9 ★★★ 65

Pipe Dream 45

Pipe Dream Arête Project 45

Pipe Dream Direct V7 ★★ 45

Pipe Dream V5 ★★ 45

Pipe Dream Warmup V0 45

Pistol and Fist V3 ★ 70

Pistol Whip Project 144

Pit, The V1 ★★ 145

Plagiarizing Apologists 198

Plagiarizing Apologists V1 198

Planted 34

Planted V4 34

Plan, The V0 ★ 141

Playhouse V9 ★ 200

Polish Happy Slap 145

Polish Happy Slap V4 ★★ 145

Pogo Power V9 ★★ 109

Pope of Mope V6 146

Pop the Cork V7 163

Pornos and Porcupines V4 ★ 170

Pornos and Porcupines 170

Post Falls 196

Potential Project 147

Precious Days of Eternity V3 ★★ 135

Pretentious Blog V4 ★★ 52

Prometheus + Var V2 180

Propaganda 44

Propaganda Left V4 44

Propaganda Project 44

Propaganda V3 ★★★ 44

Prostor's Backwards Hat V4 ★★ 49

Prostor's Wall 49

Prow Low Project, The 146

Prow, The 146

Prow, The V6 ★★★ 146

Proxima Nova V3 ★★★ 155

Public Enemy 139

Public Enemy V3 139

Pumpkin Waffle V0 108

Puppis V7 ★ 77

Purple Prose V3 53

Purple Teeth V6 ★ 56

Q

Quad City Dj V3 ★★ 48

Qualchan's Arête V6 ★ 111

Quasimodo V2 ★ 179

Queen for Queen V2 ★★★ 61

Quesadilla, The 217

Quesadilla, The V7 ★★ 217

Quizinator V2 ★ 60

R

Racing Stripes 171

Racing Stripes Project ★ 171

Rain V5 ★★ 71

Ral 9005 V3 ★ 141

Rama V3 86

Ramayana 86

Rancor, The V4 34

RBG V2 ★★ 123

Reasonable Doubt 70

Reasonable Doubt V3 ★★ 70

Reasonable Force V3 105

Rebels V2 195

Red October V3 ★ 43

Red Rover V3 56

Red Scare V4 ★★★ 52

Regular Left V1 179

Regular V1 179

Religious Guilt V4 ★ 92

Remote Rocks 109

Renaissance Man V5 ★ 54

Retrograde 30

Retrograde V1 ★★ 30

Revival Right, The V3 191

Revival, The V1 191

Revolution V10 194

Rex Kwon Do V6 ★★★ 201

Rhino, The V4 92

Riggins Run V0 68

Right Face of Widow Project 152

Right V2 145

Rip Saw V2 189

Ritter Run V2 108

Roadman, The V2 ★★ 163

Road Rock 214

Road Rock Arête V1 214

Road Rock Lip V4 214

Road Rock Roof V3 214

Rocks of Sharon 166

Romaine V3 ★★★ 81

Romancing the Stone 78

Romancing the Stone V5 ★★ 78

Roof Traverse V3 132

Rookie Move V0 ★★ 61

Rook, The 134

Rook, The V3 134

Room with a View 103

Room with a View V4 ★ 103

Roskelley Warmup V1 188

Rotation V3 ★ 213

Roundhouse Low V10 ★★ 201

Roundhouse V6 ★★ 201

Route Warm-Up Rock V0 77

Royal Arch V2 180

Rule of Thirds V1 ★★ 198

Russian Happy Slap V6 ★ 145

S

Sacred Geometry 200

Sacred Geometry Project ★★★ 200

Sacrifice, The V6 ★★ 121

Sad Shark 197

Sad Shark V4 ★★ 197

Sagittarius A* 144

Sagittarius A* V9 ★★ 144

Saintly Sam V2 ★ 86

Salivate V4 ★★★ 200

Sam Eagle V2 ★ 29

Sam Reed Memorial 100

Sam Reed V3 100

Saucer, The 160

Saucer, The V2 160

Say Goodbye to Your Good Side V6 ★★ 134

Scaredless in Spokane 63

Scaredless in Spokane V5 ★ 63

S Cargo V4 70

Scarlett Johansson 80

Scarlett Johansson V5 ★★★ 80

Scarred Ground + Var V2 185

Scary Slab Left V5 69

Scary Slab Right V4 69

Scatty Cat V4 81

Scree V3 187

Scrumptious 136

SPOKANE BOULDERING | 231

Scrumptious V6 ★★ 136
Scrum Think V0 161
Sea Foam V1 94
Secondary Face 186
Serrated V10 ★ 98
Seven Loves You 60
Seven Loves You V5 60
Shady Slab V4 ★ 210
Shake Spear V3 ★★ 42
Shark Wrestle V4 ★ 38
Sharon Stone 169
Shepard and Flock Project 36
Shepherd's Way, The V2 185
Sherlocked V3 ★ 52
Shipwrecked 200
Shipwrecked (Aka Matt and Dave
    Go to Jail) V5 ★★ 200
Shoobs 68
Shoobs V2 68
Short Roof V4 ★ 120
Shrub, The V8 ★ 138
Sickle, The V5 ★ 28
Sic Transit Gloria V7 ★ 78
Silage V8 ★ 131
Silent Steel V5 ★ 43
Sink Like a Stone V1 163
Sixty Dine-O V3 ★ 52
Skyline V1 187
Slab Problem V4 185
Slab, The V2 183
Slab V2 208
Slab V4 215
Slap Happy V3 ★ 145
Slapping the Nip V2 179
Sleepy Cougar Project 81
Sleepy Time Tea 64
Sleepy Time Tea V4 ★★★ 64
Slip and Slap 99
Slip and Slap V4 ★ 99
Slippery Sloped V2 160
SMEG-a-Squeeze V8 28
Smokey's Low V8 187
Smokey's Traverse 187
Smokey's Traverse V6 ★★★
    187
Smoking Monkey 143
Smoking Monkey V11 ★ 143
Snake Pit 212

Snake Pit Project ★ 212
Snitches Get Stitches V3 ★ 89
Snot Rocket 211
Snot Rocket Project 211
Soco Amaretto Lime V2 ★ 42
Sol Alcance V2 82
Solute, The V3 ★ 124
Something To Say V5 ★★★ 98
Son of the Beast V8 ★★ 120
Soul in Hand V8 ★★ 85
Soulless 85
Soul Shine V4 ★ 85
Soul Slinger V2 ★ 85
Soulstice V3 ★★ 85
Soul to Squeeze 147
Soul to Squeeze Sit V11 ★ 147
Soul to Squeeze V9 ★ 147
South Bank V3 53
Space Jam 48
Space Jam V5 ★ 48
Spade, The 154
Spade, The V10 ★★ 154
Sparrow Fox 65
Sparrow Fox V4 ★★★ 65
Speed of Light V5 ★ 148
Spherical Canon V4 194
Spillway 197
Squares Pace 38
Square's Pace Left V2 38
Staring at the Sun V2 148
Statue of Liberty 136
Statue of Liberty V7 ★★ 136
Step Back Three V4 164
Stepford V2 ★ 111
Steppin' Out V4 183
Stick in the Spokes V2 ★★ 156
Stiff Chocolate Project 67
Still the Louvre V3 39
Stir, The V3 ★ 95
Stoking the Fire V6 ★ 122
Stowaway V7 ★ 111
Stratus V0 129
Submarine Boulder 43
Summer of 69 V2 ★★ 52
Sum of All Sides Project 195
Sunny Arête V4 ★★★ 210
Sunny D V2 ★★★ 83
Sunny Sort of Feeling V1 ★★ 63
Sunset Traverse V7 ★★ 171

Sunshine Left V3 ★★ 83
Sunshine Right V1 ★★ 83
Sunshine V2 ★★★ 83
Sunshine Wall 83
Supafly 130
Supafly V4 ★★★ 130
Superbloom 218
Superbloom Area 218
Superbloom V5 ★★★ 218
Surf Du Block V3 ★ 143
Suspended V5 152
Sweater Puppy V6 ★★ 215
Sweet Cheeks 127
Sweet Cheeks V0 ★★★ 127
Swoop, The 79
Swoop, The V1 79
Symbol, The V3 ★ 95

T

Table Saw V7 29
Tabletop Rock 108
Tailwinds V2 ★ 37
Taking Heat V4 ★ 63
Tall Tales V3 ★★ 69
Tarantula Direct V0 184
Tarantula Right V1 184
Tarantula Traverse 184
Tarantula Traverse V3 ★★ 184
Tarantula Turd V0 184
Tara's Top V4 ★ 50
Tara's Wall 50
Tara V6 ★★ 50
Tenebrous 35
Tenebrous V4 ★★ 35
Tequila For Two V3 ★★ 106
That's So Raven 157
That's So Raven V4 ★ 157
Think Tank V0 ★ 143
Thirds 118
Threesome V3 194
ThreeStories V2 ★★ 69
Three-Story Boulder 69
Three-Toed Sloth V2 ★ 117
Thrutchy Crapness V6 ★ 150
Thrutchy Madness 150
Thrutchy Madness V4 ★★★ 150
Tidbit 133
Tidbit V3 ★★ 133

Tighten Up 47
Tighten Up V4 ★ 47
Tina's Tips V2 180
Tinie Boi 163
Tiny Eiger Right V2 188
Tiny Eiger V2 188
Tiny Temper V6 ★★★ 63
Todd's Dyno V4 ★ 50
Tomato Tutu 48
Tomato Tutu V2 ★★ 48
Tongue, The 97
Tonisha 64
Tonisha Left V2 ★ 64
Tonisha V4 64
Tonya Hardly V4 ★ 76
Too Much Sauce Tuesday V3 ★ 217
Tooth Fairy 103
Tooth Fairy V1 103
Top Boy 162
Top Boy V5 ★★★ 163
Topiary V3 ★ 133
Top Tier 47
Top Tier Project 47
Trail Head 76
Trail Head V1 ★★ 76
Traverse Project 136
Traverse, The V1 ★★ 180
Tree Amigos V6 ★ 63
Tremble 66
Tremble Part 2 Project 36
Tremble Right Project 66
Tremble V5 66
Triad 162
Triad V1 162
Triangle, The V4 ★ 87
Trimmed and Soiled V9 ★★ 29
Troll Toll V8 ★ 134
Try a Little Tenderness V2 180
Tummy Rubber V3 192
Tum Tum 115
Turd in the Punchbowl V6 143
Turk's Grease V3 184
Twisted Pull V3 ★ 109
Twisted Rock 109
Two Face V1 ★ 76
Two Hands and Two Holds V7 180
Two Off 61

Two Stories V5 ★★ 71
Two-Story Boulder 71
Two Tiered to Finish V2 ★★★ 71

U

Ugly Dog Symphony V2 69
Unbearable Lightness of Being V5 ★★ 100
Underneath Project 97
Under Yout V2 191
Unorthodox 154
Unorthodox V6 ★★ 154
Up First V1 ★ 42
Upper Area 195
Upper Beacon Area 195
Upper Beacon Hill 195
Upper Bench 189
Upper Bench V0 189
Upper West End 152
Urethral Euphoria V5 ★ 156

V

V0 and Sons V0 ★ 111
Vega 160
Vega Project 160
Vega V4 160
Vendetta 164
Vendetta Project, The 164
Vertical Marathon V0 76
Very Small Plate, The V2 160
Virginia Creeper V1 ★ 29
Vishnu V2 86
Vlogs about Clogs V0 52
Voodoo Magic 104
Voodoo Magic V4 ★★★ 104
Vow of Silence V6 ★ 135

W

Waheela V8 ★★★ 111
Wallflower Surf V1 ★★ 87
Wallflower V0 ★★ 87
Warm-Up 208
Warmup Rock 178
Warm-Up Wall 89
Warm-Up Wall (5.9 Face) V1 89
War Room, The 85

War Room, The V4 ★★ 85
Way of the Cookie, The V7 ★ 132
Way Too Much V2 ★ 113
Weird Corner V2 ★ 208
Welcome to McLellan V1 27
Welcome to the Hood 81, 82
Welcome to the Hood Project 82
We're All Pawns V0 62
West End, The 140
Whackozoid V0 218
What the Kids Want V5 ★★ 87
Whiplash V3 106
Whiskey for One 106
Whiskey for One V4 ★★ 106
Whisper and a Clamour V4 ★ 51
White Bird V2 188
Who's the Boss? V8 ★★ 132
Wicked Skengman 70
Wicked Skengman V5 ★★★ 70
Widowmaker 152
Widowmaker V5 ★★★ 152
Will Scarlet V4 ★ 172
Windstorm V6 ★★ 170
Wow, Amazing V3 186
Wrecking Ball 149
Wrecking Ball V9 ★★ 149
Wretch Project, The 66
Wrinkle Resistant V1 ★★ 127

X

Xeno 214
Xeno V3 ★★ 214

Y

Year of Regrets V1 195
Yellow Submarine V2 43
Yout V2 191

Z

Zulu Princess V8 ★ 52

SPOKANE BOULDERING | 233

INDEX BY GRADE

V0

5.8 Dihedral V0 ★ 90
90's Glow V0 180
Barn-Door Chimney V0 188
Burgled Burgers V0 79
Chill V0 178
Corduroy Summit V0 53
Corner, The V0 183
Crystal Crack V0 188
DS Store V0 41
Ears V0 ★★★ 94
Emancipation Corner V0 30
Finger Ripper Crack V0 180
Friction Boulder V0 189
Golden Ratio V0 ★ 198
Green Spotted Monster V0 83
Hyper Dark V0 119
Jenga V0 ★★ 41
Layback Dihedral V0 ★ 89
Man on the Moon V0 148
Mandible Mantel V0 ★★★ 103
Obelidear V0 ★ 43
Pestiferous Innervations V0 66
Pipe Dream Warmup V0 45
Plan, The V0 ★ 141
Pumpkin Waffle V0 108
Riggins Run V0 68

Rookie Move V0 ★★ 61
Route Warm-Up Rock V0 77
Scrum Think V0 161
Stratus V0 129
Sweet Cheeks V0 ★★★ 127
Tarantula Direct V0 184
Tarantula Turd V0 184
Think Tank V0 ★ 143
Upper Bench V0 189
V0 and Sons V0 ★ 111
Vertical Marathon V0 76
Vlogs about Clogs V0 52
Wallflower V0 ★★ 87
We're All Pawns V0 62
Whackozoid V0 218

V1

400 Lux V1 68
Angry Beaver V1 95
Baby Tooth V1 103
Balasana V1 86
Bebe Steps V1 33
Blockade V1 191
Bowl of Dreams V1 ★ 45
Building Blocks V1 ★ 90
Bumbles V1 192
Calm Coyote V1 ★ 95
Captain Phasma V1 34
Car Chase V1 105
Cassette Player V1 60
Castle V1 ★ 61
Catnapper V1 64
CHoulder, The V1 33
Cirrus V1 ★★ 129
Classic Corner V1 ★★★ 208
Cleft, The V1 179
Club G Spot V1 139
Coffee at Boots V1 108
Color Blind V1 56
Corner V1 99
Crawlerscout V1 164
Crumbling Bald V1 159
CS V1 49
Cumulus V1 ★ 129
Dance, The V1 ★★ 121
Deep Blue V1 ★ 62
Down The Back V1 39
Easy Thing V1 159

Eggs on Plates V1 ★ 33
Emancipation V1 30
Entrance Cruiser V1 27
Entrance Right V1 27
Falcon Hawk Moon Child V1 ★ 70
Fall of Troy, The V1 67
Finger Ripper V1 180
Fun and Done V1 ★★ 106
Fun Bags V1 ★ 215
Game Over V1 48
George's Slab V1 ★★ 27
Get Gold without Digging Holes V1 163
Get Shorty V1 39
Goldfish V1 96
Good Knight V1 61
Green Crack V1 ★★ 56
Halfway Point of Nine Miles Balls, The V1 45
Happy Trail V1 ★ 121
Hard Knock Life V1 70
Hidden Crack V1 179
Hip Waders V1 105
Howling Monkey V1 ★ 145
Ivy Arête V1 ★★ 29
Jack Jack V1 218
Jugs V1 215
Leaning Book V1 179
Left Exit V1 82
Lichen Me Mucho V1 180
Lounge Lizard V1 95
Made in the Manor V1 ★★★ 162
Make it Hot V1 ★ 63
Marge's Arête V1 125
Maroon Nissan V1 105
Mike's Climb V1 179
Minne Warmup, The V1 178
Modern No. 20 V1 ★ 155
Molar Hug, The V1 ★ 103
Mollie's Run V1 68
Mr. Who V1 ★★ 30
My Forgotten Man V1 ★ 44
Nise 1 V1 191
No Such Thing as a Fish V1 161
Overhung Edges V1 ★★ 208
Paradox in Purple V1 ★★ 51
Party Animal V1 ★ 87

Pencil Neck Ghost   V1   118
Perfect   V1 ★★★ 36
Petrov Defense   V1 ★★ 61
Pillar, The   V1   189
Pit, The   V1 ★★ 145
Plagiarizing Apologists V1   198
Regular   V1   179
Regular Left   V1   179
Retrograde   V1 ★★ 30
Revival, The   V1   191
Road Rock Arête   V1   214
Roskelley Warmup   V1   188
Rule of Thirds   V1 ★★ 198
Sea Foam   V1   94
Sink Like a Stone   V1   163
Skyline   V1   187
Sunny Sort of Feeling   V1 ★★
    63
Sunshine Right   V1 ★★ 83
Swoop, The   V1   79
Tarantula Right   V1   184
Tooth Fairy   V1   103
Trail Head   V1 ★★ 76
Traverse, The   V1 ★★ 180
Triad   V1   162
Two Face   V1 ★ 76
Up First   V1 ★ 42
Virginia Creeper   V1 ★ 29
Wallflower Surf   V1 ★★ 87
Warm-Up Wall (5.9 Face)   V1   89
Welcome to McLellan   V1   27
Wrinkle Resistant   V1 ★★ 127
Year of Regrets   V1   195

V2

Aggravated Assault   V2   105
Ain't No Party (Like My Grand-
    ma's Tea Party) V2 ★★ 87
Andre Agassi   V2 ★ 67
Approach, The   V2   194
Astronomer, The   V2 ★ 77
Baby Arête   V2 ★ 81
Battle Cry   V2 ★ 85
Belinda's Burrito   V2 ★ 82
Birds Aren't Real   V2   188
Bowling Ball   V2 ★ 42
Breanne's Sit Down Crack Problem
    V2   111

Broken Ankles   V2 ★★ 48
Candy Floss   V2   94
Casper   V2 ★ 99
Center Slab   V2   55
Cholo   V2   187
Chris' Climb   V2   183
Comeback Kid   V2 ★ 156
Corner Hug   V2 ★ 27
Crescent Moon   V2   94
Crown, The   V2 ★★ 95
Cubic Zirconia   V2   30
Cut, The   V2   180
Dave's Problem   V2   184
Diamond Easy   V2 ★ 93
Dirty Love   V2   149
East Lip Traverse   V2 ★ 208
Eastern Kids   V2 ★ 62
Edge takes over for Vinny, The
    V2   61
Elysium   V2 ★★ 87
Event Horizon   V2 ★★ 144
Exit left   V2 ★ 150
Fade Away Left   V2   164
Fade Away Right   V2   164
Fingertip Traverse   V2   180
Five Fingered Discount   V2 ★★
    138
Flooded   V2   192
Floozy   V2   60
From the Steep Side   V2   93
Fungineer   V2   60
Funk, The   V2 ★ 112
George Cubebanks   V2   31
Gleaming the Cube   V2 ★★ 31
Glory Fades   V2   78
Grape Ape   V2 ★ 117
Gym Socks   V2   112
Hanuman   V2 ★★ 86
Hay's in the Barn   V2 ★★ 131
Heatwave   V2   195
Hello Shorty   V2   39
Huge Georgebanks   V2   187
Iron On   V2 ★ 127
Ivy League   V2 ★★ 33
Jester, The   V2   95
Jet Black   V2 ★ 141
John's Layback   V2   188
Kevin Durant is Nice   V2   38
Kitty Hawk   V2 ★ 50

Knife Edge Crack   V2   189
La Fiera   V2   94
Left   V2   145
Lid, The   V2 ★★ 39
Lightning Bolt   V2 ★★ 35
Lil Lip Left   V2 ★ 42
Lost Glen   V2   102
Low Post, The   V2   161
Lowdowner   V2 ★★ 99
Marshmallow Peeps   V2 ★ 94
Mason's Muscle   V2   181
Matriarchal Jesting   V2   52
Midnight Caller   V2   67
Mind of a Lemming   V2 ★ 47
Molar Left, The   V2 ★ 103
Morning Arête, The   V2   185
Naked Prostor   V2   49
Nazca to Gaza   V2   31
Nine Mile Balls   V2 ★ 45
Nise   V2   191
Off the Wall   V2 ★ 163
Open Book   V2 ★★ 99
Paws then Claws   V2 ★★★ 47
Phantom Unmasked   V2 ★★ 122
Pilferers   V2   105
Prometheus + Var   V2   180
Quasimodo   V2 ★ 179
Queen for Queen   V2 ★★★ 61
Quizinator   V2 ★ 60
RBG   V2 ★★ 123
Rebels   V2   195
Right   V2   145
Rip Saw   V2   189
Ritter Run   V2   108
Roadman, The   V2 ★★ 163
Royal Arch   V2   180
Saintly Sam   V2 ★ 86
Sam Eagle   V2 ★ 29
Saucer, The   V2   160
Scarred Ground + Var   V2   185
Shepherd's Way, The   V2   185
Shoobs   V2   68
Slab   V2   208
Slab, The   V2   183
Slapping the Nip   V2   179
Slippery Sloped   V2   160
Soco Amaretto Lime   V2 ★ 42
Sol Alcance   V2   82
Soul Slinger   V2 ★ 85

SPOKANE BOULDERING | 235

Square's Pace Left V2 38
Staring at the Sun V2 148
Stepford V2 ★ 111
Stick in the Spokes V2 ★★ 156
Summer of 69 V2 ★★ 52
Sunny D V2 ★★★ 83
Sunshine V2 ★★★ 83
Tailwinds V2 ★ 37
Three Stories V2 ★★ 69
Three-Toed Sloth V2 ★ 117
Tina's Tips V2 180
Tiny Eiger V2 188
Tiny Eiger Right V2 188
Tomato Tutu V2 ★★ 48
Tonisha Left V2 ★ 64
Try a Little Tenderness V2 180
Two Tiered to Finish V2 ★★★
     71
Ugly Dog Symphony V2 69
Under Yout V2 191
Very Small Plate, The V2 160
Vishnu V2 86
Way Too Much V2 ★ 113
Weird Corner V2 ★ 208
White Bird V2 188
Yellow Submarine V2 43
Yout V2 191

V3

24/7 Redbull V3 156
A Crow Named Carl V3 76
Above Trail Head V3 76
Alfredo V3 ★ 202
All Blue Room V3 50
Anvil, The V3 ★★ 113
Anything Goes V3 ★ 139
Battle of the Bulge V3 178
Bears, Beets, Battlestar Galactica
     V3 142
Blue Water V3 ★ 104
Boa Rocha V3 107
Bodacious Boulder Left V3 ★
     199
Bold School V3 ★★ 44
Bouncer, The V3 ★ 159
Breakaway V3 ★ 156
But Who Cares V3 39
Calder's Arête V3 104

Campfire Kids V3 ★ 136
Caprica V3 77
Centenarian V3 ★ 149
Center Line V3 ★★ 208
Cerberus V3 89
Certified Chode V3 ★ 97
Chasing the Dragon V3 ★ 198
CHed Arête, The V3 ★ 33
Chimera V3 ★ 35
Christmas in Key Largo V3 70
Corner V3 ★★★ 208
Corner Store V3 ★★★ 42
Cornflake Traverse V3 ★ 183
Cow Masseuse V3 ★ 131
Cubicle, The V3 31
Dad's 50! V3 186
Darkside V3 ★ 142
Deception Stretch V3 183
Dedos Técnicos V3 ★★★ 36
Dime in a Dozen V3 203
Din, The V3 ★★ 52
Ding Dong Darling V3 118
Do it Alone V3 ★ 156
Doctor Was Tthe Mother V3
     ★ 118
Eddie's Overhang V3 ★★ 181
Egg Topic V3 85
Excavator V3 ★★ 204
Fat Lip V3 62
Fester Skank V3 ★★ 162
Final Stanza V3 ★ 46
Fingercuffs V3 117
Fisticuffs V3 ★★ 117
Flood, The V3 ★★★ 120
Flushing a Dead Rooster V3
     ★★★ 62
Fungus Among Us V3 60
Further Education V3 ★ 90
Future, The V3 ★ 157
Gmork V3 153
Golden Gate V3 ★★ 56
Haettenschweiler V3 ★ 155
Hat Trick Swayze V3 ★ 76
Hierapolis V3 ★ 72
Hot Rod Banana V3 72
Hotstopper Huck V3 104
Ice Princess V3 ★ 117
Inguinal Fortitude V3 111
Ivy Crest V3 33

Jumble, The V3 ★ 211
Kitty Litter V3 50
Lawman, The V3 ★★ 157
Lip Mantel V3 ★★ 212
Little Flatiron V3 ★ 127
Maginot Line V3 ★ 178
Marge's Dirty Bag V3 125
Marge's Dirty Clippers V3 125
Marge's Uncomfortable Bunch
     V3 125
Mason's Muscle Variation V3
     181
McLove Handles V3 ★★★ 106
Millennial V3 ★ 123
More Than You Paid For V3 ★
     197
Morla V3 ★ 153
Mouse House V3 ★ 148
Mouth V3 191
Mouthful of Lies V3 ★ 71
Neapolitan V3 ★★ 65
No Lights in the Attic V3 ★ 55
Nose, The V3 ★★★ 212
Numbers Game V3 134
Ocean Spray V3 ★★★ 30
Party Rock V3 ★★ 87
Paul's Climb V3 181
Pettifoggin' V3 161
Pistol and Fist V3 ★ 70
Precious Days of Eternity V3
     ★★ 135
Propaganda V3 ★★★ 44
Proxima Nova V3 ★★★ 155
Public Enemy V3 139
Purple Prose V3 53
Quad City DJ V3 ★★ 48
RAL 9005 V3 ★ 141
Rama V3 86
Reasonable Doubt V3 ★★ 70
Reasonable Force V3 105
Red October V3 ★ 43
Red Rover V3 56
Revival Right, The V3 191
Road Rock Roof V3 214
Romaine V3 ★★★ 81
Roof Traverse V3 132
Rook, The V3 134
Rotation V3 ★ 213
Sam Reed V3 100

236 | INDEX

Scree   V3   187
Shake Spear   V3 ★ ★   42
Sheev   V3   35
Sherlocked   V3 ★   52
Sixty Dine-o   V3 ★   52
Slap Happy   V3 ★   145
Snitches Get Stitches   V3 ★   89
Solute, The   V3 ★   124
Soulstice   V3 ★ ★   85
South Bank   V3   53
Still The Louvre   V3   39
Stir, The   V3 ★   95
Sunshine Left   V3 ★ ★   83
Surf Du Block   V3 ★   143
Symbol, The   V3 ★   95
Tall Tales   V3 ★ ★   69
Tarantula Traverse   V3 ★ ★   184
Tequila for Two   V3 ★ ★   106
Threesome   V3   194
Tidbit   V3 ★ ★   133
Too Much Sauce Tuesday   V3
      ★   217
Topiary   V3 ★   133
Tummy Rubber   V3   192
Turk's Grease   V3   184
Twisted Pull   V3 ★   109
Whiplash   V3   106
Wow, Amazing   V3   186
Xeno   V3 ★ ★   214

V4

5.11 World   V4   60
7 Little Lies   V4 ★   44
Ain't No Foolin' Around   V4   91
Always Climb Up   V4 ★ ★   80
Another Dam Problem   V4 ★ ★
      198
Apostate, The   V4 ★ ★   134
Arrow Edge, The   V4   49
Arrow, The   V4   49
Assistant, The   V4   132
Balloon Animals   V4 ★ ★   158
Barber, The   V4 ★   133
Barn, The   V4   192
Blue Raspberry and Other Lies
      V4 ★   163
Bohemian Rhapsody   V4 ★ ★ ★
      113

Brave Bull   V4 ★   117
Burrito Babe   V4 ★ ★   217
Cakes and Ale (Horseshoe)   V4
      71
Calion Ronde   V4 ★   82
Cam's Sunshine   V4   83
Category Five   V4 ★ ★   171
Cawwwwdiac Arrest   V4   76
Clarkson   V4 ★ ★   155
Contrivance of the Mind   V4 ★
      197
Dam, The   V4   133
Dead Dog   V4 ★ ★   135
Delicate Slab   V4   107
Dorm Fridge   V4 ★   133
Drive   V4   81
Eddie's Face   V4   181
Evolving Nature of Flakes, The   V4
      ★ ★   91
Ew   V4   156
Fat Natchies   V4 ★ ★   215
Felix Ignis   V4 ★   136
Fight or Flight   V4 ★   52
Follow the Leader   V4   178
For Score   V4   192
Forty Winks   V4 ★   64
Golden Ratio   V4 ★   89
Goodie Two Shoes   V4 ★ ★   134
Grass Fed   V4 ★ ★   131
Grunt, The   V4   94
Hard-On with a Hacksaw   V4
      ★ ★ ★   55
Head Wound Cave   V4 ★ ★   89
Housewife   V4 ★ ★   125
Iron Monkey   V4   145
Knife Dab   V4   209
Larry Peterman Project, The   V4
      ★ ★   41
Larry's Left Hang   V4 ★   41
Lazy Layback   V4   82
Levels   V4 ★   47
Lounge Chair   V4   146
Lovely Little Lies   V4 ★   92
Mechanical Bull   V4 ★ ★   122
Mesmerized   V4 ★ ★   186
Molar Center, The   V4 ★   103
Molar Right, The   V4 ★ ★ ★   103
Mom's Spaghetti   V4 ★ ★   202
Monkey Direct   V4 ★   183

Nevermind   V4 ★ ★   129
Ogre, The   V4 ★ ★   62
Old School Achilles   V4   185
Orca   V4 ★   143
Phantom   V4 ★ ★   122
Planted   V4   34
Polish Happy Slap   V4 ★ ★   145
Pornos and Porcupines   V4 ★
      170
Pretentious Blog   V4 ★ ★   52
Propaganda Left   V4   44
Prostor's Backwards Hat   V4
      ★ ★   49
Rancor, The   V4   34
Red Scare   V4 ★ ★ ★   52
Religious Guilt   V4 ★   92
Rhino, The   V4   92
Road Rock Lip   V4   214
Room with a View   V4 ★   103
S Cargo   V4   70
Sad Shark   V4 ★ ★   197
Salivate   V4 ★ ★ ★   200
Scary Slab Right   V4   69
Scatty Cat   V4   81
Shady Slab   V4 ★   210
Shark Wrestle   V4 ★   38
Short Roof   V4 ★   120
Slab   V4   215
Slab Problem   V4   185
Sleepy Time Tea   V4 ★ ★ ★   64
Slip and Slap   V4 ★   99
Soul Shine   V4 ★   85
Sparrow Fox   V4 ★ ★ ★   65
Spherical Canon   V4   194
Step Back Three   V4   164
Steppin' Out   V4   183
Sunny Arête   V4 ★ ★ ★   210
Supafly   V4 ★ ★ ★   130
Taking Heat   V4 ★   63
Tara's Top   V4 ★   50
Tenebrous   V4 ★ ★   35
That's So Raven   V4 ★   157
Thrutchy Madness   V4 ★ ★ ★
      150
Tighten Up   V4 ★   47
Todd's Dyno   V4 ★   50
Tonisha   V4   64
Tonya Hardly   V4 ★   76
Triangle, The   V4 ★   87

SPOKANE BOULDERING | 237

Vega V4 160
Voodoo Magic V4 ★★★ 104
War Room, The V4 ★★ 85
Whiskey for One V4 ★★ 106
Whisper and a Clamour V4
    ★ 51
Will Scarlet V4 ★ 172

V5

Admiral Thrawn V5 ★★★ 35
Anahata V5 192
Ask Carlos V5 ★ 79
Back Pedal Betty V5 ★★ 133
Backside, The V5 ★ 100
Barnacles V5 111
Bashy V5 ★ 69
Betrayal, The V5 ★★ 120
Bodacious Boulder V5 ★ 199
Breaking Wind V5 ★ 37
Chapfallen V5 66
Contrails V5 ★★ 129
Degradation V5 ★ 49
Dirk Diggler V5 ★ 180
Excuses and Exfoliation V5 149
Fannie Likes 2 Dance V5 ★★
    159
Fast Fashion V5 ★★ 99
Feedlot, The V5 ★★★ 131
Fekky V5 ★★ 113
Five is a Crowd V5 194
Fool, The V5 ★ 121
Four, The V5 ★ 147
Galaxy Smear V5 ★ 52
Gatekeeper, The V5 ★★★ 159
Headwinds V5 ★★ 37
Heretic V5 160
Hog, The V5 ★ 203
Hood Tuff V5 82
Hot and Heavy V5 45
Hypotonic V5 124
J-Hooks V5 ★★ 215
Just the Tip V5 ★ 199
Kamiakin V5 ★ 111
Kidney Stone Traverse V5 156
Laser Razor V5 ★★ 49
Lean, The V5 ★ 213
Legend of Red O'Kelly, The V5
    ★★★ 134

Lightwork V5 ★★★ 67
Lil' Dabby V5 ★★ 202
Little John V5 ★★ 172
Lousy Lip V5 ★ 209
Marge Simpson V5 ★★ 125
Misfit Angel V5 190
Moby Lip V5 51
Moshi Moshi V5 ★ 96
Nate's Lovely Elephant V5 ★
    119
New American Classic V5
    ★★★ 54
Passably Fly V5 ★ 130
Pipe Dream V5 ★★ 45
Rain V5 ★★ 71
Renaissance Man V5 ★ 54
Romancing the Stone V5 ★★
    78
Scaredless in Spokane V5 ★ 63
Scarlett Johansson V5 ★★★ 80
Scary Slab Left V5 69
Seven Loves You V5 60
Shipwrecked (AKA Matt and Dave
    go to Jail) V5 ★★ 200
Sickle, The V5 ★ 28
Silent Steel V5 ★ 43
Something to Say V5 ★★★ 98
Space Jam V5 ★ 48
Speed of Light V5 ★ 148
Superbloom V5 ★★★ 218
Suspended V5 152
Top Boy V5 ★★★ 163
Tremble V5 66
Two Stories V5 ★★ 71
Unbearable Lightness of Being
    V5 ★★ 100
Urethral Euphoria V5 ★ 156
What the Kids Want V5 ★★ 87
Wicked Skengman V5 ★★★ 70
Widowmaker V5 ★★★ 152

V6

Analog Woman V6 ★ 125
Arbitrary Agression V6 ★ 96
Arden's Middle Finger of Fury V6
    ★★★ 73
Battle Scar Galactica V6 ★★
    141

Beach House V6 ★★ 219
Blue Steel V6 ★ 56
Buy One, Get One V6 ★★ 138
Charlie's Banana Hammock V6
    ★★ 64
Cheekbone V6 62
Covenant, The V6 ★★ 120
Crosswinds V6 ★ 36
Cut and Run V6 ★★ 63
Dam Right V6 ★★ 198
Dancing with Myself V6 ★ 50
Early Onset Geriatric V6 ★ 106
Easy Out V6 ★ 92
El Luchador V6 ★ 202
Felacio V6 ★ 112
Flash in the Pan V6 146
Flying Saucer V6 185
Frankline V6 ★★★ 77
Full Settings Reset V6 66
Head and the Heart, The V6
    ★★ 192
Hypertonic V6 ★ 124
Infinity Traverse, The V6 ★ 189
Itty Bitty Titty Committee V6 140
Johnny Is a G V6 ★★ 147
Kung Fury V6 ★ 197
La Diosa V6 ★★★ 33
Lay Up V6 164
Little Dipper V6 ★★ 77
Luca Bomb V6 ★★ 46
Mere Pessimism V6 ★ 200
Mistress Misery V6 ★ 203
Mother Lover V6 ★★★ 194
No Flake V6 181
No Top V6 181
Passing the Stone V6 156
Pope of Mope V6 146
Prow, The V6 ★★★ 146
Purple Teeth V6 ★ 56
Qualchan's Arête V6 ★ 111
Rex Kwon Do V6 ★★★ 201
Roundhouse V6 ★★ 201
Russian Happy Slap V6 ★ 145
Sacrifice, The V6 ★★ 121
Say Goodbye to Your Good Side
    V6 ★★ 134
Scrumptious V6 ★★ 136
Smokey's Traverse V6 ★★★ 187
Stoking the Fire V6 ★ 122

Sweater Puppy V6 ★★ 215
Tara V6 ★★ 50
Thrutchy Crapness V6 ★ 150
Tiny Temper V6 ★★★ 63
Tree Amigos V6 ★ 63
Turd in the Punchbowl V6 143
Unorthodox V6 ★★ 154
Vow of Silence V6 ★ 135
Windstorm V6 ★★ 170

V7

Ataxia V7 ★★ 154
Baby Fett V7 ★ 108
Backstage Rodeo V7 ★ 122
Bait and Switch V7 ★★★ 93
Bald Faced Liar V7 ★ 60
Big Dabby V7 203
Big Dipper V7 ★★ 77
Black Magic V7 104
Bloody Piss V7 ★ 156
Brightness, The V7 148
Call to Arms V7 ★ 90
Campbell's Soup V7 ★ 134
Carver V7 ★★★ 98
Diamond Slab V7 ★★ 93
East Coaster Traverse V7/V3
    186
Eating at the Y V7 ★ 104
Fairwinds V7 ★★★ 36
Forbidden Bucket V7 ★ 91
Game 7 V7 ★ 48
Heart of the Storm V7 ★★★
    171
Helium Huffer V7 ★ 158
Huevos Rancheros V7 ★ 31
Jameture Night V7 ★ 117
My Boy Mazlo V7 ★ 98
Noctilucent V7 ★ 129
Nonstop Ego Trip V7 ★ 52
Pipe Dream Direct V7 ★★ 45
Pop the Cork V7 163
Puppis V7 ★ 77
Quesadilla, The V7 ★★ 217
Sic Transit Gloria V7 ★ 78
Statue of Liberty V7 ★★ 136
Stowaway V7 ★ 111
Sunset Traverse V7 ★★ 171
Table Saw V7 29

Two Hands and Two Holds V7 180
Way of the Cookie, The V7 ★ 132

V8

69 Year Old Traverse, The V8
    ★ 51
Aces High V8 ★★ 154
Archer, The V8 ★ 172
Atama no Amenonuhoko V8
    ★★ 96
Bitter Bloodclart V8 65
Bulldozer V8 ★★ 149
By the Horns V8 ★ 157
Calculated Assault V8 ★★ 159
Carver Extension V8 ★★ 99
Carver Low V8 ★★ 98
Collective Mind V8 ★★★ 143
Concussion V8 ★ 89
Dam Straight V8 ★ 198
Dig Dugged V8 ★★★ 37
Eyebrows and Anus V8 ★★ 29
Ferocious Fred V8 ★★★ 86
Flaky Little Friends V8 ★ 122
Girl Next Door, The V8 ★★ 66
Hall Monitor V8 ★★ 72
Insolence V8 ★ 91
Landslide V8 ★★ 219
Middle of the Pack V8 ★ 156
Papa Tortilla V8 ★★★ 217
Shrub, The V8 ★ 138
Silage V8 ★ 131
SMEG-a-Squeeze V8 28
Smokey's Low V8 187
Son of the Beast V8 ★★ 120
Soul in Hand V8 ★★ 85
Troll Toll V8 ★ 134
Waheela V8 ★★★ 111
Who's the Boss? V8 ★★ 132
Zulu Princess V8 ★ 52

V9

Ataxia Extension V9 154
Big Dick Energy V9 ★★ 199
Catching Feelings V9 ★★★ 66
Crime of Passion V9 ★★ 90
Cynic, The V9 ★ 200
Deadline (Epic Arête) V9 ★★★ 28

Ebb and Flow V9 ★★ 87
Girl's Best Friend V9 ★★ 192
Heartbreaker V9 ★★★ 171
Killer Queen V9 ★ 113
Levitation V9 ★ 213
Lock in a Sock V9 ★★ 123
Mass Hysteria V9 78
Mr. Wenzel V9 ★★★ 92
Pink Wine & Other Vices V9 ★★★
    65
Playhouse V9 ★ 200
Pogo Power V9 ★★ 109
Sagittarius A* V9 ★★ 144
Soul to Squeeze V9 ★ 147
Trimmed and Soiled V9 ★★ 29
Wrecking Ball V9 ★★ 149

V10

Buckaroo V10 ★★ 210
Fat Fingered Fred V10 ★ 86
Heeling Power V10 ★★ 146
Horse with no Name, A V10 ★★
    213
Mark of the Beast V10 ★★ 120
Minotaur, The V10 150
New Wave Rookie V10 ★★ 28
Revolution V10 194
Roundhouse Low V10 ★★ 201
Serrated V10 ★ 98
Spade, The V10 ★★ 154

V11

Elevation V11 ★★ 213
Love Taker V11 ★★ 170
Smoking Monkey V11 ★ 143
Soul to Squeeze Sit V11 ★ 147

V12

Elitist (AKA Mythical Beast), The
    V12 ★★★ 139
Jaws V12 ★★ 109

SPOKANE BOULDERING | 239

PROJECTS

An updated list of projects can be found at spokanebouldering.com

- 99 Problems Project 70
- Aeronaut Project, The ★ 158
- Alex Arête Project 80
- Arête Potential Project 55
- A Step Above Project 66
- BDE Sit Project 199
- Big Boi Project, The 36
- Blunt Force Trauma Project ★ ★ 155
- Bohemian Right-Handapsody Project ★ ★ 113
- Bulgy Arête Project ★ 123
- Cave 1 Project 146
- Cellophane Project 158
- Center Line Project 106
- Classic Right Project 54
- Corkscrew Roof Project, The 163
- Crescent Project 113
- Crimp Project 213
- Dissolution Project 124
- East side Project ★ ★ 210
- Fat Boy Slim Project ★ 147
- Gatekeeper Project 159
- God Project, The 33
- Hall of Impossible Project 72
- Harder Stuff Project 141
- Hard Mantel Project 199
- Hidden Project 99
- Highball Slab Project 104
- Hips Don't Lie Project 106
- Jump Start Project 97
- Kegerator Project 133
- Lakeview Project 215
- Larry Peterman Project, The V4 ★ ★ 41
- Latex Project 158
- Little Bulge Project Left 53
- Little Bulge Project Right 53
- Lonely Only Project 127
- Malicious Mischief Project 92
- Mammatus Project 129
- Masthead Project ★ ★ 111
- Mastication Project 213
- Nimbostratus Project 129
- Order 66 Project 34
- Perch Project, The ★ ★ 214
- Piano Man Project ★ ★ 135
- Pinch Project 51
- Pipe Dream Arête Project 45
- Pistol Whip Project 144
- Potential Project 147
- Propaganda Project 44
- Prow Low Project, The 146
- Racing Stripes Project ★ 171
- Right face of Widow Project 152
- Sacred Geometry Project ★ ★ ★ 200
- Shepard and Flock Project 36
- Sleepy Cougar Project 81
- Snake Pit Project ★ 212
- Snot Rocket Project 211
- Stiff Chocolate Project 67
- Sum of all Sides Project 195
- Top Tier Project 47
- Traverse Project 136
- Tremble Part 2 Project 36
- Tremble Right Project 66
- Underneath Project 97
- Vega Project 160
- Vendetta Project, The 164
- Welcome to the Hood Project 82
- Wretch Project, The 66

Nate Lynch and Shane Collins bumpin' fists.

ABOUT THE AUTHORS

Hey there, and thanks for reading our book. This has been a passion project of ours for a long time and we are very happy to have it on the shelves. We hope that it's helpful and maybe even puts a smile on your face.

In our real lives, Nate spends his time as a mechanical engineer, husband, and a father of two. Shane is a UX Researcher in the tech world and a Space Camp graduate.

Like we mention in the intro, we've been climbing together for over 10 years now, but we do more than that. Outside of climbing, we have ran ultra marathons, performed mediocrely in pub trivia, built an adjustable woody (twice), lived many quality experiences, and have shared a special friendship that made working on this book surprisingly easy and enjoyable. We hope you feel the fun we had making this, too.